D0190700

T R A V E L E R S ' T A L E S

GATHER
THE FRUIT
ONE BY ONE

50 YEARS OF AMAZING
PEACE CORPS STORIES

VOLUME TWO: THE AMERICAS

TRAVELERS' TALES

GATHER
THE FRUIT
ONE BY ONE

50 YEARS OF AMAZING
PEACE CORPS STORIES

VOLUME TWO: THE AMERICAS

Edited by

PAT AND BERNIE ALTER

Series Editor
JANE ALBRITTON

Travelers' Tales
An Imprint of Solas House, Inc.
Palo Alto

Travelers' Tales and *Solas House* are trademarks of Solas House, Inc. 853 Alma Street, Palo Alto, California 94301. www.travelerstales.com

Cover Design: Chris Richardson
Interior Layout: Howie Severson
Production Director: Susan Brady

Library of Congress Cataloging-in-Publication Data

Gather the fruit one by one : 50 years of amazing Peace Corps stories / edited by Pat and Bernie Alter. -- 1st ed.
    p. cm.
 ISBN 978-1-60952-001-4 (pbk.)
 1. Peace Corps (U.S.)--History. I. Alter, Pat. II. Alter, Bernie.
 HC60.5.G37 2011
 361.6--dc22

                    2011005702

First Edition
Printed in the United States
10 9 8 7 6 5 4 3 2 1

De a uno se junta el mistal.

You must gather the fruit from the mistal tree carefully,
one by one.

Table of Contents

Part Two
WHY ARE WE HERE?

Part Three
GETTING THROUGH THE DAYS

Part Four
CLOSE ENCOUNTERS

Part Five
SUSTAINABLE PEACE

Series Preface

THERE ARE SOME BABY IDEAS THAT SEEM TO FLY IN BY STORK, without incubation between conception and birth. These magical bundles smile and say: "Want me?" And well before the head can weigh the merits of taking in the unsummoned arrival, the heart leaps forward and answers, "Yes!"

The idea for Peace Corps @ 50—the anniversary media project for which this series of books is the centerpiece—arrived on my mental doorstep in just this way in 2007. Four books of stories, divided by regions of the world, written by the Peace Corps Volunteers who have lived and worked there. There was time to solicit the stories, launch the website, and locate editors for each book. By 2011, the 50th anniversary of the founding of the Peace Corps, the books would be released.

The website had no sooner gone live when the stories started rolling in. And now, after four years and with a publisher able to see the promise and value of this project, here we are, ready to share more than 200 stories of our encounters with people and places far from home.

In the beginning, I had no idea what to expect from a call for stories. Now, at the other end of this journey, I have read every story, and I know what makes our big collection such a fitting tribute to the Peace Corps experience.

Peace Corps Volunteers write. We write a lot. Most of us need to, because writing is the only chance we have to say things in our native language. Functioning every day in another language takes work, and it isn't just about grammar. It's everything that isn't taught—like when to say what depending on the context, like the intricate system of body language, and like knowing how to shift your tone depending on the company you are in. These struggles and linguistic mishaps can be frustrating and often provoke laughter, even if people are forgiving and appreciate the effort. It takes a long time to earn a sense of belonging.

And so in our quiet moments—when we slip into a private space away from the worlds where we are guests—we write. And in these moments where we treat ourselves to our own language, thoughts flow freely. We once wrote only journals and letters; today we also text, email, and blog.

Writing helps us work through the frustrations of everyday living in cultures where—at first—we do not know the rules or understand the values. In our own language we write out our loneliness, our fury, our joy, and our revelations. Every volunteer who has ever served writes as a personal exercise in coming to terms with an awakening ignorance. And then we write our way through it, making our new worlds part of ourselves in our own language, in our own words.

The stories in these books are the best contribution we can make to the permanent record of Peace Corps on the occasion of its 50th anniversary. And because a Volunteer's attempt to explain the experience has always contained the hope that folks at home will "get it," these stories are also a gift to anyone eager and curious to learn what we learned about living in places that always exceeded what we imagined them to be.

It has been an honor to receive and read these stories. Taken together, they provide a kaleidoscopic view of world cultures—beautiful and strange—that shift and rattle when held up to the light.

I would like to acknowledge personally the more than 200 Return Volunteers who contributed to these four volumes. Without their voices, this project could not have been possible. Additionally, editors Pat and Bernie Alter, Aaron Barlow, and Jay Chen have been tireless in shepherding their stories through the publishing process and in helping me make my way through some vexing terrain along the way. Special thanks to John Coyne whose introduction sets the stage for each volume. Thanks also to Dennis Cordell for his early work on the project.

There are two people critical to the success of this project who were never Peace Corps volunteers, but who instantly grasped the significance of the project: Chris Richardson and Susan Brady.

Chris and his PushIQ team, created a visually lush, technically elegant website that was up and ready to invite contributors to join the project and to herald both the project and the anniversary itself. He took on the creative challenge of designing four distinct covers for the four volumes in this set. His work first invited our contributors and now invites our readers.

Susan Brady brought it all home. It is one thing to collect, edit, and admire four books' worth of stories; it is another to get them organized, to the typesetter, the printer, and the team of marketers on time and looking good. Susan's good sense, extensive publishing experience, and belief in the worthiness of this project sealed the publishing deal with Travelers' Tales/ Solas House.

Finally, there are the two others, one at each elbow, who kept me upright when the making of books made me weary. My mother—intrepid traveler and keeper of stories—died four months after the project launched, but she has been kind enough to hang around to see me through. My partner, cultural anthropologist Kate Browne, never let me forget that if Americans are ever going to have an honored place in this world, we need to have some clue about how the rest of it works. "So get with it," they said. "The 50th anniversary happens only once."

—JANE ALBRITTON
FORT COLLINS, COLORADO

FOREWORD

✷

Thirty Days That Built the Peace Corps

JOHN COYNE

In 1961 John F. Kennedy took two risky and conflicting initiatives in the Third World. One was to send 500 additional military advisers into South Vietnam. The other was to send 500 young Americans to teach in the schools and work in the fields of eight developing countries. These were Peace Corps Volunteers. By 1963 there would be 7,000 of them in forty-four countries.

—*Garard T. Rice,* The Bold Experiment: JFK's Peace Corps

KENNEDY'S SECOND INITIATIVE INSPIRED, AND CONTINUES TO inspire, hope and understanding among Americans and the rest of the world. In a very real sense, the Peace Corps is Kennedy's most affirmative and enduring legacy that belongs to a particularly American yearning: the search for a new frontier.

Two key people in Congress, Henry Reuss (D-Wisconsin) and Hubert Humphrey (D-Minnesota), both proposed the idea of the Peace Corps in the late 1950s.

In January of 1960, Reuss introduced the first Peace Corps-type legislation. It sought a study of "the advisability and practicability to the establishment of a Point Four Youth Corps," which would send young Americans willing to serve their country in public and private technical assistance missions in far-off countries, and at a soldier's pay.

The government contract was won by Maurice (Maury) L. Albertson of Colorado State University who with one extraordinary assistant, Pauline Birky-Kreutzer, did the early groundwork for Congress on the whole idea of young Americans going overseas, not to win wars, but help build societies.

In June of 1960, Hubert Humphrey introduced in the Senate a bill to send "young men to assist the peoples of the underdeveloped areas of the world to combat poverty, disease, illiteracy, and hunger."

Also in 1960, several other people were expressing support for such a concept: General James Gavin; Chester Bowles, former governor of Connecticut, and later ambassador to India; William Douglas, associate justice of the Supreme Count; James Reston of *The New York Times;* Milton Shapp, from Philadelphia; Walt Rostow of MIT; and Senator Jacob Javits of New York, who urged Republican presidential candidate Richard Nixon to adopt the idea. Nixon refused. He saw the Peace Corps as just another form of "draft evasion."

What Nixon could not have foreseen was that a "day of destiny" waited for the world on October 14, 1960. On the steps of the Student Union at the University of Michigan, in the darkness of the night, the Peace Corps became more than a dream. Ten thousand students waited for presidential candidate Kennedy until 2 A.M., and they chanted his name as he climbed those steps.

Kennedy launched into an extemporaneous address. He challenged them, asking how many would be prepared to give years of their lives working in Asia, Africa, and Latin America?

The audience went wild. (I know this, because at the time I was a new graduate student over in Kalamazoo. I was working part-time as a news reporter for WKLZ and had gone to cover the event.)

Six days before the 1960 election, on November 2nd, Kennedy gave a speech at the Cow Palace in San Francisco. He pointed out that 70 percent of all new Foreign Service officers had no foreign language skills whatsoever; only three of the forty-four Americans in the embassy in Belgrade spoke Yugoslavian; not a single American in New Delhi could speak Indian dialects, and only two of the nine ambassadors in the Middle East spoke Arabic. Kennedy also pointed out that there were only twenty-six black officers in the entire Foreign Service corps, less than 1 percent.

Kennedy's confidence in proposing a "peace corps" at the end of his campaign was bolstered by news that students in the Big Ten universities and other colleges throughout Michigan had circulated a petition urging the founding of such an organization. The idea had caught fire in something like spontaneous combustion.

The day after his inauguration, President Kennedy telephoned his brother-in-law Sargent Shriver and asked him to form a presidential task force to report how the Peace Corps should be organized and then to organize it. When he heard from Kennedy, Shriver immediately called Harris Wofford.

At the time, Shriver was 44; Wofford was 34. Initially, the Task Force consisted solely of the two men, sitting in a suite of two rooms that they had rented at the Mayflower Hotel in Washington, D.C. They spent most of their time making calls to personal friends they thought might be helpful.

One name led to another: Gordon Boyce, president of the Experiment in International Living; Albert Sims of the Institute of International Education; Adam Yarmolinsky, a foundation executive; Father Theodore Hesburgh, president of the University of Notre Dame; George Carter, a campaign worker on civil rights issues and former member of the American Society for African Culture; Louis Martin, a newspaper editor; Franklin Williams, an organizer of the campaign for black voter registration, and a student of Africa; and Maury Albertson, out at Colorado State University.

Unbeknownst to Shriver and Wofford, two officials in the Far Eastern division of the International Cooperation Administration (ICA) were working on their own Peace Corps plan. Warren Wiggins, who was the deputy director of Far Eastern operations in ICA, was still in his thirties but had already helped administer the Marshall Plan in Western Europe. He was totally dissatisfied with the manner in which American overseas programs were run; he called them "golden ghettos." With Wiggins was Bill Josephson, just 26, and a lawyer at ICA.

They started developing an idea that would be limited to sending young Americans overseas to teach English. But as they worked on it, their vision broadened. The paper detailing their recommendations was titled "A Towering Task." They sent copies to Wofford, Richard Goodwin at the White House, and to Shriver, who thought it was brilliant and immediately sent a telegram to Wiggins inviting him to attend the Task Force meeting the next morning. It was Wiggins who advocated initiating the Peace Corps with "several thousand Americans participating in the first twelve to eighteen months." A slow and cautious beginning was not an option.

Three times in February, Kennedy would telephone Shriver to ask about progress on the Peace Corps. The final draft of the report was created with Charles Nelson sitting in one room writing basic copy, Josephson sitting in another room rewriting it, Wofford sitting in yet another room doing the final rewrite, and Wiggins running back and forth carrying pieces of paper.

Shriver held the position that Peace—not Development, it might be noted—was the overriding purpose, and the process of promoting it was necessarily complex. So the Peace Corps should learn to live with complexity that could not be summed up in a single proposition. Finally, the Task Force agreed on three.

- Goal One: It can contribute to the development of critical countries and regions.
- Goal Two: It can promote international cooperation and goodwill toward this country.
- Goal Three: It can also contribute to the education of America and to more intelligent American participation in the world.

On the morning of Friday, February 24, 1961, Shriver delivered the report—the Peace Corps Magna Carta—to Kennedy and told him: "If you decide to go ahead, we can be in business Monday morning."

It had taken Shriver, Wofford, Wiggins, Josephson, and the other members of the Mayflower Task Force, less than a month to create what *TIME Magazine* would call that year "the greatest single success the Kennedy administration had produced." On March 1, 1961, President Kennedy issued an Executive Order establishing the Peace Corps.

And today, fifty years later, we are still debating what the Peace Corps is all about. As Sarge Shriver thought all those years ago, "the tension between competing purposes is creative, and it should continue."

Well, it has!

John Coyne, who is considered an authority on the history of the Peace Corps, has written or edited over twenty-five books. In 1987 he started the newsletter RPCV Writers & Readers that is for and about Peace Corps writers. This newsletter, now a website, can be found today at PeaceCorpsWorldwide.org.

Introduction

AT ITS CORE, THE PEACE CORPS EXPERIENCE IS A JOURNEY OF discovery. The journey is not a simple or easy one, however. It involves a variety of experiences, some anticipated some not. Discovering a new country is the most obvious and least metaphorical. Discovering a foreign culture is also not unexpected. Then there is discovering personal, physical, and even intellectual limits. Finally, there is a rediscovery of the United States after the journey is supposedly over and we return to a country thought of as home. These explorations often change us far more than we change the worlds we travel through. The stories in this volume are attempts to describe the various signposts of that voyage through the countries of the Americas.

The most immediate encounter is with the country itself, confronting often unexpected geography and weather. Along with the sheer physicality of adjusting to a new home is learning and using a new language that does not yet come trippingly off the tongue. There are allusions to these initial explorations sprinkled throughout the stories contained here. But stories

like Alanna Randall's "The Scent of Iris" in Belize, Alan
Yount's "Over the Mountain" in Guatemala, or William M.
Evensen's "The Amazing Jungle Walking Tour" in Peru are
essentially tales of the physical environment these volunteers
faced. The almost constant struggle to overcome a sense of
separation from the local community caused by a lack of initial
language facility and by topographical isolation in the rainforests of Panama is also at the center of Jessi Flynn's "The Easter
Bunny's Culinary Skills."

Another stage in the Peace Corps voyage is the exploration
of foreign cultures and the success or failure of cross-cultural
engagement. Dealing with cultures that may not only have had
different answers to questions, but sometimes even asked completely different questions, is a theme that also runs through
many of the stories found in this volume. Bob Hudgen's
encounter with breast milk on a Bolivian flatbed truck in his
tale "What They Don't Teach You..." is a good first stop.
A more complex account of cross-cultural communication is
Ellen Urbani's recounting in "Our Samuel" of the remark-
ably different yet awfully similar methods the U.S. Embassy
and her Guatemalan neighbors used to pass on information.
Kendra Lachmiet's "Little Library of Horrors" describes how
three different cultures can collide in a small town library in
Paraguay. Finally, an example of successful cross-cultural purchasing power can be found in Krista Perleberg's Ecuadorean
"Pretty Woman."

Part of any voyage of discovery is learning your limitations
and trying to work within them or overcome them. As Paul
Vitale recounts in "Sink or Drown Proof" for Peace Corps
Volunteers, this learning could begin even before a volunteer
arrived in the assigned country, which in Vitale's case was
Ecuador. Martha Martin's "The Danger of Paved Roads" shows
how accepting or pushing limits continued after her arrival in

Costa Rica. "God and Motorcycles" by Patrick H. Hare, on the other hand, demonstrates that a volunteer's personal idiosyncrasies did not necessarily lead to negative consequences.

When is a home not a home? That's a question that many a volunteer has dealt with after returning to the United States. After two years or more of living in a foreign culture, readjusting to U.S. society can be surprisingly difficult. Brandon Louie's initial encounter with our consumption-oriented society upon his return from Nicaragua, described in his "Homeland Buffet," attests to that difficulty. For Katherine Jamieson in "Too Much of One Thing Ain't Good for Nothing," it appears that her Peace Corps experience will forever set her apart from the country in which she was born and raised.

Even after resettling in the "home country," a question remains: Did the world change us more than we changed the world? That dilemma haunts a number of returned volunteers. Ronald A. Schwarz's "Kennedy's Orphans" attempts to find an answer by seeking out many of the sixty-two men who were the first volunteers to enter training for the Peace Corps back in 1961. Wynne Dimock sets out on a similar, though far more personal, quest in "The Making of a Leftist."

We have previewed quite a few stories for you in this Introduction; however, there are many more awaiting your discovery. These tales represent fifty years of Peace Corps Volunteers traveling to and through the Americas; learning about new worlds and their cultures; sometimes changing them and sometimes leaving them relatively untouched; but always returning with an awareness of what lies beyond our borders.

Read and enjoy!

—Pat and Bernie Alter
Arlington, Virginia

PART ONE

ON OUR WAY...
AND BACK AGAIN

Sink or Drown Proof

What did rock climbing, swimming with your hands tied, and survival treks have to do with being a Peace Corps Volunteer? Apparently, in 1962, quite a lot.

MARRIED IN 1962, KATHLEEN AND I MOVED TO SAN FRANCISCO in mid-1963 after I completed my graduate studies at the University of California. I was a city planner and would return to my planning position with the Department of City Planning. Four short months later, however, in November of 1963, we found ourselves headed to New York and the possibility of Peace Corps assignments in Ecuador. These were very heady times.

We spent a few carefree days in the Big Apple before we started our Peace Corps orientation. We enjoyed the exotic restaurants, the theaters, and the vistas. It was breathtaking for two West Coasters. After one of our first Peace Corps sessions on November 22, we stepped out for a quick bite to eat. We noticed, as we sauntered down one of New York's busier thoroughfares, that there were no people. The streets were empty: literally. Then we happened upon a shop selling TVs and learned that President Kennedy had been shot and was not expected to live. We rushed back to our Peace Corps hotel

3

and learned that we were to be whisked off to our first PC training site, Puerto Rico, that afternoon, before the week of mourning could begin.

We arrived in San Juan, found our small, hospitable hotel and were taken to the Peace Corps representative's home for dinner. It was a sad occasion, but people supported one another, and we were all committed to getting on with the job that JFK had created for us.

The next day we were driven up into the tropical rainforest some hours from San Juan. The training site was about twenty miles from the town of Arecibo. We turned off the paved highway on to a dirt road and headed up a mountain. The training site was reminiscent of my Boy Scout camp in California. Camp Crozier was one of two training sites located along the road. The other site, about a mile further up the road, was Camp Radley. The camps were named after the first two Peace Corps Volunteers who died in accidents while serving in the Corps, another sobering thought.

Crozier consisted of a series of open-air cabins that held ten or more people; latrines and showers were strategically located. There was a central dining area and various obstacle courses spread out among the trees, along with an Olympic-sized swimming pool. We later learned that the first Peace Corps trainees had hand dug the hole for the pool.

The training staff that greeted us was extremely knowledgeable about swimming, rock climbing, and survival training; the Spanish teachers were native speakers who very ably started us on our journey to learn the language. Interestingly, no one at the site had much of a clue about what the Peace Corps was all about, and I doubt that many of them even knew where Ecuador was located. And, for that matter, most of the folks in Washington who were calling the shots were flying the program by the seat of their pants. But this was understandable, given that Peace Corps was less than two years old. And now its founder was dead. The one unifying theme of the Puerto Rican experience was that we were all there because of JFK and his call to do good works for people in other countries: "Ask not what your country can do for you, but what you can do for your country."

We were going to be tested in a variety of ways. We would first go through Outward Bound's training at Crozier; then, for those of us who survived Puerto Rico, we would spend several more months at the University of Denver for more language training and general orientation for our Peace Corps assignments in Ecuador. Those of us who survived the rigors of the stateside training would then be sworn into the Corps in Texas, where we had additional training, and then flown to Quito, Ecuador, for even further orientation. In Ecuador, we would finally be assigned as either rural or urban community developers. Interestingly, we learned that our assignments had yet to be identified by the in-country staff.

I have some very vivid memories of our experiences during those three weeks in Puerto Rico. One of my first was our "welcoming" to Camp Crozier. Our group consisted of fifty-eight trainees, twelve of whom were married. Three of the couples were virtually on their honeymoon. The camp administrator informed us that all of the men were assigned to cabins A, B, and C, while all the women were assigned to cabins D, E, and F. When someone asked about where the married couples would live, the administrator took great delight in repeating herself. So Kathleen headed in one direction, while I headed in another direction to find our respective accommodations. The married couples were very unhappy. But people began to realize that we were being tested. And tested we would be until we got on the last propeller Panagra flight to Quito, in March of 1964.

The training program was physically rigorous. We learned to "drown proof" ourselves in the afternoon after we had climbed rocks in the morning. Interspersed between the not drowning and the climbing were Spanish classes. I was in the beginning group of the Spanish program and had a lovely Cuban American who taught me some basic Spanish that helped me survive later in my stay in Puerto Rico. Kathleen was in the advanced Spanish class, thrived in the language program, and excelled in the swimming pool. In fact, she was one of the best swimmers of our group.

The swimming program was unusual. Rather than trying to perfect our swimming strokes, we were instructed on how to stay afloat for hours. They called it "drown proofing." The final swimming test at the camp consisted of drown-proofing with our hands and feet tied. Then one of the instructors tossed pieces of car tire into the deep end of the pool and each of us tried to sink to the bottom, grab a bit of tire with our teeth and surface. I failed that part of the test, but Kathleen did it!

There was one more swimming test. We were taken to Arecibo for a quick visit (a chance for the men to get haircuts) and then to the ocean for a drown-proofing test with Mother Nature, who happily tumbled trainees in the surf: everyone but me, who got a different kind of opportunity to stay afloat. I was the last out of the barber chair and was accidentally left behind when the group headed to the beach. When I came out of the barbershop, there was no PC vehicle and no one around speaking English. It was my first test in *hablando espanol*. I was not fluent, but managed to walk out of town in the right direction, catch a *guagua* (small rural taxi), and get dropped off near the road to Camp Crozier. As I trudged up the hill, the carryall filled with happy drowned-proof survivors came by and offered me a lift back up to the camp. I had had my own land-based drown-proofing experience, too.

Then there was the rock climbing, also a challenge. The rock-climbing instructor had found a nice, sheer rock outcrop along the highway to the Dos Bocas Dam. The face was challenging, but climbable. A belayer was at the top of the climb and made sure none of the climbers fell to his/her death. Groups of trainees were assigned the task of climbing the rocks at different times during the day, and in every case the married couples were separated. Kathleen lucked out and scampered up the rock face in the morning. I pulled the afternoon climb and had made it almost to the top when I stopped.

The rocks were very hot. In fact, the training staff handed out cotton gloves to the afternoon climbers. The problem was that you couldn't climb using gloves. The climb involved using finger/hand holds, and when wearing cotton gloves you lost the necessary friction required to hold your position to make your moves up the rock. So there I was, hot rocks and all, stuck. The instructor who was belaying me poked his head over the last rock outcrop and said very quietly, "Kathleen made it to the top this A.M." I sprouted wings and made it to the top without the gloves, swearing all the way.

Dos Bocas Dam was the site of our rappelling exercise. Rappelling was less of a hassle for me because I had previously climbed with the Sierra Club. We were asked to rappel off the face of a high dam and drop down to the base of its outer wall. On the dry side of the dam, and before the actual drop to the bottom, you had to swing out and drop down past the railing and some kind of projection. I have no memory of how far we had to drop and rappel, but in any event we had enough rope to reach the bottom in our rappelling harness and belay lines. It was a real challenge for those who had never rappelled before. On occasion, a trainer stationed at the bottom of the jump said, "Looked like that was a real challenge for you. Do it again." Kathleen was given that opportunity, but turned it down—and told the instructor were he could put the idea.

There was little contact with the outside world during our stay at Crozier. And the only recreation for most of us was at a tiny *cantina* located near the camp. Tomasito, the proprietor, knew a good opportunity when he saw one and set up a primitive outdoor bar, complete with pool table, music, and cold beer. I am sure that the trainers were taking notes about our comportment during those relaxing moments, of which there were few. Once Kathleen and I were chatting after lunch when a trainer walked by and snarled, "Don't you two have anything better to do?"

We were always being observed. We learned early in our training about something known as "peer ratings." Every so often we were given peer-rating sheets to fill out. Who were the top five trainees? Who were the best all-around individuals? Who were the five trainees having the most problems or making the most problems? It became clearer along the way that these peer ratings would play a vital role in the "de-selection" of trainees during the training program. And so many of us tried to be on our best behavior and be good guys at all times; not always easy when you are rappelling off the face of a dam or clambering up the side of a rock outcrop that has been baked in the tropical sun. The people calling the shots at the camp took the peer ratings seriously and nearly half of our group was deselected before we were sworn into the Peace Corps.

In Puerto Rico, we were also tested on our ability to survive military-style. We were divided into teams of four or five of the same gender, and each of us was issued one small can of food, a compass, and a map outlining the route for a four-day survival trek. We were expected to survive for four days by primarily living off the land. As it turned out, we really learned how to mooch. Thanks to the generosity of Puerto Ricans, we all survived.

Kathleen's group of five was left at a trail near the rappelling Dos Bocas Dam.

"We started up a jungle covered mountain, up and up and up until we thought we'd collapse from heat prostration," she wrote home. "At the top, a most pleasant *señora* greeted us with two children and invited us for coffee or dinner or anything. She was so pleasant we hated to turn her down, but we had to keep going in search of a place to spend the night. Our thirty-pound packs dug into our backs, our feet swelled with blisters, and our bodies were covered with sweat.

"We came upon an evangelical church and asked a couple nearby if we could sleep in the church that night. They said no, but eventually invited us in to sleep in a shed that housed several of their fourteen children."

Kathleen's group continued their trek for three more days, eating lots of oranges from trees that lined the trail and sleeping in classrooms in small rural communities. These communities fed them, too. In exchange for their generosity, the trainees gave the communities their meager canned goods. The gals, good with maps, handily found their pickup point and slept yet another night on the "nice cement floor" of a schoolhouse and waited for the PC carryall scheduled to arrive the next day. As they waited a full eight hours for a ride back to camp, they taught games to the school children. No time was ever wasted.

For the last phase of our Puerto Rican experience, we were assigned to families for several days to participate in community projects. Kathleen and I lived with a family and participated in a self-help housing program. In the 1960s, Puerto Rico was trying to make the rural parts of the island more appealing to keep people from moving to the big urban centers. To this end, the government built factories and established rural self-help housing projects across the island. I am not sure if they were trying to keep the people "down on the farm" or were taking advantage of the cheap labor. In any event, it appeared that the rural development program was not working; rural people continued to flock to the urban centers of the island or to migrate to America.

Before the end of our training program in Puerto Rico, Peace Corps arranged for us to meet the governor of Puerto Rico, Luis Muñoz Marin. Our best Spanish speaker made an eloquent speech in Spanish about the Peace Corps and our appreciation for Puerto Rico's hospitality. The Governor then responded in perfect English, welcoming us to the island. Kathleen remembers him as the nicest politician she had ever met: a true gentleman and a good person.

Because we had come to enjoy Puerto Rico, Kathleen and I remained there through the Christmas holidays before heading back to California for a brief visit with family and friends. We had survived the first phase of the Peace Corps training experience and were looking forward to our time at the University of Denver, fieldwork in San Antonio, Texas, and eventually, a long flight to Quito, Ecuador.

While one can rail over Peace Corp's primitive and, I might add, expensive attempts to get us ready for our two-year assignment, one has to keep in mind that Peace Corps was still in its infancy and feeling its way through the complexity of preparing primarily young, enthusiastic, inexperienced Americans for the rigors of assignments in distant lands. Training in Puerto Rico allowed us to become more aware of our own potential, overcome obstacles, and gain the self-confidence that would serve us well in the future.

In retrospect, while many of the exercises at Camp Crozier were strengthening us for the rigors of our work in Ecuador,

I think the staff used these exercises as a way to generate data they thought they needed to justify the de-selection of supposedly weaker candidates. If any criticism is merited about our training program, it should be directed at the de-selection process. We lost so many good people because of their inability to kill a chicken, jump off a dam, or comport themselves properly in front of the psychologists, psychiatrists and trainers who, in most instances, had never ventured beyond a U.S. border.

These days, all of Peace Corps' training is conducted in either the region or country of service, and I am sure that Volunteers who have gone through in-country training still have criticisms about their training experience. But I think the introduction of in-country training and the use of "self-selection" rather than de-selection has better served the Corps and disrupted far fewer lives than did the training system back in the 1960s, when everything was new.

Paul Vitale served in Ecuador from 1964-66. He was one of the first Returned Peace Corps Volunteers hired by USAID, joining the Foreign Service in 1966. He served in Quito, Rio de Janiero, Lima, and Washington, D.C. In 2001 he and his wife Kathleen founded Endangered Threads Documentaries, a nonprofit educational organization that documents endangered indigenous art forms.

WYNNE DIMOCK

The Making of a Leftist

Present at the revolution…or perhaps not.

MY FIRST CLUE SHOULD HAVE BEEN THE BUMPS AND RUTS OUR seemingly indifferent driver took a bead on as we were propelled toward our assignment in northeast Brazil. Bouncing along in the back of the Commission jeep, I felt more like a projectile on a launching pad. But, hey, wasn't this just part of the adventure? And who could not want us? We were Americans and were there to help!

The bumps and ruts continued. For over a hundred of us up and down the Sao Francisco River Valley, work with the valley Commission was oddly illusory, or simply non-existent. Our varied assignments to work in villages all along the river were to be modeled after the Tennessee Valley Authority program implemented in Brazil before WWII, when America was eager to convince Brazil to sell rubber to the USA rather than to Germany. A generation or so later, we arrived with motives of our own: idealistic dreams, the lure of adventure and, more importantly to our government, the prevention of another "domino" falling to Communism in South America. Little did we know that Brazil was becoming ripe for the revolution of 1964. Northeastern leftists and many of the Commissioners themselves wanted Americans out of their country.

The Commission hospital I was assigned to had few patients and no real treatments. Seemingly in charge were two ancient Brazilian nuns in full habit, one of whom—Sister Isabel—brandished a red-polished toe protruding through a hole in her sock. Whenever I asked about work, she would drag over a rocking chair and offer me a big grin, saying, "Rest!" This, while the death rate for infant diarrhea in Brazil's northeast was staggering. I was puzzled.

In the meantime, we were being told various stories about delays in equipment and projects not yet ready to go. For many, the frustration became intolerable. Our neighbors began to tell us stories of Volunteers "vagabonding" throughout Brazil, while Peace Corps friends told us of drunken fly-swatting contests throughout the river valley. Countless Volunteers were eventually sent home as too "immature."

Another jolt: after joining one of the "vagabonds" who offered me a free seat on her plane trip to Recife, we encountered anti-Americanism in the coastal city most noted for left-wing activities. Wandering along the beach, we stumbled into an art show where we saw explicitly angry graffiti. One depicted a scowling Uncle Sam with a large syringe drawing blood out of a prostrate Brazil, while dropping a "crumb" in "Brazil's" mouth. Critical as I was of my own country, I was shocked to see the USA so maligned. Yet we had also begun to hear stories of American aid workers living isolated and lavish lifestyles on nearby beaches. Unwittingly, I aligned myself with their distancing and kept a camera between me and all that I saw that day.

What were we to do? There were six of us who had become close during training, and four of us had no substantial work. I had started going out on home visits with local health workers to fine-tune my Portuguese and learn about local health practices. We also began writing letters to our Director. Fortunately, in those early years of the Peace Corps, we were an item of curiosity to others who traveled the world. Hans Mann, a German photographer working for the American Embassy, looked us up and helped champion our concerns. Merle Miller, a flamboyant American writer planning a documentary on agrarian reform in northeast Brazil, insisted, "You must meet Rene Bertholet!" Those words would launch the beginning of the most remarkable experience of my life.

A dinner with Bertholet and Merle Miller was arranged nearby in a surrealistically lush hotel setting. Three of us were mesmerized, listening to stories of the European refugees Bertholet brought with him to Brazil to escape their WWII nightmares. As their own agricultural cooperative thrived, Bertholet and a few of the others became restless. Dreams of agrarian reform brought them to the northeast in l959, where thousands were living illiterate, slave-like existences on large sugar plantations. With financial help from several European countries basking in their rapid recoveries following post-war Marshall Plan funding, Bertholet bought up 100 square miles of land and quickly signed up peasants aching for a better life. With support from the new cooperative, Pindorama, families cleared their land, built their own mud homes, and started growing the "passion fruit," *maracuja*. Selling their harvests to the cooperative juice factory paved the way for them to become fledgling landowners.

While Bertholet's descriptions were compelling, his intensity and French accent sealed our fates. Through his sharp, hawk-like face, he deftly addressed our longings. "I want around me young people who are tired of 'ze' affluent life." We were thrilled, and within weeks were working in

Pindorama, the most successful model of agrarian reform in northeast Brazil, then and now, forty plus years later.

Bob, a civil engineer, would work on roads and bridges. Judy, his wife, was a nutritionist and would begin by educating the Brazilians about the Food for Peace products. Mark, our romantic philosopher/car mechanic, would do the upkeep on all the cooperative vehicles, including our jeep. As an R.N., I was promised an M.D. from somewhere for "professional backup," as the Peace Corps had requested. Once a week was the most that could be arranged.

Three of us were priviliged to actually live with Bertholet long enough to get a feel for some of the "pros" and "cons" of an heroic life. Prone to high drama, middle of the night excursions with his driver into nearby cities to arrange money or political support to stave off one more crisis, he lived a somewhat itinerant lifestyle with no apparent permanent place to live. When we invited him to share a part of the house he had allocated to three of us, he insisted—shyly—on the smallest, most spartan room of all.

Judy and I started work the day after our arrival, with appointments made for us by Bertholet in teachers' homes equipped with schoolrooms, benches, and chalkboards. He introduced us, and we began demonstrating the preparation of the Food for Peace dried milk, and bulgar, a high protein grain. It was not often that an event centered on women. They were curious, friendly, and receptive. Cow's milk was more expensive and less accessible. We would later contend with problems of infant diarrhea as women would dab a wet finger in the dry milk and then in the baby's mouth. And, unknown to us, the lack of vitamins A and D, which were to be added to the milk, was an American oversight creating some infant eye problems we only became aware of later. But that first day was clearly a fun day as well. One woman was shocked to find out we were Americans; another told us our fortunes.

This beginning was timely for the colony. Bertholet had a two-year contract with the USA to receive milk, bulgar, oil, cornmeal, and flour, but the distribution was delayed by a contract dispute. Americans wanted the right to inspect such distributions whenever requested, while Brazilians wanted the USA to "request" such inspections.

Was some sensitivity missing?

Bertholet would have no more of these delays. Waiting for permission to distribute the food, he had cleverly lent flour to Penedo bakers in exchange for a return of flour when the USA contract was finalized. He also had flour made into *bulachas*, a hard biscuit, which would last up to six months. At a time of year when new colonists were arriving, beginning land-clearing and home-building, Bertholet needed to have food for them to buy on credit until the first crops were harvested.

Soon we were overwhelmed with packaging the food for the colonists. Bertholet had written the authorities telling them he had no choice but to distribute the food immediately. His decision was made for him by the reality of people having nothing to eat while available food was spoiling. We opened the warehouse doors to long lines of colonists greeting us with smiles of relief on their faces: a good day!

Word of medical help in Pindorama spread like wildfire. Twenty people showed up for the first of Dr. Jose's weekly visits. It wasn't long before people were knocking on my wooden window. How did they discover which was mine? I was soon working twelve to fourteen hour days and was thrilled, mostly. Each day was fascinating; fortunately, Judy, Bob, and Mark were always available when I needed some extra hands, or courage!

I think back on all my "patients" with nostalgia and awe. What grueling lives they lived, and yet, many played musical instruments and kept songbirds in homemade birdcages, simply for their enjoyment. Stories of their lives and our encounters with their health issues cannot be trivialized with generalizations about issues related to childbirth, the "evil eye," the value of "fatalism" for them, or their sheer resilience. It is primarily their conditions of being "undermined" that still concern me.

So, what has been the impact of the Peace Corps on my life? Inestimable. Political activism became my avocation. It could also be said that I was "radicalized," which to me merely means supportive of basic change with more equity for the "have nots" in the world. Following my arrival back home, radical change briefly became the norm with the anti-war and civil rights movements of the late sixties and seventies. In the spirit of the times, many Volunteers began examining their Peace Corps experiences and studying the foreign policy practices of our government. The Committee of Returned Volunteers (as opposed to the official Returned Peace Corps Volunteers) began publishing articles in 1970 about American interventionism throughout the world, questioning the Peace Corps itself as a potential tool of "cultural imperialism."

In *Brasil*, an eighty-four page booklet edited in 1970 by the CRV and the Chicago Area Group on Latin America, ex-Volunteers stated, "Many went overseas with a belief that they had something to offer to the struggle of people around the world to make a better society for themselves...instead, they learned that the USA government time and again aligned with the forces of repression and reaction, and that, as Americans they could not help in other peoples' battles when they had not yet won their own."

A prescient comment was made in a 1979 *Ramparts* magazine when a Brazilian activist was asked what we in the United States could do to help those struggling against the Brazilian dictatorship. "Expose what they are doing. Expose and denounce the participation of the United States in the repression in Brazil, in training our torturers." And finally, "We think that the main contradiction in the world today is not between capitalism and socialism, but between the giant monopolies and the people they exploit."

Now, decades later, have the proverbial chickens come home to roost? What has been the impact upon the United States of fifty years of the Peace Corps with almost two hundred thousand Volunteers in over one hundred and forty countries?

That question has yet to be answered. But we do know that our country now has between eight and nine hundred military bases throughout the world. We have a military budget two and a half times that of the rest of the world combined! As Martin Luther King Jr. courageously stated before his assassination, "A country that continues year after year to spend more money on military defense than on programs of social uplift is approaching spiritual doom."

Wynne Dimock served in Brazil from 1964-66 and now lives in Colorado, where she continues her work as a political and community activist, even as she considers switching her focus to fulfill a lifelong dream of playing boogie-woogie on the piano.

W. W. WALES

Pablo's Christmas

There are no time limits on helping people,
as this determined Volunteer demonstrates.

AS A PEACE CORPS VOLUNTEER, STARTING IN 1961, I SERVED AT
the Escuela Agricola Americana in Valle de Zamarano,
Honduras. I worked in the farm equipment department of
the school, instructing students from fourteen different Latin
American countries. My service ended on November 23, l963,
the day after President Kennedy was assassinated.

One Christmas Eve in 1962, we were at the local *bario* having a beer, and I had a young boy Pablo, maybe three or four
years old sitting on my lap. I asked what Santa was going to
bring him, and he replied, "Santa never comes here."

I replied, "When Willie gets back to the United States, I'll
make sure Santa comes to see you."

"O.K.," he said, satisfied for the moment.

Back home in the fall of 1967, having remembered my
promise to Pablo, I talked to the manager of the local radio
station, WIKB, in Iron River, Michigan, my hometown. They
agreed to help in any way possible. I also got in contact with
the local VFW Post 3134. With the fine cooperation of these

two groups, a Christmas donation was set up. The radio station spent much time explaining the program and asking for donations.

The station announced that donations could be dropped off at my place of business, or two VFW posts in Iron River and Crystal Falls. The response was overwhelming; in three weeks we had collected six tons of toys and clothes. Many people went out and bought new gifts, wrapped them, and donated. It seemed like everyone, including kids, became conscious of the drive. One woman called the radio station and told them about her son.

He had gone out trick-or-treating; when he came home, she asked what he was going to do with all the candy. He replied, "I could bring it down to Willie at the Farmers Mart, and he could send it to the kids in Honduras." This gift opened up a new part of the drive, with many bags of candy being donated for "Willie's Kids."

The next hurdle was how to get the items to Honduras. I heard of a truck driving school in Lansing, Michigan, that trained semi-drivers, and their last assignment was to take a cross-country tour. I contacted them, and they agreed to pick up the items; however, there would be a fee for transport from Iron River to Lansing.

I had recently gotten a letter indicating interest in helping with the cause from a Mr. Charles Stillman, Chairman, finance committee, Time-Life, Inc., who was a director at the driving school. He informed me that he and a number of staff at the magazine wanted to help in any way they could. He then forwarded a check for $50 to help with the transport expenses. The school then picked up the items and drove them to the Port of New Orleans.

Another director of the school, Mr. George Gardner, Jr., of United Fruit Co. was also contacted, and he graciously agreed that when the goods got to New Orleans, a United Fruit ship would make arrangements for getting the gifts from New Orleans to Puerto Cortez, Honduras. Escuela Agricola Americana then picked up the gifts from the port and transported them to the school.

They got there in time for Christmas. Literally hundreds of people showed up for Christmas. Sr. Armado Pelin, photographer at the school, took many photos of people getting gifts. He sent me photos of the gifts being distributed. I started receiving phone calls from major news media questioning me about the drive. Clippings arrived from all over the world from interested readers. For its role in the drive, WIKB was awarded the Ernie Pyle Award in the state of Michigan. The award is given to the news media that best serves in Community Service. The most meaningful was an editorial reading: "The world needs more people like Willie Wales, who are willing to spare a moment for their fellow man, it is a pleasanter place because he took time to help make it so"

But just as meaningful was the letter that came from Honduras.

"*Feliz Navidad*," they said. "Merry Christmas."

W.W. Wales graduated from Michigan State University, studying farm equipment and sales. He spent two years in Honduras (1961-63) as a farm equipment Volunteer. He is now retired and spends his winters in Florida. His granddaughter and her future husband have both applied to the Peace Corps.

MARIA ALTOBELLI

Some Never Forget

*Returning to Bolivia, a non-Peace Corps spouse finally
gets to see what all the fuss was about when her
husband served in the time of Che.*

THE BUS LURCHED TO A STOP, AND I FELT A JAB IN MY RIBS. "HEY,
Ducks, we're here."

My husband was already halfway up the aisle of the bus as I
blinked awake and peered at the dark, nebulous shapes outside
the window. I shrugged. *So this is what it looks like.* I had heard
about the town of Ascensión de Guarayos since Paul first went
for what proved to be a three-year stint in the Peace Corps in
1966, yet it wasn't until 2004 that we decided to visit Bolivia
together. The five-hour bus ride from Santa Cruz had been a
spur-of-the-moment decision.

Once the bus pulled away, I spotted some bushes across
the road. "My bladder's ready to burst. Wait right here. It will
only take a sec."

Paul grabbed my blouse and jerked me back. "No way.
You're not peeing on my soccer field." He stopped and stared
at the field across from us. "I can't believe it's still there."

Oh, Lord. The soccer field had been Paul's first project after
waiting six months to get fluent in Spanish and learn how the

town operated. This was hallowed ground, and I had been ready to pee on it. "O.K. but that hotel better be open or I'll be peeing right in the middle of the plaza."

"Trust me. Tourism isn't a big thing in Ascención de Guarayos. Someone will be waiting for us. It's not that far away."

The sleepy caretaker opened the door and handed us the key. I bolted to the room and made a bee-line for the bathroom. Once the wave of relief dissipated, I looked up at the shower head. "Hey, wait a minute. I wanted to take one of those electrical spark showers you always talked about taking in La Paz. You know, the ones where you played Russian roulette with electrocution every time you took a shower. No fair."

Paul followed my gaze. "Well, no one ever actually got electrocuted that I know of, but they were tricky. This is better. Trust me."

The next morning, we sat on the curb in front of the hotel while a contingent of little boys congregated around us. We made chit-chat until Paul asked, "You guys go to school?"

They boys nodded almost in unison and stood up a little. "We go to the Pablo Kundzins School."

"What?" Paul stared at the group. "I'm Pablo Kundzins."

Eyes bulged and mouths opened. The tallest boy swallowed. "*¿De veras?*"

"Really. I'm Pablo Kundzins."

With that, each of the boys ran off in a different direction.

I nudged Paul. "Looks like you might as well be Superman, Batman, and Kalimán, El Hombre Increíble all rolled into one." I watched as the last boy rounded a corner. "Get ready. The word is out."

"*¡Cállate!* Put a lid on it."

I jumped up and pulled Paul to his feet. "C'mon. I want to see that school. Let's go for a walk."

Sure enough, a couple blocks from the plaza, we saw it—the *Escuela Pablo Cuncins*. Paul's Latvian name had been impossible for the Guaraní-speaking population, but this looked close enough to me. "Hey, you're a legend in your own time."

"Enough. Just drop it."

I turned to poke and tease Paul again and caught a fleeting glimpse of a smile so kept my mouth shut.

By the time we got back to the hotel, a small crowd had gathered in the lobby. In the conversation that ensued, we found out that some years back, the government issued an edict that all numbered schools in Bolivia be given a name. One group in town wanted the school named for a popular music instructor from the Guaraní. Another group supported a local teacher who worked his way up the ranks and became a well-loved politician. Since neither group was willing to budge an inch, they ended the dispute by naming the school for the Peace Corps volunteer who had helped raise the money for the school and then worked alongside the parents on the construction.

A man draped his arm over Paul's shoulders. "We figured it was a safe bet. Hell, we thought you had died in Vietnam."

Back in our room, I flopped on the bed. "Hey, Viejo, pretty good for a Conscientious Objector—dying like that in Vietnam. Bet your draft board would have loved to hear about that."

"All my draft board wanted to do was put me in jail." He paused. "Bet they would have settled for dead though." Paul sat in the room's one chair. "You know, it's strange what happens when you bring a road into town. This place used to be so isolated. I got in and out on horseback or hitched a ride on a supply plane. I'm not so sure all the changes are good."

I slipped off my shoes. "What do you mean?"

"When I was here, the Guaraní leaders walked from Mass across the plaza to the *cabildo*, that big town hall-type building across from the church. Each of the leaders had a silver-topped staff, and everyone crowded into the *cabildo* after them. There the townsfolk decided what should be done in the community during the week. It was wild—all these different groups trying to convince the elders that their plan was best. Once all said leaders agreed and yelled out a word I forget, everyone pitched in and did the work, whether it was their project or not."

"Well, how do you know they aren't doing that now?"

"Today's Sunday, right? Did you see any procession? While we talked with those kids this morning, I watched people come out of church. They stood around in little groups or wandered off. Naw, I'd say the *cabildo* system is dead." Paul shook his head. "Win some and lose some. We better get some rest. It's going to be hard fitting all the invites we just got into the time we have left."

I rolled over to make room for Paul on the bed. "I take it we won't be going back to Santa Cruz later this afternoon then?"

Days of get-togethers, meals, conversations and parties later, we packed before dawn and snuck off for the bus station in the dark. Paul checked the station clock and looked down the road. "This is the only way we're going to do it. We'll never make our plane if we meet any more people."

As we sat in the cramped seats of the Santa Cruz bus, a short, stooped man limped down the aisle and stopped in front of Paul.

"Do you remember me?" he asked.

We had been awake for almost our entire stay in Ascención and our eyes could barely focus. Paul looked at the hunched man in rumpled clothes in front of us. "I'm sorry. I don't. Help me out."

"Maybe you would remember my wife, the one who had so much trouble with her pregnancy."

Paul reached for the man's hand. "Manuel Ortumpi! Yes, yes. I remember."

Good Lord. Even I remembered. I had heard the story of his wife enough times. She was pregnant with her first child. The baby refused to be born, and nothing could be done for her in the town's meager facilities. The only way to Santa Cruz was in a plane owned by the Evangelical minister who wanted the equivalent of $250 before he would even think about revving the engine.

Two hundred and fifty dollars represented an impossible sum. In those days, most families lived on $75 a *year*. The minister turned a deaf ear on the husband's pleas and promises of future payment, so Paul and Manuel went door-to-door collecting a few bolivianos from each household. The priest emptied the poor boxes in church and dug into his own pockets. Paul added the rest of his month's Peace Corps pay. They were still over a hundred dollars short.

Paul went to find Yeguaroba, a young man who was one of the respected members of the community. Paul explained what had happened. "Maybe you could come along with us and act official."

Yeguaroba nodded. "Let me get my gun. You're carrying quite a bit of money. We need to protect it."

When Paul, the frantic husband, and Yeguaroba got to the minister's house, Paul dumped the pile of rumpled bolivianos on the desk. "This should cover it."

The minister started to count through the pile.

Yeguaroba fingered the trigger of his ancient carbine and looked official. Even menacing. "We have enough." He moved the gun upward. "I think you should start the plane."

The baby died while still inside the young mother, but the Santa Cruz doctors saved her life. However, when Paul left Ascención de Guarayos, she was still in delicate health.

"I just wanted you to know," Manuel Ortumpi said. "My wife recovered. We have three grown sons."

The two held onto each other's hands a long moment. "Thank you," Manuel said simply. With a last handshake, he walked off the bus and was lost in the crowd pushing to get on.

The motor started up. After a couple blocks Paul let out a deep breath and eased back into his seat. I looked out the window. "This doesn't look like the way out of town. Wait a minute. Oh, my God. Hope you're ready for this."

Paul opened his eyes as the bus stopped. Hours before school started, dozens and dozens of students stood in front of a school in their uniforms. The ones in front held a banner that read "Escuela Pablo Cuncins."

"You better get out. Don't think the bus driver plans to move until you do something."

Paul pulled himself up with a sigh. Passengers behind the driver peered out the window. Students bounced about from one foot to the next as Paul walked over to the group. He embraced the teachers and clapped his hands, looking at each of the students. With a few shouts of *¡Olé!* and *muchas gracias*, he bowed and then raised his arms, giving the V sign to everyone in the group before re-boarding the bus. I listened to the sound of *adiós* as the town faded from view and heard the voices in my mind for miles.

*Paul Kundzins served in the Peace Corps in Bolivia for three years from 1966-1969 and then went on to a life of travel and teaching. He and his wife Maria Altobelli (*Female Nomad and Friends: Tales of Breaking Free and Breaking Bread Around the World*) now live in Pátzcuaro, Mexico. In 2010, they attended the latest reunion with members of Peace Corps Bolivia in the time of Che.*

Homeland Buffet

*Wide-eyed and naïve all over again, an RPCV comes
home to a land no longer entirely familiar.*

He broke down in front of a Brazilian barbeque restaurant in the Century City Shopping Center. The kind of
place where you pay based on how much your food weighs.
Apparently this had become a popular method of consumption.
Why not just weigh the patrons before and after eating and really
put it all out there on the table? It was his first day back in the
United States after twenty-eight months. One for every year of
his life. It hit him early with the force of a freight train—the
mass of the masses times the acceleration of the pace of life. He'd
arrived that morning, a three-hour flight from Guadalajara to
Los Angeles—two names that might as well appear within the
same borders. Did, at one time, long ago. The River That Runs
Between Rocks and the City of Angels. Now, worlds apart. Less
than 1,500 miles, but traversing distances within himself that he
didn't even know existed until that very moment.

His last act in Latin America had been to bribe a government
official. He and his travel companion had failed to visit a participating financial institution and pay the required Immigration

Entrance Fee before attempting to exit Mexico. Unfortunately, the nearest banks wouldn't be open until after their flights had departed. Fortunately, a kind immigration officer was more than willing to waive the fee in return for a small donation; and he did it with a smile and a geniality that made the process seem like the most natural, wholesome transaction ever performed on God's Green Earth. Even on this, the last day of his journey, Latin America had lessons to teach and counsel to give. It had its own way of saying goodbye, with the nod of an old friend and the wink of a soothsayer. "The Best Moments Are Yet to Come," was the optimistic reassurance given by a tequila advertisement in a duty-free shop window. "*Vivir Es Increíble*," said an insurance company from the side of a gateway across the tarmac. Neither of them seemed like particularly trustworthy experts on the subject of life and happiness, but he accepted their parting thoughts with gratitude.

It had been a sunny morning in Mexico—with the urban haze hanging low over the dusty, brown mountainscape—but Southern California welcomed him with cold, wet dreariness, arms firmly crossed in front of her chest. He strained for a view of his long-lost homeland, staring intently out the plane window, but his gaze was greeted with nothing but an impenetrable murkiness. The land refused to reveal itself. The jilted lover would not be so easily coaxed from her covers. They finally broke through the cloud soup as they made their final approach, low over the Pacific Ocean. The somber coastline, skyscrapers in the distance, boats rocking in the whitecaps. It felt as though the psychic energy from his combined excitement and anxiety would surely send the plane plummeting into the dark waves below. But somehow they remained aloft, the runway was reached and he found himself safely on the ground. The much-anticipated and dreaded re-entry; he hoped that all of his forms were in place. Back in the United States.

The plane released them into a dilapidated, second-class terminal, far from the shiny hustle and bustle of LAX's celebrity traffic. It had all the charm of a drafty industrial warehouse, seemingly saying, "Welcome to America! You are all suspect! Please prepare to be grilled and cavity searched!" All exposed air ducts and piping with nowhere to hide. As he approached the stern, mustachioed Homeland Security agents and customs officials, he knew exactly how the pipes felt. Was a thick, bushy mustache a required piece of the security uniform or what? Like a cobra's hood that bluntly states, "Don't fuck with me." Even after two years in Latin America with some of the most mustache-loving people he had ever met, it struck him as absurd. Or was it simply mustache envy—the disappointing fact that his particular combination of Asian and Caucasian genes did not equal much in the finicky arithmetic of facial hair? His turn finally came, and he was whisked through without any trouble or fanfare. Where are you coming from? Guadalajara, Mexico. How long were you gone? Two years. What were you doing down there? I was a Peace Corps Volunteer in Nicaragua. Welcome home, said in a flat, unwelcoming tone. Thanks.

The physical baggage he claimed at the carousel, but the rest of it he tucked below a downward gaze and held close to his chest. Emerging from the secured zone, he hoped to see a familiar person anxiously awaiting him amidst the sea of strangers and strangeness. He needed the face of a friend. Someone was supposed to pick him up but, disappointingly, hadn't arrived yet. There were many smiles, but none greeted him. Welcomed home with a classic, modern-day dilemma in a world of convenience: How to get in touch with someone with no cell phone and no cash? He was forced to attempt to make contact the confusing, inefficient and expensive way—via public phone. He shuddered at the thought, as the descriptive "public" in the American lexicon usually referred to all things crappy. Certainly that fact hadn't changed in a two-year absence. Besides, public telephones always seemed to be the most complicated machines in every country, undoubtedly kept that way by the powerful cell phone lobbies. Still, short of stealing someone else's phone—an option he contemplated only briefly—he didn't have much choice.

Stepping over to the bank of phones cautiously, his only seventy-five cents in hand, he was met with nothing but frustration. His friend was an L.A. transplant who still had an out-of-town phone, and an irritating, robotic message was quick to inform him that long-distance calls cost an entire dollar. Fuck. He was a quarter short, and the only other cash he had was a handful of Mexican pesos that he'd decided not to convert in Guadalajara. Now he needed to unlock even the slightest value from those foreign bills.

He optimistically approached the currency exchange window, foolishly believing that he should be able to get at least twenty-five cents for the three dollars worth of pesos in his wallet. Another wide-eyed, naïve newcomer.

"How much money would you like to convert?" asked the young, female attendant.

"Umm, twenty Mexican pesos?" he attempted.

But the transaction fee for such a small amount was too much, and it couldn't be done. This is what the girl explained to him as her male partner gave him a dismaying look of pity-tinged apathy usually reserved for homeless beggars or grotesquely disfigured people. "How about...forty pesos?" was his pathetic attempt to sweeten the deal, but this, too, was rejected. He tried to explain that he just needed a quarter to make a phone call, but they looked as if they'd heard that line a thousand times before. He was just their latest encounter with foreign desperation. *Fuck this country!* he swore to his inner self.

Down but not out, he returned to the pay phones, determined to unlock their mysteries and escape this hell. Eventually he managed to purchase a calling card with one of his credit cards. He spent another eternity studying the microscopic instructions of both the card and the phone, during which time his public awkwardness and inability actually prompted an airport attendant to ask him if he needed any help. She didn't specify the exact kind of help that she had in mind, but her look, like those of the exchange shylocks, said it all. Finally, he managed to get a call through. The amount of time that this whole process took firmly categorized him as either a complete foreigner or severely mentally handicapped. He felt like solid amounts of both. Not an hour back on American soil, and already he was totally overwhelmed and incapable of keeping up. His friend was on the freeway and casually asked him to call back in a few minutes, unaware of the nearly impossible feat being requested. He courageously agreed and hung up with a sigh.

Moments after the second call, he found himself in a Cartier-edition Lincoln Town Car belonging to his friend's grandmother. If his actions and demeanor hadn't proven beyond the shadow of a doubt that he didn't fit in, the sight of the two of them in this car certainly sealed the deal for any onlookers. The sense of relief at the sight of an old friend flooded him with joyous feelings of the good old days. Still, he couldn't escape the troubling sensations encountered in the airport. Home safe, but the whole sound part yet to be determined. Barely skirting the atmosphere and already his heat shield was showing signs of structural instability. An inauspicious new start for an already shaky country-citizen relationship.

Every bit of the experience was so very surreal, just like the anticipatory imaginings of countless lazy, Nicaraguan afternoons. Only this was no creative REM projection, no artist's conceptualization. The Real Deal, despite its sense of unreality. It was a day of firsts, celebrated as if he were a newborn. His first Eggs Benedict back in the United States. His first traffic jam. His first sight of a Nintendo Wii. His first pint of microbrew. His first glimpse of a world he had left behind that had not stood still in his absence.

For the first time in two years, it seemed as though it was everyone else who had changed and he who had remained the same. He felt like a space traveler, returning home after a journey spent at light's speed to find that all his friends were successful young professionals. And married. And having children. While he was away, nothing had seemed more important than his life and work in Nicaragua. He was the one growing exponentially while everyone back home was packaged away in cryogenic stasis, right? He hadn't even come back to visit, so sure of his own odyssey. But now, with those first tentative steps out of his capsule, he sensed the tables of significance and importance turning, leaving him alone on the wrong side.

That afternoon reminded him of a gift he had received for his first Christmas away from home. It was a framed photograph of his father, his mother and his three siblings, the one that they sent out to everyone in their official holiday cards. A picture of a beautiful, happy family. His family. But he wasn't in the picture, because it had been taken after his departure. And seeing his friends again, seeing his country again, felt just like looking at that picture. It felt like staring at a world that had moved on after his death, or a world in which he had never existed at all. Feelings of mortality, on top of everything else. Fucking-A.

And then there were all of the little things that he had missed. So seemingly insignificant, and yet their cumulative power formed a loop that he had been completely left out of. One rage-of-the-moment after another in a fad-frantic popular culture that waited for no man. No place on Earth could highlight this better than L.A. What the fuck was a Pinkberry? Or a Red Mango? Or a Beard Papa? And was there seriously a restaurant called Pink Taco? When had it become fashionable to christen every new establishment with a euphemism for female genitalia? Where do you want to eat tonight, Honey? There's the Purple Clam? Or we could try that new Vietnamese place, the Vagina Hut? The painfully outdated issues of *People* magazine that had littered their Volunteer office in Estelí did not prepare him for any of this.

Everything had to be explained to him and he had a million questions. What is this "Twilight" you speak of? O.K., now why is that so popular? What's a "Rock Sugar?" Why the hell would anyone want to walk around with a Bluetooth headset on all day long?

What do they think this is, the future? Why don't they all just shave their heads while they're at it and really embrace the whole Lobot look? He was like Johnny Five, attempting to soak up all that was Americana in a single read. At this rate, a short circuit was inevitable.

Despite the upheaval in his head, his stomach seemed to be adjusting quite well to the American smorgasbord. There was so much he had missed, so many culinary genres that had been impossible to find in Central America. In the spirit of the day, his friends decided to introduce him to the latest craze in Southern California fine dining: a pay-by-weight Brazilian *churrascaria* located in a nearby shopping center. Just pile on as much as you want, weigh the plate and enjoy, was how they described it. His own mental plate already filled to overflowing, just the thought of this intriguingly fantastical wonderland was the slice of *picanha* that broke the scale. The day's experiences amounted to a gargantuan, Kobayashi-sized meal, and he couldn't possibly digest it all. Apparently one of his companions had even figured out a way to beat the restaurant's system. The plan required a two-diner team and precisely coordinated meat-to-vegetable weight ratios; and though he normally would have relished such a discovery, his eyes simply glazed over with incomprehension.

So they took him to the mall for dinner. An experience not unlike teaching a child to swim by throwing it into a pool. Especially if the pool was full of electric eels…and the child was intoxicated. A questionable method of instruction, but leading to some priceless facial expressions! The lesson began the moment they entered the cavernous parking complex. In a stroke of genius straight out of the most mundane of science fiction novels, every parking space was marked with a colored light designating it as either empty or occupied. No one had informed him of this particular technological breakthrough. So simple, and yet it hit him like a hoverboard. If just the parking garage was enough to blow him away, he feared that he was in way over his head.

The group surfaced in the cosmetics department of Bloomingdales. The parking lot was intense, but this was beyond overpowering. A sterile beauty lab that assaulted all of his senses. It was a shot of Botox to the brain, a room that did not speak in whispers. Every counter had its own shrill scream. You are not attractive enough! You are not young enough! You are not rich enough! You smell like you've been bathing in a river for the past two years! It was the voice of L.A. for him, but way too concentrated. He exited as quickly as possible, practically running for the doors that led to the well-lit outer walkway.

They walked a bit further, chuckling as they passed a Pink Taco, and then it appeared. All of a sudden he was there. Standing before the fabled Brazilian restaurant—his long-lost friends at his side, the materialistic futurescape surrounding them, a building-sized picture of Paul Blart the Mall Cop looking on—it all hit him at once. He had arrived on a flight half a day earlier, but this was the moment when he truly came home. Maybe if the fanciful eatery hadn't actually existed, he would have been able to discount everything—all the newness, all the uncertainty. But it was there, all of it right there, writ large in florescence and staring him directly in the face. Tears welled up in his eyes and he let them come. Tears for the unfamiliarity of all that had been familiar. Tears for what was and what could have been. Tears for an uncertain present and an even more uncertain future. It wasn't the plethora of options that did it. It wasn't the inherent excess or the oblivious affluence. It was that all of it—the excess, the options, the affluence—was him. It was the realization that, for all his air of internationalism and his trash-talking, long-standing status as a disparaging, self-hating American, this was his country and this was his culture. This was his home, and, for all its faults, he had missed it. That's what caught him by surprise as expectant diners placed their meals on the scale beyond the full-length windows.

The tears were short-lived, but that moment would never truly cease to be. He left the establishment an hour older and 2.37 pounds heavier, but in many ways he would always be that young man standing teary-eyed in a mall in front of an ethnic chain restaurant. A bright and shiny world of possibilities before him, weighing it all like so many assorted meats and vegetables.

Brandon Louie was an agriculture Volunteer in rural Nicaragua from 2006 to 2008. His post-service hobbies include couch surfing, mooching, appreciating refrigeration, taking hot showers, not taking things for granted, and trying to figure out what the hell he is going to do with his life. His favorite Spanish word is cabuya, *especially when used like* "booyakasha."

KATHERINE JAMIESON

✳

Too Much of One Thing Ain't Good for Nothing

Simplicity may indeed be a gift, but in the United States it can be difficult to find, at least for this Volunteer returning from Guyana.

TRAVELING IN THE BACK OF A PICK-UP TRUCK IN THE REMOTE interior of Guyana, South America, I stopped in a small Amerindian town near the border of Brazil. The savannah stretched before me, dotted with straw huts and bony cows, the Kanuku mountains rising up in massive peaks at the edge of the horizon. Villagers offered cups of *piwari,* an alcoholic drink made from fermented cassava, but I drank little, mindful of the sun beating down and the half empty canteen swinging from my backpack.

As we were pulling away, I saw a young girl running toward the truck. Her thin, tan legs kicked up a cloud of red dust as she flew by the town's one church, its whitewashed cross glowing against the clear blue sky. Breathless, she reached the cab of the truck, and the driver slowed, rolled down his window. *Sir, you could take this to Aloma?* she asked, between gasps. *In Lethem?* Her outstretched palm held a folded piece of white paper, already tinged pink from her the sweat of her hand. *Yes, girl,* he said smiling, *she'll have it by nighttime.* She stood back as we pulled off, jouncing down the one-lane, unpaved highway for the next five-hour stretch of our journey.

The image of this girl returns to me now, more than ten years later, and I see her squinting against the harsh light, waving and waving. In the driver's hand, the faint outline of her childish handwriting is visible through the thin paper. I marvel at her faith in a stranger to deliver her message; then Aloma, I must imagine, pressing another precious note into another driver's palm. A circle of carefully inscribed words journeying back and forth, from hand to hand, across a silent plain.

Today, as I read through hundreds of e-mails, switch to call-waiting on my cell phone while elbowing my way through crowded streets, I feel lonely. I want the well-chosen words of a friend written on paper instead. I want the delight of a letter delivered without postman or stamp or electronic chime. I want the intimacy, the simplicity of those days; the time in my life that did not seem bracketed by demands, ruled by an unforgiving clock, cluttered with meaningless messages.

For two years, I had this simplicity. I had been warned of the poverty in Guyana, and I braced myself to live without air conditioning and hot water, with uncertain electricity and swarming mosquitoes. It was amplified when many of my possessions—flashlights, water purifiers, shoes—succumbed to the tropical rust and mold. I had no car or bicycle and depended on the speeding minibuses for transportation. A piece of foam on a wooden frame served as my mattress, a pipe jutting from a dank cement cell, my shower.

But these privations were minor compared to those of the families living in makeshift shacks in the squatter areas, crowding two or three in a bed. Their real destitution shamed me. The teenage girls at the vocational school where I taught barely had money for uniforms, yet they managed to keep them bleached and ironed every day. Often one of them would come running after me yelling, *Miss! Miss! You forgot, Miss!* waving my ballpoint pen in the air. What I lost, they protected. What I assumed would always be available to me, they never took for granted.

For two years I studied under the tutelage of a non-throw away economy. A place where my host mother dug my empty toothpaste tube out of the trash, cleaned and transformed it into a kitchen appliance. A place where people did wash by hand, tubs and tubs of sheets and towels, shirts and pants, all soaked, scrubbed, and hung to dry on a line under the sun. A country where everyone knows how to clear a drain with a straightened wire hanger, and any trash is picked through over and over again for scrap metal, roofing, the missing piece needed to resurrect a radio or car.

What I had not realized is what a relief simplicity can be. Yes, life in Guyana was harder sometimes, less convenient, and much slower. I was forced to be patient. The birthday checks my mother sent took three months to clear in the bank, which at the time seemed completely reasonable. I began to enjoy the freedom of my limited and unchanging wardrobe (style was largely unaffordable in Guyana and people washed so carefully they were able to wear clothes from the 1970s). I had no computer, no newspaper subscription, only the books I had lugged with me. And my salary, though well below the U.S. poverty line, was more than enough for food and housing and entertainment.

The gift of Guyana was the gift of limited options. One movie playing in town? Well, that was the one that you saw. One dinner plate at the rum shop on the corner? Well, that was what you had to eat that night. One beer, one kind of cheese, no apples, two radio stations. Before Guyana I had always imagined that more choices were better. I had never expected to find relief in what I couldn't have.

My return to the States was rocky. Plastic metro cards strewn about the New York City subway platform seemed a wild extravagance. Why couldn't they be re-used; where would all this excess go? I remembered the story of a Guyanese friend's uncle who, when he first moved to the U.S., had supported himself by pulling electrical equipment off the curbside, refurbishing and reselling it. For years I could not stop myself from picking through similar piles for perfectly good books and clothes that would have been preserved for decades in Guyana. The wise words of Guyanese women echoed back to me, *Too much of one thing ain't good for nothing!* In my home country, there seemed to be vastly too much of everything.

I tolerated the windowless cubicles and the high cost of living and the people who sold me groceries without looking at my face because I thought that this was the cost of life in the States. But the thrills I thought awaited me never appeared. I had access to everything I had been "missing" for two years, but I now found that I did not need or even enjoy much of it. Material wealth was available to me again because of my social class and nationality and race, but it could not satisfy the yearning I felt for the quiet years I had spent in the developing world. Yet it was impossible to explain this to anyone; my nostalgia was illogical in a country where less is rarely good, never better.

My life became a desperate search for the elusive "simple." It was no longer just a matter of walking down the dirt road to the open-air market, answering the cries of the countrywomen, *What ya shopping sistah?* and accepting a ripe mango from the same sinewy hand that had picked it that very morning. I became a follower of "Voluntary Simplicity," the lifestyle component of the environmental movement. But I soon realized that the philosophy was missing the point of the real simplicity I had seen in Guyana. I was paring down to feel better about myself, to reject the consumerist society, but it was not just about material things. What I craved was simplicity of mind, to regain the stillness and silence of those long, hot Guyana days, days where nothing was needed and nothing was extra.

Ultimately, the search for simplicity led me back to myself. In desperation, I went to a meditation center thinking I might find an escape there. In the hours of silence I tried to quiet my thoughts, and Guyana returned to me. But what I realized was that it was not so much the country itself I missed, but the kind of mind this landscape had allowed me to develop. For the two years I lived in Guyana, I had had the blessing of few possessions and distractions, and so I dwelled in the natural beauty, dwelled in my friendships, dwelled in my life. It was this dwelling that I was so painfully missing when I came home. Meditation allowed me a return to the mind of those days, showed me how to recreate some of that simplicity in the midst of my now busy life.

Guyana haunts me still. The girl on the road, her little note in the driver's hand, haunts me. But my meditation practice has shown me that simplicity is always available, though now I must consciously choose it where once it was granted to me by circumstance. Each morning I light a candle, I burn incense, I lower my eyes. In my mind, I wait for the girl's note to be delivered, I wait to be able to grasp its meaning. *Stop waiting*, her words whisper from the page, *you choose your life*.

Katherine Jamieson was an Urban Youth Development Volunteer in Guyana from 1996-98. She is a poet and non-fiction writer who has been widely published. She currently lives in Brooklyn, New York, and works as a holistic health counselor and yoga instructor.

PAT ALTER

*

A Life

*There is more—and less—to a Peace Corps
experience than meets the eye.*

I WAS IN HIGH SCHOOL WHEN I FIRST HEARD ABOUT PRESIDENT
Kennedy's Peace Corps. The idea of living abroad and help-
ing people appealed to me. In my final year of college, I met a
graduate student who had served in the Peace Corps in India.
With his encouragement, I applied, requesting to be sent to
India to work in family planning. Peace Corps offered me
Paraguay working in health education. No matter. I took it.
The graduate student wished me well, gifted me a tape player
along with tapes of music we both liked and promised to write.

My group trained for a summer in Escondido, California,
with a couple of Spanish immersion trips into Baja, and then
flew into Asuncion and onward to our sites. Mine was Pilar,
a town of 12,000, located on the Paraguay river, a long day's
bus ride from the capital, Asuncion or, way more exciting, an
hour's flight by DC-3, sharing the space with smuggled cigarettes and landing on a grass runway.

I was assigned to the Regional Health Center and lived
on my own in a tiny rented house. For my second year, I

was moved to a much smaller health center, in the town of Itacurubí de la Cordillera, 1,900 inhabitants, located along Paraguay's main road to its border with Brazil and a mere two-hour bus ride to Asuncion. I lived that year as a paid guest in the home of a widow and her cousin. I enjoyed my work in both towns, adapted to life without running water in both and without electricity in one, made Paraguayan friends and traveled every chance I got. On one trip up north, far off any paved road, we stopped in a small general store and were surprised to see an American Mennonite woman in nineteenth-century dress standing behind the counter, selling hardware and home-baked cookies.

The graduate student made good on his promise to write and even flew down to visit me midway through my assignment. When I returned to the U.S., I threw my readjustment allowance into the travel kitty and joined him on a six-month trip overland from Europe to India, a nine-month Hindi language program and a three-month trip back home through Asia. We've been together ever since, through thirty-one years of foreign service postings. It all began with Peace Corps.

Pat Alter served as a Public Health Volunteer in Paraguay from 1970-72. Following her service in Peace Corps, she continued her travels to Europe, Asia, and Latin America both as a private tourist and as a State Department spouse. She currently works as a librarian at Arlington Public Library. She is co-editor of this volume.

PATRICIA EDMISTEN

Nothing Is Ever
the Same Again

After two years in Peru, the entire world looked forever different.

Palm Beach, Florida

Irritation welled on Worth Avenue.
Valentino, Hermes, Sterns, Teller.
Heavily made-up Palm Beach women,
their planned, casual elegance,
engaged the sharps and flats of my mind.
Was it aggression or insecurity?

Attracted and repelled.
How would I look in that fuchsia and emerald
gown?
In a mansion with Atlantic view?
In a yacht so fine I could sail to Tierra del Fuego?
But what of infant mortality and human rights
abuses?

Perhaps their wealth is quietly effective,
like irrigation projects in Ethiopia:
trickle-down economics for the poor.

Hypocrite!
I lunch at L'Europe: choice chicken chunks,
garnished with walnuts and papaya.
Why not be a guiltless capitalist,
gourmet, and clothes horse?
Wear my wealth like the poor wear their
destitution:
openly.

—Palm Beach, Florida, Winter 1989

Burqa on the Plane

Does it make him feel good
that no other man has seen your delicate white wrists
covered with gloves,
the fine lines on your forehead
concealed by black muslin,
the alabaster ankles
circled by cubits of your fortress gown?

I worry this Thanksgiving eve,
while you are in the restroom:
Do you wear explosives under all that yardage?
Will the smoke alarm detect your cargo
before we become meteorites
destined forever to circumnavigate the Earth?

How do you pee in that wee water closet?
How do you properly position yourself
to not wet your robes on the floor?

Ah, you return.
Your husband smiles at you.
He turned around many times during your absence,
wondering, I thought, why we were still in the
air.

He is eating; you do not partake.
Only your eyes are hungry.
Forgive my suspicions, sister.

—Fourteen months after September 11, 2001,
North West Airlines flight, Los Angeles to Memphis

The Old Man at the Beach

I saw him from a distance,
an old man walking on the shoreline,
the water sloshing through his rubber sandals.

As he passed, he looked at me,
smiled broadly, and said,
"The water feels so good on my feet."

He went on, and I,
overcome with bittersweet aching,
loved him and all mankind...

—Pensacola Beach, August 2003

Patricia (Silke) Edmisten serviced in Peru from 1962-64 and currently shares her time between Florida and North Carolina. The Peace Corps (and the Catholic Church) turned her into a royal pain in the ass.

MELISSA BASTA

* ✷ *

Pearl of the Antilles

In 2004, the Peace Corps Haiti program was closed.
But the volunteers who served there remain ever open
to Haitians for their strength and bright smiles.

I WAS ONE OF TWENTY PEACE CORPS TRAINEES SENT TO REOPEN the Peace Corps Haiti program after it closed in the 1991 coup d'état. On the flight from Miami to Port-au-Prince in September of 1996, there was a collective air of excitement among our group. It was the kind of young, excited energy that comes with new beginnings, new friends, new places, and new projects. I was twenty-six and overflowing with American confidence.

As we made our final approach, Haiti looked green and fresh from the air. When I stepped off the plane, that air was hot and thick, the airfield littered with broken-down planes, trucks, and scraps of old machine parts. We were greeted on the tarmac by the Peace Corps Country Director and the U.S. Ambassador to Haiti, then whisked through the logjam and chaos at the airport, and taken to a VIP lounge where we were addressed by Haitian government officials. They charged us to begin efforts to break the long-established cycle of poverty in

47

Haiti; their words were endearing, their appreciation for our commitment to volunteer, inspiring.

Once I stepped outside this exclusive comfort zone to begin my Peace Corps service, I was instantly reminded that Port-au-Prince is synonymous with poverty. Its smell hung heavy in the humidity, the air made thick by exhaust fumes spewing from rundown, battered cars and trucks clogging the roadways. We boarded a small fifteen-passenger bus and began winding our way through Port-au-Prince toward Route National #2, the beginning of a six-hour drive to Les Cayes.

As we drove through the countryside, the scene played like a silent movie before my eyes: crumbled buildings, washed out roads, overcrowded trucks piled high with people and goods, children without clothes or shoes carrying buckets of water half their size, pigs feeding on top of trash piles, ratty street dogs scavenging. I stared out the window watching in complete silence and disbelief. All of my research and reading had not prepared me for the reality of Haiti. My feelings of excitement began to fade and flip-flop: from fear to guilt, compassion to anger, sadness to determination. My senses were overloaded; my stomach in knots. My confidence was shaken. The words "break the cycle of poverty" played over and over in my mind, and the thought of getting off the bus terrified me.

Eventually, the long journey to our training site ended, and I did get off the bus in southwestern Haiti. The next morning, I woke to the sun rising and the roosters *cock-a-doodle-doing*. In the bathroom, I was greeted by a dead cockroach, belly up by the toilet. I entered the shower where ice-cold water fell straight from the ceiling onto my head, quickly washed away both the dead mosquitoes that had collected in the basin overnight and any lingering drowsiness I might have enjoyed.

That was the beginning of many cold bucket baths, dead bugs and early morning roosters. I remained in Haiti for nearly three and a half years where I learned to look beyond the poverty to uncover the treasures hidden in the hearts and smiles of the Haitian people living in the countryside. My Peace Corps experience and time in Haiti was humbling and life-changing. And when it came time for me to leave, I realized that I would carry Haiti in my heart forever.

On June 1, 2010, I returned to Haiti, six months after the 7.0 earthquake that destroyed the capital city of Port-au-Prince, crippling the entire country. It was my first time back in eight years. My plane was filled with missionary groups, doctors, nurses, government officials, journalists, development workers, and Haitians returning to their homeland to provide much-needed care, to reconnect with friends and family, to make sense of the destruction and understand how to move forward and recover.

The mood was heavy, and the flight silent. As we approached Haiti, I felt weighted down by my own feelings of guilt and disappointment. Guilt for not staying more engaged in Haiti over the years and disappointment that this catastrophic event would be the catalyst for my return. On our final descent, I stared out of the window, looking down on entire communities reduced to rubble. I could see where the waters of the rainy season ran in rivulets off of the mountains into the ocean like weeds spreading from the land and clouding the blue Caribbean waters. From the sky, it looked as though Haiti were bleeding into the ocean.

There was no new beginning to be excited for on this arrival, no VIP meet-n-greet or air-conditioned bus to shuttle me halfway across the country. Haiti and its people had been shattered into a million tiny pieces. With a heavy heart and a small backpack on my shoulder, I got off the plane, passed through customs and walked out into the street alone, looking for the car and driver I hired to meet me at the airport. I stood surrounded by hard Haitian faces casting curious stares. I held their eyes and threw out a *"Bonjou, kouman w ye?"* and a *"Sak pase?"*—both common Haitian greetings that softened their faces and rewarded me with bright Haitian smiles.

My car arrived as the rain began to fall, and we sped off into the sea of destruction. Again, I found myself riding through Port-au-Prince staring out a window in silent disbelief. My surprise this time, however, was not about the unusual sites of Haiti that had struck me when I first arrived and then become familiar. Rather it was the magnitude of destruction that surrounded me at every turn. Whole streets that I had known were unrecognizable. And I could only imagine the horror that unfolded during the seconds, hours, days immediately following the collapse of every single structure we passed. As we navigated the streets filled with people, rubble, cars and debris, my eyes blurred with tears, and all I could think was Haiti is calling me back, and I will be there for her.

The next morning, I was up before the sun, anxious. I had made plans to meet Jimmy who was a shy, teenage boy in my Haitian family the last time I saw him eight years ago. I was meeting him on a street corner in Champs de Mars, once home to the city's main park: a beautiful stretch of grassy green open spaces featuring Haitian monuments, the National Palace and several historic, French-colonial government buildings. As I approached the corner, there he stood, a grown man, in the heart of the country's capital city, which lay in piles of broken concrete around him. A sprawling tent city blanketed the park. I jumped out of the car and ran over to him. There we stood in the middle of the morning chaos that spilled out of this makeshift city, now home to some 15,000 people displaced by the earthquake. With tears rolling down our cheeks, we hugged hard and then laughed at how we had both become *gran moun*, old people.

That week, we visited what was left of the apartment he had shared with six other family members in Port-au-Prince. We stood before the flattened building with its bits of twisted rebar reaching for the sky as he explained how he had been in the street when the earthquake struck and how, at the time, he did not know if any of his family was inside when it collapsed. We visited the shell of a building he now lived behind, a small space he and his family and friends share with two other families. On some days the space is home to as many as twenty-one people; water there is available just three days out of the week. Then, we headed home, leaving Port-au-Prince for the countryside following along the fault line all the way to Vialet, a small rural community that sits on Route National #2 just west of the capital, and where I lived as a Peace Corps Volunteer alongside Jimmy's family for two years.

I have made this drive a hundred times, but never while dodging the wounds inflicted by an earthquake. On this day, however, I could not help but think about how this would be my first visit home without Bos. Bos was Jimmy's father, my counterpart and closest friend during my time in Vialet. He had died in 2005, and it was Jimmy who had called to tell me the news.

As we entered the front gate, it was like I had never left, except for the tarp tent that had been erected behind the house and a painful reminder that Bos was not there. While the children had grown and people had aged, everything felt the same. The welcome was warm, and like old friends, we picked up where we left off. Madame was preparing food, the girls were busy organizing dishes and setting the table and the boys were getting water for bath time. I sat with Madame while she cooked, visited with the girls in the back, played with the children who came to see the *blan* and sat on the front porch with the boys talking until it was time to go visiting. Just like the old days.

After a hearty meal of rice and beans, we set out to visit friends and family. When we entered the gate to grandma's house, I looked up to see a large sarcophagus before me that had not been there before. Jimmy explained that it was where both Bos and grandpa had been laid to rest. I was not prepared for the sight, and his words hit me like an arrow in my chest, as I walked across the yard to kiss grandma who could no longer walk or see. Sitting with her, I remembered how her home had been a place full of people, children, and activity. Today, she sat alone on the front porch, staring blankly toward our voices, her house now rundown and empty of people. In that moment, to me, she was Haiti personified. Alone and crippled by years of a hard life.

She told me how Madame still brings her dinner some nights because she no longer cooks, that she has stopped going to church because it is too difficult for her to get there, and how she could use some medicine for her legs to help ease the pain. In the moment, I felt powerless. We left her sitting alone as the sun vanished from the sky.

My return to Vialet left me discouraged and deflated. I thought I would return to find some visible signs of community development. There were few signs of progress: in fact, Vialet and its people looked as though they had suffered more from the last decade of political unrest, natural disasters, and poverty than any damage caused to the town by the recent earthquake.

After such a long absence, this return would have been hard in any case. But everything—the sights, our emotions—was intensified by the shadow of the earthquake. And yet, while there was so much sadness woven into the fabric of this journey, in the end, I left feeling strangely hopeful for Haiti. I reconnected, and through that connection I was reminded that there is a strength and resiliency unique to the Haitian people.

I felt it from the young and old everywhere I travelled, from tent camps to schools and from hospitals to mango fields. It is this strength that has given me renewed hope for Haiti, and the belief that with consistent, sustained support, Haiti will one day reclaim its title as The Pearl of the Antilles.

Melissa Basta, who served in Haiti from 1996-2000, lives in Fort Collins, Colorado, with her husband Joe (an RPCV who served in the Dominican Republic) and their two children. Several weeks after the earthquake, she organized a fundraiser and silent auction to which she donated her own collection of beautiful Haitian voodoo banners.

RONALD A. SCHWARZ

Kennedy's Orphans

*Columbia 1 was the very first group of Peace Corps Volunteers to
go on their way and come back again. Find out what happened
to them since their return, almost fifty years ago.*

*In February 2008, thirteen members of Colombia 1 participated in a
reunion of more than 150 ex-Colombia Peace Corps Volunteers in
Cartagena. We raised glasses of wine, whiskey and aguardiente. We
thanked Colombians for their generosity, and for teaching us that life's
greatest reward lies in trying to make it better for others.*

MIDNIGHT, SEPTEMBER 6, 1961: SIXTY-TWO MEN FROM ALL COR-
ners of America boarded a train at New York's Penn Station.
Destination: the White House. We were members of Colombia
1, the first Volunteers to enter training for the Peace Corps.
After two months at Rutgers University, we were on our way
to meet El Presidente. After briefings at the State Department
and a session with Vice-President Lyndon Johnson, we arrived
at the White House. Richard Goodwin, one of Kennedy's
special advisers, led us on a tour of the premises. He cautioned,
"The meeting with the President is on hold."

Goodwin appeared ill at ease. He had recently returned from
a conference in Uruguay where, in the early morning hours,

he met a bearded, fatigue-outfitted figure: Che Guevarra. Che conveyed his thanks to the USA for the Bay of Pigs invasion, noting that it "had been a great political victory [for Cuba]... and transformed them from an aggrieved little country to an equal." Che told Goodwin that there was an intrinsic contradiction in the Alianza [Para el Progreso] and that by encouraging the forces of change and the desires of the masses, we might set loose forces which were beyond our control, ending in a Cuba style revolution.

Che's message may have been on Goodwin's mind as he guided us through the corridors of the *Casa Blanca*. Our mission as Volunteers was community development. Our assignment: to encourage the forces of change and help *los campesinos* take control of their own development. Unlike Guevarra, we, Kennedy's Children, had given little thought to the revolutionary implications of our assignment.

As we entered a dimly lit East Room, a buzzer sounded. The President was on his way. When Kennedy, hand buried in his jacket pocket, descended the stairs, the rumble of conversation was transformed into an electric silence. JFK appeared tired and distracted. He whispered to his brother-in-law, the Peace Corps Director Sargent Shriver. Then he spoke to us about his hopes for the Peace Corps and the Alliance for Progress, his initiative that acknowledged U.S. responsibility to the hemisphere, but that also required its wealthy elite to accept tax and land reforms, and its governments to invest more in education and health.

Kennedy conveyed his lack of confidence in the foreign policy establishment. It was not a new theme. During his election campaign, he criticized the "ill-chosen, ill-equipped, and ill-briefed ambassadors." JFK had read *The Ugly American* and wanted more Americans who, like the book's hero Homer Atkins, worked at the grassroots and spoke the local language.

The President shook our hands and said, "I look forward to your return and want to hear what it's really like down there." He glanced at Shriver and added, "I don't know if this Peace Corps is going to work, but if you have any complaints, don't write me, send them to Sarge."

On paper, there was nothing exceptional about the men in Colombia 1. Almost half had only two years of university education. One, Matt Deforest, a truck driver from Illinois, only a high school diploma. Meeting us in the flesh on our first day at Rutgers, reporters noted our enthusiasm, but none described us as "the best and the brightest." The lead sentence in the June 1961 article in the *New York Herald Tribune* read, "Looking more like the freshman football team than America's latest weapon in the Cold War, the first contingent of eighty Peace Corps Volunteers sat in creaky wooden bleachers in the middle of the Rutgers University campus."

We were, however, men whose values were shaped by World War II victories and post-war prosperity. For us, the Peace Corps was an adventure and an opportunity to help others. None of us viewed the assignment in terms of how it might advance our careers.

The Peace Corps selected a handful of Latinos for Colombia 1. They included Martin Acevedo, John Arango (both of Colombian ancestry), Henry Jibaja (Cuban parents), Enrique Morales, John Montoya, Dennis Salgado and Thomas Torres, all of Mexican descent. The youngest Volunteers, all nineteen, were Phil Lopes, John Montoya, Terry Grant, and Dennis Grubb. A few were Army and Marine veterans and two, Bill Woudenberg and Dennis Salgado, had served in the Korean War. Steve Honore, a physics major and perhaps the smartest of the group, was the lone Black American. Texas and California provided the largest number of Volunteers, and the conservative South just one, Buck Perry from Tennessee.

Year One

The day after meeting President Kennedy, we boarded a chartered, propeller-driven, Avianca Super Constellation to Colombia. We landed in the early morning, under the cover of darkness. About a hundred people were there to meet us, mostly Colombian soldiers armed with automatic weapons. The troops formed a tight corridor from the tarmac, as we passed through customs and to buses waiting to take us to Tibitatá, a Rockefeller-funded agricultural research station.

Our uniformed reception reflected caution, not ceremony. Colombia in 1961 was a wounded nation recovering from thirteen years of political violence that claimed more than 300,000 lives: one person in twenty killed. Large areas of the country were prohibited zones for travel and Volunteer placement. As young men, however, our optimism and primitive faith in JFK's leadership inoculated us from anxiety and fear. Colombians welcomed us with warmth and enthusiasm largely due to the charisma of JFK, and his Catholicism. We were ubiquitously referred to as *los hijos de Kennedy*—Kennedy's children. We were hailed in the press.

On our first weekend in Bogotá, we met "*los oligarchos.*" Our project directors had arranged for us to spend a few days in the homes of the Colombian elite that dominated political life, owned the huge farms and factories, ran the universities and controlled the media. While they appeared to support the aims of the Alianza, some agreed with Che's analysis that it would ultimately undermine their positions of power and privilege. A woman hosting one of the Volunteers in her mansion told him she expected "to be against the wall within a few years."

We also encountered skeptics, university students and critics on the left, who viewed us as agents of Yankee imperialism and, for some, an arm of the CIA. During the first two weeks, we were visited at Tibitatá by a succession of cabinet ministers and President Alberto Lleras. And, we had an audience with the Cardinal, at his quarters.

The Director of the Peace Corps in Colombia was Captain Chris Sheldon. In May 1961, four months before he arrived in Bogotá, his sailing ship, the *Albatross*, sank in a Caribbean storm. His wife and five students perished, and the tragedy was later immortalized in a book and a movie, *The White Squall*.

The Colombia 1 project was administered by CARE. The CARE Director was Mert Cregger who had mined gold in Colombia before he joined the organization. When Colombia 1 arrived, CARE's activities focused on food and tool distribution. Community Development was in their portfolio, on paper.

The depth of the CARE/Peace Corps experience was mirrored on the Colombia side. The Community Development Agency, Acción Comunal, had a short history, a new director and a small, inexperienced, poorly paid field staff. On a scorecard for "potential political disaster," the Colombia One-CARE-Peace Corps-Acción Comunal structure earned an easy 10.

After a month of in-country training, we were sent in pairs to villages and towns throughout Colombia. This coupling of Volunteers was necessary because most of us had difficulty advancing a conversation beyond *buenos dias* and *quiero una cerveza*. Our directors did their best to ensure that at least one of the two Volunteers in a village could sustain a conversation.

My initial Peace Corps site was the small village of Santa Cruz, north of Bucaramanga. The setting was out of a Juan Valdez commercial: green hills, cut by trails used by farmers and mules to transport sacks of coffee beans to market. My partner, Phil Lopes, and I settled into a large room in a house occupied by an extension agent of Los Cafeteros. We painted walls, built furniture, bought horses and began stage one of the community development process: getting to know the people and identify their "felt needs." This effort involved long walks and mounted visits to peasant farms, hundreds of cups of thick, rich coffee (*tinto*), uncountable bottles of beer, and endless conversations about President Kennedy. His status, in the minds of most Colombians, appeared to be somewhere between the Pope and a rebel Jewish carpenter.

In December 1961, a few months after we had settled into our villages, JFK visited Colombia. The reception, composed mainly of peasants and workers, was exuberant. President Lleras provided JFK with an explanation, "It's because they believe you are on their side." Kennedy's visit was widely covered on radio and in the press. It boosted the image of America, added a notch or two to our status, and for the next eighteen months his visit to Colombia was a win-win discussion topic in bars and *tiendas*.

In our encounters with *los campesinos*, we preached the gospel of community development, organized committees—Juntas de Acción Comunal—and inspired collective action for schools, roads, health centers, athletic fields, and aqueducts. The Alliance for Progress also raised expectations of financial aid. We sometimes encountered officials and community leaders who saw us as ambulatory checkbooks. In fact, we had no cash, materials, or equipment. As Kennedy's children, however, we had access to Colombian authorities and felt no hesitation in requesting support from the Cafeteros and government agencies.

The mobilization of villagers and the formation of committees generally went smoothly. The *campesinos* humored us and often went through the motions of a democratic vote. In fact, everyone except us knew who would run the *juntas* well before the scheduled "election." In principle, the project called for us to work with Colombian counterparts, *promotores*. In practice, the results were mixed, and many of us carved out our own niche. Our major obstacles were our own impatience, the inevitable delays, and our frustration with unfulfilled government promises of materials and equipment. Priests and local political bosses who tried to hijack the "democratic process" presented another set of problems. Most, however, gave us their support or blessed us with indifference

Communication between Volunteers and staff was, by today's standards, primitive. Some towns had telephones, but it took a day or two, with luck, to complete a call. CARE and the Peace Corps in Bogotá contacted us via a telegram that usually arrived within two or three days.

Another method of communication was a mimeographed newsletter, the ALVOLS. The last in my file is No. 121. ALVOLS outlined monthly reporting requirements, how to purchase a horse and saddle ("the returnable property of CARE"), life insurance forms, conference schedules, and health tips. ALVOL 51 (July 16, 1962) notes, "New snake bite serum will be issued to each Volunteer. If you have old snake bite serum, please discard it on receipt of the new supply." Reminders to boil water and use condoms were favorite topics, largely ignored.

For a group of youthful American males, Colombia provided relentless opportunities for distraction. The music never stopped, the women were beautiful, and the beer cost eight U.S. cents a bottle. Most months, a city held a three-to-five day carnival, some with bullfights and the best matadors from Spain, Mexico, and Colombia. All featured large salsa orchestras who played until dawn under mammoth tents. At the fiestas, we made our cultural contribution to Colombia: demonstrations of how to do "The Twist." Air transport was cheap, and by staying in our villages for three consecutive weeks we "earned" a week of leisure. We cashed in with astonishing regularity and achieved notoriety as *los cuerpos de paseo*: the vacation corps.

The Peace Corps administration contributed to our rounds of recreation by holding periodic conferences. It was their way to learn what we were doing, how the program could be improved, and our psychological condition. One conference, timed to remove us from possible violence during national elections, took place in the cities of Santa Marta and Cartagena on the Caribbean coast. The venue for the Santa Marta conference was the Aguila beer factory and during breaks we had the option of coffee or *cerveza*. Meetings lasted until midday, and afternoons featured water skiing and touch football at the beach. Evenings were a time for poker, meals and drinks at a seaside café, and excursions to local brothels. One nighttime adventure at the brothel "Las Americas" featured a drunken brawl and high-speed police chase through Santa Marta. Fortunately, the incident was never picked up by the press.

The month following the coastal conference, tragedy stuck Colombia 1. A handful of Volunteers were returning from their Easter vacation in the Chocó, a vast jungle region bordering the Pacific coast. The first plane out, an AVISPA DC-3, was overbooked and had seats for only two Volunteers, David Crozier and Larry Radley. The plane was reported missing and a search quickly organized. The Colombian government and the U.S. Army sent several planes and helicopters and, after a few days, the wreckage was spotted near the top of a steep mountain ridge. It was impossible to land the chopper, and the proximity of trees to the helicopter blades made descent by cable too risky. An attempt to reach the site by climbing the mountain and cutting through the jungle also failed.

On April 29th, seven days after the AVISPA plane was reported lost, a team of five led by a Colombian Air Force officer and a U.S. Army captain made a hazardous descent from a helicopter hovering over the crash site. They built a landing pad and were joined by three Peace Corps Volunteers, Ned Chalker, Steve Honore, and Barney Hopewell. Ned's report of the scene reads, "The people were unrecognizable. There were no whole bodies. Heads and arms and other pieces much too terrible to describe were lying around." The Peace Corps had its first fatalities. Chalker, Honore, and Hopewell confirmed the identity of their fellow Volunteers by their Sears boots. Before departing, the rescue team constructed several wooden crosses. The remains of all passengers are still at rest on the mountainside.

Following the death of their son, the Croziers' gave the Peace Corps Director, Sargent Shriver, a copy of a letter from David. Shriver kept a framed copy of a quote from the letter on his wall. It reads, "Should it come to it, I would rather give my life trying to help someone than to have to give my life looking down the barrel of a gun at them." The Peace Corps acknowledged David and Larry's sacrifice by naming two training camps in Puerto Rico after them, Camp Crozier and Camp Radley.

Year Two

The following year, our second in Colombia, was far different from the first. Culture shock faded, our command of Spanish improved, and we adapted to the Colombian way of doing things. Our towns and villages became homes rather than places to escape from. My monthly schedule, in my second site, Silvia, Cauca, included forty to sixty hours traveling on foot and horseback, twelve to fifteen nights sleeping on a bench or table, a few village meetings, hours of labor on a construction site, and a visit to Popayan to discuss plans or request materials from a government official. Weekend activities included work on a school or road project, soccer practice, league games, and dancing and drinking at a local bar or club.

The variety and number of projects started and finished by Colombia 1 Volunteers was far greater than anyone, including ourselves, would have predicted. The official report of completed projects includes 44 schools, 65 classrooms, 29 rural roads (200 miles), 27 aqueducts, 4 health centers, 26 cooperatives, 100 sports fields, several hundred latrines, and the formation of hundreds of community action groups. An even greater number of projects are listed as "in progress." Some figures reveal traces of statistical sorcery.

We got more credit than we deserved for projects that were mostly managed and completed by *campesinos* and local leaders. Most observers agree, however, that the Colombia 1 program exceeded expectations. Our most important contribution was just being there and trying to get something done. As Americans working in rural villages, we brought attention and publicity to Acción Comunal. Our efforts, and those of later Volunteers, helped transform it from a stumbling bureaucracy into a national development organization, one that still exists. David Hapgood and Meridan Bennett, two ex-Peace Corps staff, noted in their book that "Without Peace Corps help, Acción Comunal might have disappeared in 1962, when it was still shaky, insecure and overextended." Gerard Rice, writing about the early years of the Colombia program states that "it was a significant success." Another author notes that "Members of this first Colombia group... wrote in action the basic Peace Corps textbook on community development."

Year 47

At this writing, forty-seven years have passed since our arrival in Colombia. And, in spite of being scattered throughout the USA and the world, members of our group keep in touch. Tom Mullins began a newsletter in 1965, and it was kept alive by Mike Willson, an executive with KFC. Today we use the internet.

As part of the initial wave of returned Volunteers in the early '60s, members of Colombia 1 played a role in Peace Corps management, recruitment and training. Several held positions in Washington, D.C., others served as staff in Bolivia, Brazil, Chile, Colombia, Costa Rica, the Dominican Republic, Ecuador, Honduras, Peru, Turkey, and the Philippines. Four were appointed Country Directors. Many held jobs preparing Volunteers, and collectively we trained about 5,000, mostly for programs in Latin America.

In 2003, after the death of Jim Puccetti, a Volunteer leader and one of several to marry a Colombian, I began an odyssey to investigate what happened to the Volunteers of Colombia 1. I spent most of two years flying between my home in France and their homes in the USA. What surprised me was how little they had changed. All cited the Peace Corps experience as one of the most important events in their lives. Their life stories confirm these assertions.

Korean War veteran Bill Woudenberg, now seventy-seven, lives in a small apartment in Weehawken, New Jersey. He works part time as an architectural draftsman, his profession at the time he joined the Peace Corps. "Woody" is also an artist and winner of a few prizes. In Colombia, he invented a loom to weave bamboo for use in latrine construction. Years later, working for an international NGO, he applied the technique to the manufacture of reinforced concrete products used in grain and cold storage containers. Factories using the technology were built in Bangladesh and Togo and employed several hundred workers. The technology, under his supervision, was also applied to the construction of the international airport and the national museum in Bangladesh. Reflecting on his experience, Bill told me, "In the Peace Corps I learned I could survive. I never worried about a career. I'm probably the poorest guy in Colombia 1, but I've had a good life, no regrets."

Henry Jibaja, born in the USA to Cuban parents, was one of the few Volunteers with a degree in agriculture. Looking back on his Peace Corps days, Henry recalls, "We get to Colombia and they send me to Buenaventura, twenty-six feet of rain per year, one of the few places in the country where there is *no agriculture*." After a job with Ralston Purina, Henry returned to Colombia with his Guatemalan wife as an Associate Director for the Peace Corps.

In 1972, Sargent Shriver hired Henry Jibaja to organize the Office of Economic Opportunity (OEC) headquarters in Florida. Henry played the key role in setting up VISTA in Florida and for twenty years was director of the statewide volunteer coordination agency. He had opportunities for higher positions, but that meant moving to Washington. Henry preferred to stay in Florida to avoid working with political appointees. He explained, "Dealing with them is awful, dealing with Volunteers is wonderful."

In Tucson, I spent a few days with my first village partner, the Honorable Phil Lopes. After the Peace Corps, Phil finished college and completed a master's degree in anthropology. He returned to the Peace Corps and served as Director in Ecuador and Co-Director in Brazil. The other Co-Director in Brazil, his wife Pam, is also an ex-Volunteer. Their youngest son just completed a few months in Darfur, Sudan, and later worked in Bolivia with USAID. Phil helped establish Pima

Community College and the University of Arizona College of Public Health. He is now the Leader of the House Democrats in the Arizona House of Representatives and a sponsor of legislation to protect the rights of Native Americans and improve health care services.

Sitting in his living room, I asked Phil what he had accomplished recently. He handed me Section B of the latest *Arizona Daily Star*. The headline read "Pascua Yaquis get housing boost." The article outlined a new state law that gives a property tax exemption to off-reservation homes owned by low-income tribal members. Phil Lopes was listed as the primary sponsor. I began to offer congratulations, but Phil interrupted, "Those Yaquis, they have good lobbyists. I wouldn't have been able to get it through committee and the House without those lobbyists. I don't have the guns."

John Arango, whose father was born and raised in Antioquia, Colombia, spent his early post-Peace Corps years as Director of the Peace Corps Community Development Training Center at the University of New Mexico. He later served as Peace Corps Director in Ecuador and Panama (under Ambassador Jack Vaughn, the Peace Corps' second Director). A picture on a wall of his New Mexico home shows his wife Polly receiving an award from President Clinton for her work with disabled children.

In a long career as head of Algodones Associates, John focused on obtaining rights for illegal immigrant access to schools. He also played a part in the American Bar Association's successful struggle to obtain mandatory funding for legal services for the indigent. The case was successfully argued before the Supreme Court. He now serves as Director of New Mexico Legal Aid, a statewide, non-profit organization with twelve offices that employs thirty-five lawyers. Discussing his activities, John mentioned that during a national meeting of lawyers concerned with defending the rights of the poor, "every one of us was a former Peace Corps Volunteer."

More than half of Colombia 1 spent part of their careers in international development and humanitarian activities. Collectively, they have worked in more than one hundred countries with the World Bank, the Inter-American Bank, the UN, the European Union, USAID, CARE, the Red Cross, and other public and private agencies. They initiated and participated in the establishment of low-cost housing programs in Central America, small industry development in Nigeria, rural service centers in the Philippines, the reform of Kenya's health sector, a furniture factory in Brazil, a toy factory in Colombia, disaster relief programs in Latin America, and a Famine Early Warning System for sub-Sahara Africa.

As economists, administrators and consultants, they have designed and managed hundreds of projects and loan portfolios in and for developing countries. After earning a doctorate in economics, Fred Jasperson spent his adult years with the World Bank. Dennis Grubb ran projects to set up stock markets in India and Sri Lanka. Bruce Lane, often working in collaboration with fellow Volunteer A. L. Wahrhaftig, produced films on Mexico and Afghanistan and is currently putting together a documentary on Colombia 1.

In the USA, Colombia 1 Volunteers have been leaders in education, public service, and the private sector. Tom Torres worked with Model Cities and Head Start; he served as Director for the Administration of Native American Programs for Hawaii and the Outer Pacific Islands. Mike Lanigan managed disaster relief activities for the Red Cross in the USA, Puerto Rico, and Peru. Tom Bentley and his ex-Volunteer wife Elizabeth helped create the Indochinese Cultural and Service Center in Oregon. John Luoma invented and manufactured a mini forklift for use on construction sites and through his church is involved in international charity work. Buck Perry stayed in Colombia to set up a Peace Corps Educational TV project. Now settled in the deep South, Buck and his wife Evelyn (a Volunteer in Colombia 3), manage their own electronic services business. Steve Honore, served as Peace Corps Director in the Dominican Republic (1978-81), and in 2000 received the Peace Corps' Franklin Williams Award for Outstanding Community Service. More than a half dozen others from our group, including Jack Elzinga, George Kroon, Darrel Young and A. I. Wahrhaftig, are professors at U.S. universities.

Most members of Colombia 1 continue volunteer activities in their communities. Two, Michael Murray and Ned Chalker, currently spearhead major urban development projects, *pro bono*. After his retirement as president of a major manufacturing company, Stewart-Warner, Michael Murray dedicated himself to public service in St. Louis. He was a founding board member for the $100 million reconstruction of Forest Park. The park is larger than New York's Central Park and includes a golf course, facilities for boating, tennis and ice-skating, a zoo, a planetarium and two museums. He is now President of the Board of the Metropolitan Park and Recreation District, a.k.a. The Great Rivers Greenway District. It features a connected series of greenways, parks and trails that cross state lines and will eventually encircle the St. Louis region. Commenting on his experience, Murray wrote, "DeTocqueville had it exactly right when he observed how important citizen involvement is to our democracy."

Ned Chalker retired from the National Institute of Education (NIE), and in 2000 founded the National Maritime Heritage Foundation (NMHF). The Foundation is working in partnership with the District of Columbia and the

Department of the Navy to build a national capital tall ship, *Spirit of Enterprise,* and create a Washington Maritime Center. The projects are part of an urban redevelopment program for Southwest Washington. The NMHF also plans to host an Operation Sail and invite ships from the USA and the world in 2012. Ned, who grew up in the small town of Chester, Connecticut, spoke about his experience in Antioquia: "I met all these people who after you got to know them were just like the people I grew up with, except they spoke Spanish."

As I prepared to interview Ned in May 2004, he handed me a recent printout from a blog site, Pharyngula. The author, Ed Darrell, was a George Bush Sr. political appointee, and Ned's boss at the NIE in the 1980s. It reads: "I had a wonderful 'program manager' named Ned Chalker—*the guy who got things done....* He had connections all over Washington. Ned was one of the original Peace Corps Volunteers, and many in his network were the early recruits. They could all do anything, including make the government run well and cheaply, and they were all waiting in second- and third-tier civil service jobs for someone, like a John Kennedy, to come back to power and ask them to...make their nation good, grand, and proud."

It has now been fifty years since our meeting with El Presidente. JFK's dreams for Latin America, and those of Che Guevarra, continue to inflame passion and policy in the hemisphere. Kennedy's name and vision of a democratic, peaceful, and socially responsible society continue to inform political debate in the USA.

Dr. Ronald A. Schwarz is an anthropologist and international development consultant. Following his Peace Corps years, he returned to Columbia to conduct research and establish an international training

*program for university students. Between 1990 and 2002, he
directed a consulting firm, Development Solutions for Africa, based in
Kenya. He has been a faculty member at Williams College, Colgate
University, Tulane University and the Johns Hopkins University.
He is the co-editor of three books on anthropology and author of 50
reports to the World Bank, USAID, the U.N., the European Union
and other development agencies. His rule of thumb for consultant
reports: "Keep them weighty enough to flatten a cockroach." He is
currently writing a book on Colombia One,* Kennedy's Orphans,
from which this story is excerpted.

PART TWO

WHY ARE WE HERE?

LARRY LIHOSIT

The Mapping Odyssey

For this Volunteer, one thing just kept leading
to another, that led to another...

JEFF BENIK WAS AN INDUSTRIAL ARTS TEACHER IN A BRAND NEW American International Development-funded high school which had plenty of American-made machinery, but needed a Peace Corps Volunteer to help set up a classroom, arrange the shop, write class plans, and teach Honduran teachers. The Hondurans, our hosts, had recently had more problems than a cat chasing its tail; problems which Jeff was supposed to solve quickly. He was to set up a multiple-use shop for wood, leather, metal work, drafting, and automobile repair within a large room stacked high with machines that nobody had ever seen or used; classes had already begun. Several young Americans had failed before we even arrived in this country. There were no painted danger signs, no tool cabinets, no storage areas or safety devices, no class plans for projects, no grading system, no rules of operation, no nothing; just a room full of machines, a long list of interested students, a group of Honduran teachers willing to learn and bearded Jeff Benik dressed in orange bell bottom trousers, a white t-shirt which read "Oakland Athletics," and some cheap sandals.

My situation was similar. A national planning agency was to create La Ceiba's first general plan in a city founded fifty years earlier, and my assignment was on-site liaison. In the third most populated city in the country, the mayor had supplied me with a building filled with garbage, no furniture, no telephone, no office machines like typewriters or calculators, no materials like paper, pen, no nothing. Luckily, we had consulted Honduran *jefes* in the capital before coming so that we knew where to start. That first month, while Jeff supervised painting and construction of tool cabinets, the city's carpenter built me furniture, while the city's paint crew cleaned and painted my new planning office. In the meantime, I worked in the field. Each day I walked a different section of the city with several maps rolled up and stuck under one arm while the tropical sun made me sweat like a stuck pig. My red pen scribbled notes about land uses, my green pen the availability of water, my black pen sewer lines, and my blue pen electricity. This was all new to me, so after a couple of misunderstandings with city workers, I wrote a letter to my planner buddy back home, asking him to send me a few books for reference because this town had zero bookstores, and even in the capital city, the bookstores were more like empty tool sheds.

At night Jeff and I were never bored even without a television (or telephone, or any electronic contraption like an iPod, cell phone, or computer games—which had not yet been invented). Living on the Atlantic coast in a city famous for hospitality, fine beaches, good beer, and a carnival, we had lots of visitors. First, it was the two Canadians that Jeff met in a general store who were on their way overland to the Panama Canal where they hoped to build a raft or buy a small boat, learn to navigate, and sail to South America alone. Jeff invited them to stay with us for a week or so and sleep on the concrete floor in our tiny and nearly empty living room. They had just left when a short, broad-chested Chicano with a long mustache tried to sell me his scuba diving tanks on the main street while one street down, his blond, tall dancer girlfriend begged in Spanish. There was some kind of small misunderstanding with the Los Angeles police department which originally got them moving south a year before in a thirteen-year-old luxury sedan. According to him, the car took them all the way to Oaxaca, Mexico, before there was a misunderstanding with the Mexican police, but luckily the judge liked his car so much that he not only let them both go free, but bought the car for a discounted price and ordered a police escort out of town. They stayed with us for more than a week.

Through an arduous process of trial and error, Jeff and I learned which cantinas served snacks with a round of beer (*botanitas*, sometimes called *bocadillas*), which places had the best jukebox music, which street vendors had the tastiest tacos and *papusas*, and which dance clubs were the best for men on a strict budget. We settled on Ginnette's Hall, a dockworkers' bar, which only played R&B and reggae on the jukebox and only served grapefruit juice without ice and a set-up of cane liquor called *aguardiente*. A beautifully tall and curvaceous black woman taught us how to dance. We made friends, most naturally.

The Peace Corps was unaware of our popularity and kind enough to give me a stipend for supplies. I boarded the five A.M bus with dogs and goats, bound for the capital. Four days later, still smelling of capital city *aguardiente*, but carrying a suitcase full of supplies, my real drafting began. The information that I had so carefully collected was drawn onto vellum paper. Without rapidiograph pens and India ink, I was forced to use varying widths of permanent markers. I became quite expert at laying down a line quickly before the ink could bleed. Afterward, I colored the land-use map with water-base markers. In fact, the photos taken of me posing near my giant land-use map are still my favorites.

Four months passed before a parade of capital city pros flew in. My hair was wet, my sleeves rolled up over my perspiring forearms as the director of the Honduran national planning agency and his six section chiefs gave me a presentation of their schedule of studies, stopping once for a soda pop and a second time to admire my maps, which an architect copied quickly onto another map while looking up to explain that they had used an aerial map and could not get the same detail. They were most surprised by my utility maps, especially the sewer inventory, since the mayor had claimed no such thing existed. I explained that an old man who had been cleaning the sewers for seventeen years had taken me to each manhole, each cleanout, and each grate where we had measured and taken notes. They stayed for ten days, copying all of my maps.

Just before they left, I opened my new wooden desk drawer and presented them with a full box of notes about housing in La Ceiba, which two Honduran city employees had helped me put together after inspecting hundreds of homes. The director skimmed a few pages, listening to my prepared speech before taking his gold rimmed glasses off, setting them on my desk and telling me point-blank that it was damn good. His six chiefs agreed (which they always did anyhow) and told me to write a report. Write a report? The Peace Corps only taught me to speak Spanish, not read and write! They kept on, smiling and slapping my back until they convinced me and this marked the beginning of a very serious stretch of work that would last long after they had flown back to an air-conditioned capital city office.

It was Jeff's Peace Corps Volunteer girlfriend, Sandy Elliott, who got me on the right track, loaning me a huge dictionary in Spanish. Another Volunteer gave me an engineer's dictionary in English and Spanish, another sold me a dog-eared, ripped book of verb tenses, another traded me for a new intermediate grammar text. This cost me a Guatemalan travel poster and two Mexican wool sweaters.

Weeks later, the Peace Corps Associate Director, Armando Votto Paz, stopped by without notice. He drove a new shiny four-wheel-drive jeep and was on a mission to visit another Volunteer who lived up in the mountains. Armando smiled as he turned the pages of my first draft (in Spanish). He told me that not too many Peace Corps Volunteers in the Community Development program had ever written a report in Spanish before, so why not take a day off? We jumped into his jeep, leaving a spray of red dirt in our wake.

It was a wise respite. The next month was filled with grammar and spelling after the city secretary loaned me an antique manual typewriter with a sticky letter "y." I pecked out a second draft, slow like an old dog sniffing a new tree. While Sandy edited, I drew maps to illustrate it.

The smallest detail became a strange odyssey. Photocopy machines were hard to find. Even the city's fifteen clerks typed in triplicate with carbon paper. Every single store and office owner in town met me until I discovered a lone machine that only took North American quarters, which the owner sold for one dollar per quarter. The copies, the best in town, were wet and smelled like rotten eggs, but my spirits were high. In the evenings, Sandy and her roommate, Dee Dee, fed me homemade cookies and fresh coffee while Sandy underlined passages. Even though the report was only ten pages of typewritten text and fifteen pages of tables and maps, this was like riding an unsaddled horse that nobody had mounted in six months. A saying by William Burroughs kept me trying. He said that there are two kinds of writers; those that write and those that talk about writing. The writers, he said, why they're like bullfighters while the talkers are more bullshitters. Bullfighting was more my line.

By the end of my first year in the port city of La Ceiba, the general plan and my bound housing report were presented to the city at a formal meeting. Soon, I had a job interview in the capital city at the Ministry of Government and Justice where a panel of three Honduran men and one woman asked me questions in Spanish for a half an hour. My Spanish must have improved because they all smiled, as did Armando the next day when he told me that they had invited me to join the team. My actual work was mysterious, but then so is religion. They did say that writing urban plans was not in this deck of cards, but municipal problem solving was, even though they were not quite sure exactly how that hand might play out and I, the foreign cowpoke, was not either: the joker's wild.

Larry Lihosit—aka Lorenzo—served in Honduras from 1975-77 in Group 3, within the Community Development contingent. Immediately following his service, he entered a graduate program in urban planning offered at Mexico City's Universidad Nacionál Autónoma de México. The author of several books, pamphlets, and articles, he also contributes regularly to the e-magazine Peace Corps Writers. *He still practices urban planning in California's Central Valley. This story originally appeared in his memoir,* South of the Frontera.

KENDRA LACHNIET

Little Library of Horrors

*Even in a library in Paraguay, the mixing of three very
different cultural attitudes can lead to major consternation
and disappointment.*

I SAT QUIETLY IN THE TEACHERS' INSTITUTE LIBRARY, SUR-
rounded by paper-covered shelves held up by bricks, which
I liked to call "spider-condos." Books were stacked high on
tables, and a cabinet sagged with the weight of pretty folders. A
tangle of pretty ribbon held the folders together. In the corner
lay a box full of teaching materials made by students during the
last volunteer workshop. They had never been used.

I had worked many hours trying to finish registering the
books and indexing them so they'd be ready by the following
Monday. My hand was cramping from writing longhand—and
in my prettiest letters—"Ministerio de Educación y Culto,"
the source of the majority of the inventory. Each book was
logged in the register and on an index card for the card catalog. I suggested to the librarian that we might want to photocopy several pages and cards with the words "Ministerio de
Educación y Culto" already written on them. She would have
none of that!

"Why do you Americans always insist on working fast and taking shortcuts?"

How do you explain this aspect of American culture in a country where there are no ATMs, McDonald's, microwaves, or drive-through windows? Multi-tasking was definitely not valued here.

"We just like to get things done," I tried, feebly.

"What will we do when we're all finished with registering the books?" she asked. The hand holding the nail polish paused in the air. She sounded worried.

"We can teach the students how to use the library. Then we can do what most librarians do—check books in and out, keep the materials organized, try to find other resources so we can get more books. There are lots of things we can do. By the way, how are we going to organize the cards? I think maybe we should just do a subject catalog."

My original idea was to merely color-code the books with a piece of tape to indicate the subject, but that idea was rejected after the librarian attended a three-month conference on the Dewey Decimal System. The workshops were provided by the Japanese. Anything provided by the Japanese overrode anything I could offer. Besides, she'd earned a pretty certificate.

"We're going to organize them by the date that we received or purchased them."

"By date?" I have never heard of a catalog organized by date the book was received. "How will the students be able to find a specific book?"

"They'll have to learn how to use the Dewey Decimal System."

"Do you think they will? Are you going to do a workshop for them?"

"No. They'll figure it out."

"So, we're not going to do any workshops once the library is organized?"

"No." No wonder she's worried about what comes next.

"Well, you will have to inform each student, then, of how the library functions. How long do you think books should be checked out?"

"The student can decide. They can just tell us when they will be done with the books."

"So, if someone wants to check out a book for the entire school year, that's O.K.?"

"I guess. They won't though. They only use them for a couple days."

"O.K." Whatever. "Well, you should at least have a workshop showing students and professors how to take care of the books and how to put them away. Maybe we should just tell them to leave books on the table when they're done, and we can put them away. I've seen professors shove books behind the rows because they don't know where they go and don't want to admit it."

"No, that would be too much work for us. They can put them back themselves." So much for finding sufficient work to keep her employed.

The librarian left, excusing herself to go work on the upcoming Folklore Festival, a really big deal in Coronel Bogado. Although I enjoy this festival, I realize that I'm really not much help in the construction of temporary houses and brick ovens. I'm more of an observer. I really wanted to get as much done as possible in her absence.

I worked quickly, crossing out mistakes on the cards with a neat, but unruled line, hoping they would go unnoticed. It's not like anyone was actually going to be using the card catalog. I silently fumed over the answers the librarian gave. Not only had I spent hours doing repetitive chores that could have been done much more efficiently, but now it also seemed fairly meaningless. I raged over the countless cards that, because of one error, had to be discarded. It wouldn't have been so bad if the librarian hadn't insisted on using a ruler to cross off all of the information on the card before tossing it in the trash can "because the Japanese said it had to be done that way." I doubted if she'd understood correctly. The Japanese could not possibly be that anal. It seemed like more of a Paraguayan trait, or maybe just a librarian trait, or just a "Monica" trait. It was all starting to piss me off. "*Tranquilo, no más*," a multitude of Paraguayan voices whispered in my head. I was ready to smack the next person that said those words to me, even if it was just the voices in my head.

It was getting more difficult to maintain my "pretty letters." It felt like I had to do something, but I couldn't remember what. Then it came to me: biology! The biology books tormented my mind. Monica had insisted that *Biología 1* belonged in physical science, *Biología 2* in biology, and *Biología 3* in general science. When I questioned the logic behind it, she said that the book was to be placed by the subject covered in the first chapter. I had tried to convince her that students would be able to find what they needed faster if we just put them all together, in order, under the biology number. She would have none of that, repeating her mantra, "The Japanese said it had to be done this way." Of course. Would she even notice? I doubted it. I snatched the books off the shelves, checked the dates the books had been received by the institute, found their respective cards, and defiantly tossed the cards in the trash. (I would have to remember to bring the discards to the trash pile so Don Francisco could burn them before Monica returned.) I grabbed the forbidden bottle of White-Out and revised the book labels, then placed them in numerical order under biology. Score one for the *yanqui*.

I was nervous. The clock read 3:30. I had only a half hour to finish the job before Monica's return. I realized that the library was quite a spooky place when everyone was gone. It was too quiet. I could hear the clock ticking. The sound of scratching came from a box in the corner. A cockroach? I snuck over. There was a mouse munching on the paper maché puppets I had made for the endangered animals workshop. My puppets weren't as "pretty" as the ones you could buy at the store. Of course, those puppets were way too expensive to be handled by students (or afforded by teachers), but they were way prettier, and that's what's important. My puppets were being chewed to extinction by the *ratoncito*. I felt it was a fitting demise and went back to my work. *Buen provecho,* Mickey.

I finished with the cards and labeling of the books. It was time to put the books in order. I worked quickly, realizing that time was running out. The children's books were a dilemma. Monica had labeled every one of them with the same number instead of putting them into a separate category of children's fiction. I alphabetized them by author. The slow, steady clicking of the professors' high heels was the timer, clicking off the last seconds of my efforts. I slumped in the wooden chair and kicked the trashcan under the desk just as Monica burst through the door. I was anxious to see her expression.

"Wow!" she shouted. "It's done! How pretty!"

I was pleased by her reaction, but held my breath as she scanned the shelves. Would she notice the three *Biología*s?

"It's very pretty."

"*Gracias.*"

"Very, very pretty."

"*Gracias.*"

"But let's make it prettier!"

"What?"

Monica proceeded to pull books from each shelf. First, she grabbed all of the smaller books from each shelf. Shoving the others to the right, she placed them on the left. Then, she snatched all of the larger books. Shoving left, she placed them on the right. Now each bookshelf was organized by size.

"Look! It's much prettier this way!"

I stood in shocked silence, a tear rolling down my cheek. She wasn't finished.

Next, she started pulling the majority of the children's books off the shelves, depositing them on a pile on the top shelf with a stack of folders and magazines.

"What? Why?" was all I could manage.

"These are less than twenty pages, so they're considered 'magazines.' Magazines go on the top shelf."

"But they're children's books. Most children's books are less than twenty pages. They won't even be able to see them way up there!"

"They're considered magazines," she repeated. "The Japanese said it had to be done that way. Why are you crying?"

"It's just that it's so pretty."

"Exactly. Let's go. You should go see how the Folklore Festival is coming along. It's very pretty."

I'm sure it is.

Kendra Lachniet served in Paraguay from 1992-94. She has been back to Paraguay twice since her service ended; and it's still very pretty. She was, however, shocked when she saw "Mba'echaipa" (Guaraní for "Hi, how are ya?") written in the big golden arches of a McDonald's billboard.

MARTHA MARTIN

The Danger of Paved Roads

The addition of a motorcycle to this author's household
was not necessarily a good thing.

I WOKE UP THAT MONDAY MORNING DREADING THE MOTOR-
cycle ride ahead of me. It was a long way to the elementary
school in Las Brisas, and the only redeeming quality of that
particular journey was a lot of it was on the new paved road.
It was the only paved road in the Coto Brus region of Costa
Rica, a hilly coffee-growing area next to Panama.

I am a short woman and was not very strong back then,
so I was taken aback by the motorcycle that I was given by
the Ministry of Education to ride to the schools I visited in
the Sabalito school district. It was only a Yamaha 100, but I
couldn't touch the ground when I was sitting on it unless it
was leaning to one side or the other. Peace Corps had strict
policies about motorcycles, so the fact that our group of school
and community gardens promoters got them at all is still a
mystery to me.

I didn't like going to the school in Las Brisas. I had visited
the one-room school several times each month throughout
the previous school year. Now summer vacation was over;

the week before I had visited all of my schools to do tool inventories and measure gardens for the long-awaited chicken wire. The director of the school, Don Angél, was a garden enthusiast, and the students loved working outside in the garden, but the soil was the worst of any of my schools. Almost everything we planted died before anything could be harvested. Every visit to the school was a sad one, with director and students showing me the dead or dying plants and asking me what might have happened to them. Sometimes the problems were pretty easy to solve, like the time the students lifted the recently planted seedbox full of soil that had been sterilized with boiling water only to have the bottom fall out. Most times I had no idea. The soil was acidic volcanic soil, almost void of nutrients and organic matter, as tends to be the case when rainforest is destroyed and land is farmed in Central America. Add to that the high humidity, and it was a recipe for agricultural disaster.

My husband Paul and I lived in a small cement-covered cinderblock house with a tin roof, across the street from the only evangelical church in the town of Sabalito. We had electricity and running water and a flush toilet with a septic tank in a shed in the back of the house, so we had it pretty good compared to our colleagues in Africa. The electricity and water were almost always on, though on occasion one or the other would go out for an extended period of time. We bought tanks of propane at a local store and carried them home on our motorcycles to power our two-burner propane stove. It sat on a rough handmade table in the kitchen. We had gotten both from the previous Volunteers in Sabalito, a couple and their two daughters. We used it to heat water, scald milk, cook rice and beans, fry eggs and warm leftovers from the day before. We bought our milk in one-liter plastic bags.

On that Monday morning, I boiled water for coffee and heated up some rice and beans—leftovers from the day before—in a cast iron skillet and dumped them onto a plate. I looked at my new motorcycle helmet searchingly while I ate and wondered yet again how Peace Corps had found helmets that so closely resembled the headgear worn by astronauts on moonwalks. After drinking a very strong cup of coffee with milk, I put the helmet and my backpack on and went outside to start up my motorcycle.

The ride began uneventfully, with my typically slow, cautious pace down the rocky dirt road to San Vito. I was so relieved to arrive at the paved road without any mishaps. I could speed up and enjoy the breeze in my face and get to Las Brisas quickly to see the latest agricultural disaster. Then I'd be on my way home, puzzling about what vegetables might be successfully grown there; the radishes alone had prospered, but no one seemed to want to eat sautéed radish greens.

I sped down the road, making close to forty kilometers an hour, which was very fast for me.

Much to my horror, when I was almost halfway to Las Brisas, a big, rangy dog appeared out of nowhere and started running beside me, nipping at my heel and trying to bite my right leg.

I am terrified of angry dogs. When I was still in elementary school I rode my bike to a friend's house to play with her. When I got to the door that led into the kitchen, her bulldog was waiting there, looking straight into my eyes. Then he jumped up and bit my face. With blood gushing down my face and tears streaming from my eyes, I ran back to my bike and rode home as fast as I could to tell my dad what had happened. So though I love dogs, I have a great respect for them when they are in a biting mood.

I kept accelerating my motorcycle, trying to go faster and faster so that I could outrace the angry dog. Unfortunately he figured that out also and he ran in front of my motorcycle to try to stop me; I slammed into him, knocking him off of his feet and falling heavily off my motorcycle onto my left arm. Because I was going very fast as I was trying to get away from him, I slid along the asphalt with all of my weight on my left arm, scraping it hard against the surface of the road. My whole left side was bruised and beaten up, but the dog seemed O.K. He got up right after I hit him and ran off to his master, whom I hadn't seen before. He had been walking with the dog when I rode by and probably had been laughing the whole time.

It was only after my fall that I was able to take a good look at the dog, a big German shepherd mix like most of the dogs in Sabalito.

His master, a short, stocky fellow with a big smile, said, "I don't know what I'm going to do with this dog, Señora. Everytime someone goes by on a motorcycle, he chases him."

I don't know why I didn't suggest the obvious, which was to put the dog on a leash. Perhaps because I didn't know any words for leash except chain, and I hated to see dogs chained up in their yards.

He helped me get my motorcycle started again. The engine always flooded whenever I had a wreck, so restarting it after a such a big fall was a tricky business. Once it was started he helped me get back on and said, "Now, Señora, you can continue on to Las Brisas to help the students with the garden."

After giving it some thought I decided that he was right, because the teacher and students were expecting me. I was sure that they were eagerly anticipating my visit.

But a few miles later, there was a construction crew working on the road not far from the new bridge over the river. I stopped my motorcycle and one of the workers looked up. I said, "What's happening?"

He said, "Señora, you can't go past. There's construction work going on and no one will be able to get through for at least two hours."

"Seriously?" I asked.

He nodded and grinned.

At that point I just gave up on the idea of getting to Las Brisas. I dragged my motorcycle around and started back home, much more slowly than before. Much to my dismay, one of my spark plugs burned out and I had to stop my motorcycle yet again. I was so relieved that I was out of sight of the construction workers when it happened; they wouldn't have been able to watch me change it. I'm sure that they would have found the sight of me changing a spark plug quite amusing, and I was in no mood to have anyone laugh at me again that particular day.

A week later, I still was feeling sore after my fall; but even worse, my left arm had begun to swell and it got more and more swollen every day. Nothing like that had ever happened to me before, so I really wasn't very worried about it until it got so large that I could barely fit my shirt sleeve over it. It was also starting to hurt quite a bit. When I asked Paul what he thought, he said, "Gee, it is getting kinda big and red. Maybe you should go see Dr. Huertas." I was always in trouble for spending too much time going to see Dr. Huertas in San José, so I was uncertain about going without at least calling first.

I called the Peace Corps Medical Office in San José on Wednesday to ask for advice.

The person who answered the phone, after listening to my symptoms, said, "Señora, you should go to the social security hospital in San Vito. You can't take the bus to San José to have Dr. Huertas at the Clínica Bíblica look at it because a car bomb just went off yesterday and seriously injured three Marine guards on their way to the Embassy."

I found out later that the bomb had been planted by terrorists because President Carazo had allowed two U.S. warships to dock in Limón and everyone thought that the warships were headed for El Salvador, a country to the west of Costa Rica that was in the midst of a civil war.

"Yes, Señora, and other bombs exploded near the Embassy, and Embassy officials have gotten death threats, so the Embassy and the Peace Corps office are closed, and you are advised to stay out of San José."

This was a lot for me to take in. Costa Rica was known as the Switzerland of Central America and didn't even have a standing army. Police officers didn't carry guns. Costa Rica was a very safe place.

So I ended up going to the social security hospital in San Vito. I had never been there before. I rode my motorcycle and asked directions when I got lost. In Costa Rica people give directions based on buildings or stores or other landmarks, such as "then when you get to the *pulpería*, go past two more houses and turn right…" I have never been able to follow those kinds of directions. I love to find my way with maps, but I never had a map of the streets of San Vito. It was really too small a town for that, I guess.

It took the two hospital administrators a good bit of time to complete all of the required forms so that I could be seen by medical personnel. But once I had finally gotten finished with that part of the visit, I was able to see a doctor. The expression on his face when he saw how swollen my arm was one of alarm and shock. That scared me more than anything else.

He said, "Señora, what were you thinking was wrong with your arm when it kept getting more and more swollen?"

He asked a lot of questions, like how long it had been that way, and what had happened to make it infected. He seemed very worried about the infection, and I gathered that he thought it was pretty dangerous. He actually got angry at me because I hadn't sought medical attention sooner.

"Señora, you have put yourself in a very dangerous situation. You are very close to having blood poisoning..."

His face turned red at that point and I think that he just stopped just short of calling me stupid.

He kept insisting that the swollen arm must be very painful, and I kept telling him that it was really not that bad. Never in my entire life had anyone been so concerned about my health. Somehow what seemed like a minor infection to me had turned out to be a very serious one indeed.

He gave me two bottles with different kinds of pills and some antibiotic ointment and then rushed me off to another part of the hospital to get my first antibiotic shot. Because I was allergic to penicillin, he had prescribed Lincocin instead.

His concern and interest in my condition quickly faded from my mind as I went on to the next part of the hospital process.

It began when I walked up to the two short, stocky women with black hair swept back neatly under white triangular hats and dressed in impeccable white uniforms. They were the hospital nurses who ran the shot clinic. They looked at each other when they saw me and spoke to each other in whispers before taking my prescription. I had a feeling that they didn't like the looks of me at all, a small woman with blue eyes and curly brown hair wearing blue jeans and boots and carrying a crazy motorcycle helmet in a town where women usually wore dresses and nice shoes to the hospital.

"Señora," said the shortest one, "why did the doctor prescribe Lincocin? You'll have penicillin, just like everyone else here." Penicillin was what everyone got in a country where medical care was free. It was by far the cheapest antibiotic available.

"But no, I can't take the *droga penicillina*; I'm allergic to it! It gives me itchy red spots all over my body!"

Unfortunately I kept calling penicillin a *droga* as I was trying to describe my allergic reaction to it.

Finally, the taller of the two nurses said, "Señora, we don't have any *drogas* in this hospital. We have only *medicinas*."

It was only after I had described repeatedly and in great detail the red splotches and itching that I got all over my body when I took penicillin that they finally agreed to give me the more expensive antibiotic.

I had to have a total of five antibiotic shots; the first was given at the hospital. I was really surprised that the nurses wouldn't let me wait at the hospital to make sure that I didn't have an allergic reaction to it. I suppose that I had thoroughly convinced them that I was a drug addict and a hippie, too, and they wanted me out of there as fast as possible. The other four shots were given to me by the pharmacist in Sabalito. The nurses gave me four vials to take to him, and fortunately I was able to get the final four shots in my arm and not my backside, which would have been very embarrassing to me since somehow a pharmacist was not quite a doctor or nurse in my mind.

I got a lot done between the week of my motorcycle wreck on the asphalt road to Las Brisas and the visit to the social security hospital in San Vito, strangely enough. Because I was not feeling well, I didn't join Paul on a trip to Palmar Norte to meet up with a bunch of fellow Volunteers. Instead I took a letter to the manager of the coffee cooperative in Sabalito on Friday morning asking for a donation of 600 pounds of fertilizer for schools in the Sabalito school district. Six hundred pounds sounds like a lot of fertilizer, but I visited fifteen schools on a regular basis, and there were more than that in the district. The coffee cooperative was an easy walk from our house, just past the soccer field that served as the town plaza and past the post office and down the first cross road to the right, directly across the street from the Escuela Gonzalo Acuña, one of the schools where I worked.

The manager was very nice to me and suggested that I go to a meeting of the Board of Directors that afternoon and present the request. Paul spoke Spanish very well, but I did not, so the prospect of reading the letter to the Board was a very scary one. However, the manager promised that he would ask the secretary to read the letter and said that all I would have to do would be answer any questions that the Board members had.

So that Friday afternoon, just five days before my visit to the social security hospital, I appeared at the meeting of the Board. I waited outside the room where the members were meeting until it was time for my letter to be read. I was very nervous, wondering if I would even understand any of the questions that they might ask me. When it was my turn, I entered the room and sat at the place I was directed to. The Board members were seated around a big table. The secretary sat off at the side of the room and read the letter. After he was finished I answered a few questions.

"Señora, so why didn't the Ministry of Education give fertilizer to the schools?"

"Well, they were going to, but they ran out of money. They did buy tools, and soon the chicken wire will be shipped from the warehouse in San José so that we'll have fences to keep the animals out of the gardens, but there wasn't enough money in the budget for fertilizer."

"Señora, so what is the importance of fertilizer?"

"Oh, the soil is so poor, and we are trying to grow vegetables for the school cafeterias. Imagine trying to grow coffee without fertilizer. *Es muy difícil. Imagínese!*"

After answering a few more questions I was told that I would need to return to the cooperative on Saturday morning to get an answer to my request.

When I returned to the cooperative on Saturday I was told that the request had been approved and that all of the fertilizer would be delivered to the office of Doña Marielos, the supervisor of the Sabalito school district, on Monday or Tuesday. The teachers would be able to pick their share up when they came to Sabalito for their next paychecks at the end of the month.

It was probably my most important accomplishment as a Peace Corps Volunteer. I had managed to connect the business community with the educational community in the small town of Sabalito; now the coffee cooperative had begun to work with the schools to help improve the lives of the children who were most in need, the ones who relied on the free meals they got every day as part of the school lunch program.

The fertilizer was delivered to Doña Marielos' office the day before I went to the social security hospital for my shots. My arm responded well and the swelling subsided quickly, leaving only an aching elbow to remind me of unchained dogs and the danger of paved roads.

Martha Martin was on the road in Costa Rica from 1979-81. She is now an Admissions and Academic Consultant at the School of Management at George Mason University. She just ran in her third Marine Corps Marathon for a personal record and is currently working on a creative non-fictional account of her years as a Peace Corps Volunteer.

SARAH HAWLEY

Tree Business

*One Volunteer in Nicaragua learns a lifelong
lesson in cross-cultural profit sharing.*

WAR GAMES OF HUNTING DOWN MANGOS FROM THE TOPS OF
trees were left in the battlefield. Empty porridge bowls hung
silently in the kitchen. Errands requested by parents stood on
hold as fifteen girls pleaded with screaming hands, bouncing
to play.

We played.

In the 256-habitant mountain village, we played in the sun-
shine, under clear skies and in the rain. We played *Chocolate
Pinolio*, *Perrito Perrito*, and *Rojo y Verde*. We played with balls
and Frisbees. We danced to *regatón*, *ranchero* and *típico*. We pretended to be a wedding with a thief for our socio-drama debut.
Quinceañera dresses out of toilet paper were added to the mix.
We picked animals out of clouds and read storybooks, and all
the while an agro-business grew.

As a freshman Peace Corps Volunteer just learning to crawl,
I tried hard to accomplish something before my first site visit
from our agriculture program director. One of our objectives
was to work with a youth group on gardens, tree nurseries, and

95

money. I looked in every direction except south, holding my head high and determined to build trust with the older kids. Determined not to fail. We got together for a few games of kickball and just to hang out. Time came to look for firewood, haul water, and shoot birds with sling shots. They just began to set dates for events and more kickball games, and I sat waiting.

On the side, I had a group of young girls who always showed up even on unplanned days. It did not enter my mind to work with these girls on agricultural projects, but as the older kids stopped being interested, the girls jumped at the idea with eagerness.

We planted a tree nursery at my house with only about twenty bags. We built a little rock wall and covered it with thorns. I did most of the watering and eventually moved the bags closer to the house. Then the pigs came and destroyed them all. Seriously. They ate the leaves, knocked over the bags, and spilled our work all over the ground. The kids laughed and picked up some of the black dirt from the treeless bags to start over.

Round two began with scrap wood, rusty nails, thorns, and my host dad's help in setting the posts. A fence was constructed, and this time we filled 100 bags. My host mom had started a compost pile, so we took advantage of the moist dark soil. For two days the kids got their fingernails dirty seeing who could fill the bags the fastest. A few girls came to plant the *moringa, tan marindo*, acacia, and avocado seeds, while it became my job to water the trees regularly. Months passed, the trees grew, and pigs came to test our fence. Saramelia mentioned ever so shyly that we should sell the trees to help with the construction of the children's feeding station.

She was only nine years old.

Notebook and pen in hand we set out to collect three cordobas per tree (five cordobas for avocado) and to record what each person wanted to buy. About forty trees were requested and no cordobas given because the buyers wanted to wait for the product. Through my urging, the kids offered to help plant the trees. After about two weeks of waiting, the kids collected their courage to deliver the trees. New seedlings soon sprouted in the community as well as a small group fund.

The girls liked having money and my hope to use the funds for a group excursion took flight. We sold popcorn with bubble gum in each bag as the prize. Tang fruit juice filled plastic bags and was hauled to the baseball field and sold, with the change added to their box. Some girls carted a used clothing store around to houses.

Then came the time for a decision to be made regarding the use of the funds. Not many liked the excursion idea because of what their parents might say or the fear of leaving the village to visit a strange place. "We want it to buy notebooks," they cried. I was hesitant because I knew they would just buy candy and help for the feeding station would be dropped to the thorn bushes.

Just shy of 300 cordobas was the end result for the year, and seventeen kids awaited a paycheck. I gritted my teeth while divvying out ten cordobas per child, which was their decision. Their hard work—so many hours—all handed to the corner store. With the leftover money, it was my turn to do the begging. I pleaded to save the funds for an end of the year picnic of spaghetti, tomato sauce, cabbage salad, and juice. This we could agree on. It took some personal reminding that they were the owners of the money, the ones who did the work and the reason for this group project.

The girls dusted off their empty porridge bowls and came to my house. We laid out our yard-long black, plastic picnic blanket, as Oliver Twist re-emerged. Seventeen kids waited patiently for their slab of food. The headmistress, myself, with a black plastic ladle in hand, only hoping that through this first year of my service I was able to fill some part of their lives with encouragement and just maybe teach them how to plant a few trees.

Each smile as they devoured our picnic lunch amongst cries of "When can we do this again?" opened up the opportunity to start over next year. Some even did buy notebooks.

Sarah Hawley served in Nicaragua from 2006-09. Currently, she is teaching second grade at a Spanish Immersion Elementary school in Mississippi as part of Teach for America. Sarah has enrolled at Delta State University pursuing a master's in Elementary Education. Last month she returned to visit her host family in Nicaragua and helped build an improved oven.

RICHARD MORTENSEN

✲

Anabegonda

An anaconda goes missing. Guess where it winds up.

IN 1972, AS A NEWLY MINTED PEACE CORPS VOLUNTEER FRESH
out of training in Puerto Rico, I was assigned to Belize Junior
Secondary School #2, which had been built on cleared and
filled jungle land along a tributary of the Belize River. As I
stared out at the freshly scrubbed faces in their newly starched
white shirts, blouses, olive green pants and skirts, sweat poured
from every gland and pore of my body, as both the temperature and humidity neared the 100 mark. "What am I gonna
do with these kids?" I thought, as the first-day jitters gained a
foothold on my youth and inexperience.

The classroom itself was the best that soon-to-be-semi-
independent British Honduras could do with the few meager
pounds and schillings Great Britain managed to send her way.
There were some wooden tables, wooden stools, a few tat-
tered science books from the West Indies Science Project, and
a few pieces of hand-me-down science equipment from Belize
Teacher's College. And still those eager young eyes stared with
anticipation at the tall skinny white kid from "da States."

With the hurricane shutters open, the sounds of birds and monkeys hung over the lush green canopy of the surrounding jungle as the river coursed its way through the dense foliage. "Let's go for a walk" I said, "and tell me about this place you call 'da bush'."

Thus began my two-year odyssey as a science and math teacher in what was to become Belize during my tenure. Two years of exploring the jungle classroom surrounding the physical structure of BJSS #2 resulted in a collection of insects, rodents, snakes, small mammals, and even an occasional fish, most of which we were able to observe for a few days before returning them to their habitat. I learned what my students knew, and they learned of the intricate balance between their lush country, their lives and the critters they share it with.

On one of our river foraging expeditions, we managed to "capture" two relatively small anacondas. These monsters can grow to fourteen feet or more, but ours were a mere eight feet. Belizeans, like much of humankind around the globe, are terrified of snakes, and it was no small feat to persuade them not to "stone" these slithery characters. After much discussion and an abundance of screams, we managed to bring the two safely back to the school and provide them with temporary housing in two large cages that had been constructed on the grounds. Over the next few days, a begrudging awareness began to develop within my students as they came to better understand the passive nature of the snakes (unless provoked or hungry!), and the role they play in controlling Belize's rampant rat population. Most of the students even managed to hold the snakes, although I suspect the opportunity to have their photo taken was the underlying motivator!

Sadly, on the morning of the fifth day, one cage was found destroyed and one of the snakes hacked to death with a machete. No evidence of the second snake was anywhere to be found, and we hoped the snake had avoided a similar fate and made it back to the river.

Later that morning, the classroom was disturbed by a terrified, screaming young girl who told me there was something in the girl's outhouse and would I please "come quick, mistah!" With thirty or so excited kids trailing behind, I made it to the outbuilding and found most of the rest of the school crowded around the opening, cautiously peering inside. Curled up inside the cool porcelain commode and relishing the occasional splash of water, was our wayward anaconda. I can only imagine what went through the student's mind as she prepared to park herself on the "throne" only to discover it was otherwise occupied! With a little help, we managed to maneuver the wandering serpent back to the river and as it slithered away, one of my clever young wisps was heard to note, "Anabegonda!"

Richard Mortensen served as a Peace Corps Volunteer in Belize from 1972-74.

LES YOUNG

Ecuadorian *Béisbol*

Whether played in a cornfield in Iowa or a town in Ecuador,
baseball can certainly be a model for good sportsmanship.

BY APRIL THE RAINY SEASON IS OVER IN ECUADOR, AND CHIL-dren are in school again. Soon the baseball season will begin, and La Comisión de Béisbol appears serious about reviving youth baseball in Guayaquil, the country's largest city. To my surprise, they secure uniforms and equipment for four teams, ages fourteen and younger. *El Universo* and Radio Crystal promote the new Liga Infantil, and on a beautiful Saturday morning, the left-field bleachers are filled with boys eager to play.

There are men present that I don't know, some of whom played baseball in Guayaquil during an earlier era. Even another foreign coach is there. Eufemio is from the Dominican Republic. I am from Norwood, North Carolina. A year ago I was co-captain of the North Carolina State 1963 Wolfpack team. I'm now a Peace Corps Volunteer.

After a brief try-out period, La Comisión de Béisbol selects the teams and announces the coaches. I'm stunned to learn that I am not among them.

What's going on? Am I not the best baseball coach in Ecuador? *El Universo* suggests as much in article after article. Compounding my confusion, no one in the stadium speaks English, except me. And my Spanish fluency is narrow.

Motioning to centerfield, Señor Sáenz, the president of La Comisión de Béisbol, gathers the boys not selected and says to me, "Let's take these boys out there to play." Now I get it. They want me to coach the boys no one else wants.

Señor Sáenz calls to the stadium keeper, "Juan, where are the balls and bats Enrique brought yesterday?"

"In the clubhouse, boss."

"*Bueno*, bring them here." We walk to deep centerfield, and Juan arrives with the balls and bats. They're homemade—short bats turned from lightweight wood and hand-stitched balls, soft enough to catch barehanded—perfect for these boys who've never touched a baseball before.

We begin tossing and catching, and Señor Sáenz returns to the infield. I show them how to throw the ball overhanded, catch with their hands formed like a basket, and hold and swing the bat properly. Fly balls require more attention. I develop a technique for catching them: palms up, hands touching with fingers spread apart. And I demonstrate, over and again. As the ball arrives, lower your hands and body, and bend your knees, reducing the chance the ball will bounce from your grasp.

The eight young boys pay close attention and learn quickly, and I begin to experience that wondrous feeling a teacher gets when a student masters a subject hitherto a mystery. When practice is over I ask, "Do you want to play again next Saturday?"

"*Sí! Sí!*" they reply.

Delighted with their enthusiasm, I say, "Then bring a friend with you. It takes more players than this for a game."

These boys remind me of a childhood disappointment of my own. One day I overheard some of my older friends discussing a try-out for a ball team. Fourth graders were not invited. I was too young, but that did not deter me: I went there anyway, mitt and mask in hand. I knew I could play ball as well as any fifth- or sixth-grade boy, better than most. To my disappointment I didn't get to try out. With tears in my eyes, I walked home from the ballpark that Saturday morning. My parents must have noticed. The following season there was a three-team league in our little two-stoplight town, and I played second base for the Reds.

The next Saturday morning I'm thrilled to find thirty boys waiting for me at the stadium, enough for four teams. The weather is beautiful, not a cloud in the sky. It's this way from April to mid-December, year after year, perfect baseball weather. Guayaquil, a bustling port city, is located just two degrees south of the equator and fifty miles upriver from the Pacific. Farther east, but not visible from Guayaquil, the Andes dominate the landscape with brilliant snow-covered peaks.

We practice for a while, and then I align the boys by height and count-off by fours, hoping this will yield relatively even-strength teams. They each take names—*Los Gatos* and *Ratones, Las Cobras* and *Mangosta*: the Cats and Mice, Cobras and Mongoose.

I appoint the tallest boy on each team as *el capitán* for the day, and he assigns positions to his teammates. Each week new captains will be named, extending the privilege eventually to all. To further simplify game-day organization, a pre-fixed batting order is established. The first baseman always bats first, second baseman second, shortstop third, the easier to remember the batting order. No written line-up is required; I record runs on the ground with a length of *caña*: a bamboo strip.

As the first game is played, the other two teams watch patiently, waiting their turn. I know I must do the pitching. Let the batter swing until he hits the ball. No strikeouts, no walks. For smaller boys I pitch from closer range. I pitch underhanded, when needed, until the batter can hit an overhanded pitch.

Another rule I decide to break concerns substitutions. Everyone on a team is entered in the batting order and everyone plays in the field. If a child comes to play, he gets to play.

Some of the boys hit the ball immediately. Others have trouble getting their bat on the ball. Miguel is among the latter. After a series of missed swings, I notice a frown. I approach Miguel and say, "Try to see the ball bounce off your bat. That's impossible to do; no one can do it. Yet, the longer you watch the ball, the better chance you have of hitting it solid. Do you understand?"

"*Sí,*" Miguel replies. He swings again and comes nearer to the ball.

"*Bien,*" I say. "That's better, but swing harder. And keep your eye on the ball." Miguel connects with the next pitch and races to first base, his teammates cheering and jumping up and down. Safe! A base hit! A smile as bright as the Ecuadorian sunrise appears on his face, and on mine too. "*Que bueno!*" I roar, loud enough to be heard throughout the park.

On another Saturday little Alonzo kicks at a pebble and says beneath his breath, "No! Not Carlos. He'll make an out."

I stop the game and gather everyone around to talk about sportsmanship. "Listen," I tell them. "We are here to have fun, and everyone gets to play. Putting down another player has no place here. Encourage each other, don't tear each other down."

I beckon to Alonzo, and we walk a few paces away. Bending to one knee and looking him in the eye, I choose my words as best I can, "Do you understand why I stopped the game?"

"*Sí*," he looks down. "I should not have said that about Carlos." Then, returning his eyes to mine, "I'm sorry. I won't do it again. I promise."

"*Bien*. I didn't think you would," I reply. "Now, let me tell you what's going to happen. There's a penalty for poor sportsmanship. I don't like doing this, but I must. It's important that you and everyone else know this rule. The penalty is: You lose your next turn at bat. Do you understand?"

"*Sí*," Alonzo answers, putting forth a brave face, no tears, no pleas for leniency. He's such a tender boy, not more than twelve years old, but he looks younger. All Ecuadorian children look younger than their age. I'm sure he wants to cry.

"*Bueno*." We turn back to face the others and I announce, "Play ball." I pat Alonzo on the back as he returns to his teammates, and I to pitch to Carlos. Some of the boys may be confused, not having heard Alonzo's comment, but it will become clear to them when Alonzo forfeits his next turn at bat. I'm confident I'll not have to impose this penalty again.

Little Carlos doesn't hit the ball hard, but he runs like crazy, his hustle making up for his small stature. Who knows? One day Alonzo may be pleased to have little Carlos as his teammate and friend.

Within a few weeks our league grows to six teams. Week-by-week more boys arrive, many walking great distances to the ballpark, some barefooted, others in shoes molded from injected plastic, no socks. We continue forming new teams, playing our games in deep centerfield, as the older boys play on the regulation diamond. By the end of the season our league contains fourteen teams, and Pepe, a new Peace Corps arrival, helps with the coaching. Later Pepe informs our Peace Corps Director, "I want to coach Les' league next year." I'm happy to know this. My two years in the Peace Corps will end before the next baseball season.

Prior to my departure Pepe asks, "Tell me, Les, what is the secret of your league's success?"

I think for moment, careful to get it right. "We are talking about beginners, right?" Pepe nods agreement. "Let's see. One, have the same adult pitch to both teams, and forget about strikes and walks. Two, never allow grownups to compete with each other as coaches. And three, insist on good sportsmanship."

"That's about it," I conclude. "Follow this and you'll be fine. Keep it simple. Keep it fun."

Then, before our discussion drifts elsewhere, I add, "There's one thing more. Let 'em all play."

Les Young successfully coached béisbol *in Ecuador from 1963-65. For the next seventeen years Coach Young was the leader of his hometown's summer baseball program for beginners, seven- to ten-year boys and girls. Most of his Ecuadorian* béisbol *rules applied, but unlike his Guayaquil youngsters, the North Carolina youth did not play barehanded. Today, Coach Young enjoys reading and writing and continues to reside in his hometown, Norwood, North Carolina.*

Celebrity

*Sometimes you can serendipitously fall into a project
that not only transforms your view of yourself, but
also of the world in which you live.*

DURING MY TRAINING IN TEGUCIGALPA, THE CAPITAL OF Honduras, another Volunteer asked me if I was interested in a double date with a couple of Hondurans. We met them downtown, and they led us to an expensive car. In a country where the per capita income was measured in hundreds of dollars, such a car was unusual. The Hondurans took my Peace Corps friend and me to a private club where you had to knock on the door and give a password to get in. The place was dark and choking with cigarette smoke. There was recorded music, a bar, and lots of young people drinking, talking, dancing. Our language skills were still not that great, and I wondered if we would get out alive.

My anxiety increased when my date later drove us back to his house. There was a giant gate and an armed guard. All I could think of was how we could get out of there. The house was huge. It had seven bathrooms. On one counter, I saw a photo. My date pointed and said that it was his father. His father stood next to an important American diplomat. I asked him,

"How did your father get a photo with him?" He explained that his father was the Honduran President. Our relationship would go nowhere. My father was only an attorney.

Our assignments went better, although in smaller quarters. After we finished training and were sworn in, I was placed with Joanne Gondel in Masica for about a month. They only had one school and there was not much for us to do, so the Peace Corps sent Joanne to Tela and me to La Ceiba. Dolores Demayo (Dee Dee) was a professional teacher who had originally been sent to La Ceiba as a teacher trainer. She had never spoken Spanish before arriving and had asked for help. Since I majored in Spanish in college and also spent six months in Mexico City before the Peace Corps, someone thought that we might make a good team.

Dee Dee already had a house, a two-bedroom, two-bath wooden delight located one block from the ocean. It was what we called a "Peace Corps House." One after another, Volunteers had been renting it for years, maybe since 1963 when Peace Corps had its first program there. Dee Dee inherited it from someone, which meant that it was furnished and had pots, pans, and everything else to run a household. There were four of us who shared the rent, fifty dollars each. I don't think we even had a written rental agreement.

Our assignment was to train preschool teachers, first in La Ceiba and, later, in other communities along the north coast. The schools were called "kinders," and the students were five years old or younger. When Dee Dee arrived, the curriculum consisted of the children singing, breaking for a snack, then singing some more. Our job was not to teach children, but to teach teachers how to make inexpensive learning materials and how to set up corners of the classroom with toys used for learning. "Learning Centers" were a popular concept in the United States during the 1970s. Instead of seating the children and trying to teach everyone at once, the teachers divided the classroom up into little groups that would go to different tables where they had specific tasks and games. After so many minutes, the groups rotated. The teachers did not lecture, but walked around the class helping when the students had questions.

Dee Dee did most of the work, and I made the jokes in Spanish while drinking coffee. She had been a teacher in the United States and had contacts. She was able to get free materials from all over. Schools would send us all these workbooks that they didn't want. Sometimes we went to the ritzy neighborhood called Narajal, knocking on doors and asking Hondurans to donate magazines. We collected the old magazines, cut them up and pasted the pictures to old computer cards, which had been donated by I.B.M. in Tegucigalpa. We used these for matching games. Empty oatmeal containers filled with rice or beans became maracas. How long would these really last in the humid tropics? How long before a rat ate through the container?

We made puzzles out of cardboard. Dee Dee and I would cut and cut, making examples for the teachers to follow. About once a month, we would travel to a school where we held a teacher's workshop. The teachers drew puzzles and then cut. One puzzle was a picture of a boy. We had an example of a completed puzzle. They all started to work on their puzzles, doing exactly what we did. If the boy had a red hat, every single teacher colored in a red hat. At one conference, I even mentioned, "You can color this however you want. You could even color his legs green." A few minutes later, I walked around the room to check on the teachers' progress. Every puzzle included a boy with green legs. It was weird trying to change a mindset. These were kindergarten teachers who had themselves studied a total of six years.

We used to open the workshop with an introductory exercise to get to know each other and to put everyone at ease. All the teachers would explain three unusual talents or skills that they might have. This was our icebreaker. The teachers took it very seriously. A lot of teachers told us that they could iron. Many were proud of the fact that they could ride a bicycle. One teacher told a group that she could type on a typewriter. The class stopped. The group whispered, "You can type?"

Over our more than two years, we went to many different places in Honduras, even Trujillo, which you could only reach by plane or ship. In our workshop there, I told the teachers to gather newspapers for a project. They all looked at me blankly. There was no local newspaper. Limited copies of another city's paper arrived once a week on a plane. How could they?

It was easy for us because we were foreigners. We could get paper, oatmeal cans, even books from the United States. Our counterparts were barely eking out a living and had no access to such resources. We were like celebrities. Everyone knew us and treated us special.

Sandy Elliott served in Honduras from 1974-77 as part of Group 27. She lived in La Ceiba, the third most populated city in Honduras, which is located on the Caribbean coast, and served as a teacher trainer in various Honduran localities. After the Peace Corps, she returned to her home state of California and works for a county court helping with information technology.

JEFF BENIK

The Missing Hand

As the author recounts, there are occasions when things unexpectedly seem to come together—and when they do, the memories are sweet.

BEFORE I ARRIVED IN MIAMI BEACH, FLORIDA, FOR PEACE Corps orientation, la Republica de Honduras had accepted a loan from USAID to purchase all the equipment necessary to set up four industrial arts pilot programs. American Peace Corps Volunteers were recruited to set up the shops and teach Honduran teachers. There were four of us who trained for the work, each of us to manage four schools. Two Volunteers dropped out before leaving Miami. A third made it to Honduras, but after someone broke into his room late at night, his wife insisted that they return home. I was left as the last remaining industrial arts trainer.

I taught at Manuel Bonilla, a recently constructed middle school and high school. There was a large, open, and empty room with stacks of boxes ten feet high off to one side. Nobody there had a clue how to open the boxes. No safety lines had been painted on the floor. Tables with vices had not been set up. There were no tool cabinets. All of the equipment was still neatly boxed. It had not even been inventoried. The shop was to contain wood, leather, metal, and automobile repair equipment. Aside from setting up a shop, I needed to set up rules and sample lesson plans. For instance, the people who were to be my students had never even seen a table saw, a band saw, or a lathe.

My first task was an inventory. My Honduran counterpart and I wanted to try our best to safeguard and keep track of all of the machines and hand tools throughout the school year. Next, we set up the shop. I drew a to-scale plan, and my counterpart and I assembled machinery and painted safety lines on the floor. I built lockable cabinets for the hand tools. Every tool had its outline painted on the backboard so that it was easy to put away and very obvious when missing. I didn't want things walking off.

From day one of classes, students were assigned to industrial arts, but we could not do anything because I first had to teach the teachers since they had no training in the field. Aside from familiarizing them with the equipment, I had to set up lesson plans and teach them how to teach. It was a long process.

My shop was not set up before the start of the famous La Ceiba carnival held during the third week of May. The population of the town doubled. The population at my house quadrupled. Peace Corps Volunteers laid out sleeping bags across the floors of each room. It was an all-night party that included the entire city. The streets were a pulsating mass of dancing flesh. For six nights, neighborhoods each sponsored a dance in the street with live music. The last night, bandstands were set up on each corner from the ocean to the main highway. There must have been at least sixteen bands. The band or bands that made it to sunrise won a cash prize. It was drunken debauchery at its best. I loved it.

A few months after the carnival, I finished my shop. I sent out invitations for a two-day workshop. The purpose was to introduce safety procedures, basic machinery operation, and teaching techniques. The invitation was sent to fifteen other schools, education leaders, and even the President of Honduras. At least thirty people attended the workshop. The president could not make it, but sent a personal letter of thanks.

For teaching safety, I had constructed a wooden hand. During my table saw demonstration, I purposely took off the safety guards. I talked nonchalantly as I pushed a board through the saw blade, cutting off my wooden prop hand in front of my startled audience. Then we had a lively discussion about what I had done wrong.

Just before going home, I traveled to three other schools with industrial arts programs. All three had been set up using my conference as their model. It really made me feel good. My Peace Corps experience had been a success.

Jeff Benik was part of Group 30 in Honduras from 1975-77 and served as a teacher trainer in La Ceiba. He recalls that on returning home to California, he wondered at the obsession with Mork and Mindy. *After two years of solving the world's problems in Parqe Central where locals took walks, talked politics and sports, flirted, ate, and drank, living vicariously through the TV seemed meaningless and shallow.*

SARA BETH LAIRD

✳

Everyday Greetings

In evaluating a Peace Corps experience, as in most things,
success can be defined in more than just one way.

AFTER A YEAR AND A HALF, I AM JUST NOW CONSCIOUSLY NOTICING
patterns that I follow daily. Recently I took the time to reflect
on my typical "day in the life" and was astonished to realize how
many people I interact with on a daily basis. In St. Lucia, and
especially in my rural village of Choiseul, you don't just walk
past a person; you actually greet them. Greetings come in all
shapes and forms, but some greetings I have realized are part of
a daily social routine and are missed in my absence.

The greetings begin with my early morning exercise. I leave
my house around 5:30 A.M to go walking, and immediately I
wave to my neighbors, Ma Haynes and Mr. Haynes, who are
sitting on their front porch. I simply wave because it is too
early for me to talk yet, as I just rolled out of bed and into my
tennis shoes. But if I accidentally don't look over their way as
I pass by, they make sure I see them by clapping or banging
on something.

Next, I come across Norbert, who lives in a little galva-
nized shed behind another house. He likes to whistle to get

115

my attention. I greet him and move up the road to Johnny Boy's house where I'm usually serenaded or quoted poetry while walking by. From there I walk up the hill and pass by Adelina, the shopkeeper, who usually greets me in her night-gown while combing Shania's hair, the little girl she is raising.

On my way back home from exercising, there's Chappy, who I greet as he goes on his way out to the garden, and Mrs. Raymonise who is usually sweeping her front yard and calls me *doudou* ("darling" in Kwéyòl). And if there is a day that I don't exercise, believe you me, they notice, and sometimes let me hear about it!

Later in the morning as I head down into the village for work, I greet a whole other set of people, since I am heading in a different direction from my house than my early morn-ing path. The usual people include the man who is always wearing brightly colored pants walking up the hill, Roger the guy who likes to wear pants on his head, the old man with the cane sitting on the stoop of a house, the guys who are repairing vehicles in front of my office, the lady with the dogs outside of the meat shop, the environmental health offi-cer who shares our office space, and finally Mac Arthur, my community partner.

After spending some time in the office, I go deeper into the village to run errands, and I come across another group of people whom I've grown accustomed to greeting. There are the men at Millan's rum shop, Joan and her husband Winston who hang out of their front window, and the people on the corner by the supermarket where I turn to go up the next street. Around the corner, I greet one of the resident *jumbies* (witch doctor) and then the two ladies who are always sitting outside of their shops on stools chatting. Next I come to the post office where I am warmly greeted by the postmistress who gets even more excited than I do when I receive mail.

After doing my errands, I head back out of the village saying goodbye to everyone I greeted on the way in and head back up the hill to my home. At the top of the hill, I have an internal debate as to whether I should go in and say hello to the shopkeeper at the supermarket. I know that if I go in it is always so hot that I will leave soaking wet, but I also know how much she enjoys my stopping by so she can pick on me for a little while and have a good laugh for the day. So, I usually decide to brave the heat and drop in before heading home.

When I first came to Choiseul, I did not know anybody and wondered how long it would take to get acquainted with the people. But now, I can look back and see how many relationships actually developed and how I truly became a part of the community. This daily exchange has become such a routine, and an expected one at that. If there is ever a time that I don't go into the village for some reason, maybe I have a bunch of meetings in Castries or elsewhere, the next time I go down people ask me where I have been. So, I've learned that I must inform people if I won't be around for a while, especially if I'm going to be off of the island for more than a few days. In a way, it is comforting to know that people are always watching for me and waiting for that daily greeting. It is strange to know that the most I've ever said to some of these people is "Good morning," but they feel that they know me, and I'm fairly certain that I'll be missed by them when my two years are finished.

It all just goes to show that you never truly know the impact that you will have on someone's life while in the Peace Corps. I came in thinking that I would change the world and actually see some difference in the way things were before I left. And it may be strange to say that something as simple as greeting a person every day can achieve anything, but I truly believe that it does. Though at times I miss the anonymity that comes so easily in America, I know that I will miss my everyday greetings that I give and receive so freely here in Choiseul. May I never take for granted what impact a kind word or gesture can make in another's life.

Sara Beth Laird (aka Sandy Grace) served from 2003-05 as a Small Business Development Volunteer on the island nation of St. Lucia in the rural fishing village of Choiseul. She came into the Peace Corps with a Texas accent and background in corporate training, which proved very useful as she sought to teach business skills to others in her village. She now lives and works in San Antonio, Texas, once again as a corporate trainer.

MATTHEW DUFRESNE

Who Stole My Cheese?

A little matter of some missing cheese leads to larger considerations of honesty, respect, and forgiveness.

"WHO COULD HAVE, OR WOULD HAVE, STOLEN MY CHEESE?" I asked Roger. "Don't these people realize that I have come from a long ways away to help them and this is what they do to me?"

Roger was speechless, but I knew he was feeling the same way I was. Like me, he was an outsider, but instead of being from Minnesota, he was from Managua, which could have been right next door to Minnesota as far as the people from this small town knew. No, no, this just can't be, is all I could think. My community wouldn't steal my cheese from me. It must be someone playing a practical joke, right? Right? I was hoping so.

At the time of the cheese incident I had been living and working for about six months as a community health educator at the local health clinic in Acoyapa, Nicaragua. I felt as though I had a good grasp on the language, an understanding of the culture, and a good relationship with my community. I was always out and about in my community, and wherever I went I'd always hear the warm greetings of "*Hola, Don Mateo*" or "*Cómo está, doctor?*" My community loved and appreciated me, didn't they?

Roger had recently graduated from medical school in Managua and was performing his required year of community service in Acoyapa. Roger and I had hit it off since we were the same age and had similar ambitions and backgrounds. Plus neither of us was from Acoyapa. We often worked and hung out together, practiced English and Spanish on each other, and frequently commiserated with one another. Roger and I saw eye to eye on most things, and we morally supported one another through the challenges of being in a new town, being away from family and friends, and in trying to understand small-town living.

It had been a slow afternoon at the clinic that day, so Roger and I decided to go out for a walk in town. We ended up getting back after closing time and found the clinic locked up tight. I peered into the window of the clinic and saw that my bike was safely inside, but I didn't see the piece of cheese I'd purchased earlier that afternoon from a couple of local kids who always sold their goods around the clinic. I had bought that tasty piece of cheese for dinner later on that day, and now that it was around dinnertime I was hungry and really looking forward to it.

Just to be clear, this was no everyday piece of cheese. This was fresh *quesillo* that had been made that day. So when I noticed the cheese was not on the back of my bike where I had left it before my walk with Roger, I was upset. My first thought was that the clinic staff was playing a joke on me and had hidden it. They were always playing practical jokes on one another, so I figured that this must be the case.

Roger and I walked up the street to find the nurse who was on-call that night to get the key to the clinic so that we could retrieve our belongings. Roger and I joked about how someone must be fooling with me and that we'd find my cheese once we got inside and started to look around. I told Roger that we'd likely find the cheese with some note from the jokester. Ha-ha! When we got up to the on-call nurse's house, we knocked on the door and asked for the key so that we could get our stuff. It just so happened that this nurse was the biggest jokester of everyone in the clinic, so I told her about not seeing my cheese waiting for me on my bike. She feigned ignorance about any knowledge of my cheese. Hum, this must all be part of the joke. I was sure that I'd find my cheese soon enough now that I had the key to the clinic.

Roger and I went back down to the clinic, let ourselves in and started to look for the cheese. Fifteen minutes later, after looking high and low, we hadn't found a trace of my cheese. At this point I started thinking that someone must have stolen my cheese. "Who would've stolen my cheese?" I asked Roger. The ever cool-headed and logical Roger suggested that maybe one of the clinic staff might have taken it home with them for safekeeping. This seemed plausible enough, so Roger and I went to go ask around for my cheese.

Of course it was dinnertime for everyone, but I figured that since it was supposed to be my dinnertime, too, and since I was looking for my dinner that people would understand my interruption of their mealtime. So off we went knocking on one door, then another and another and another. As we went from house to house, it became apparent that no one knew anything about my cheese.

"Who could have, or would have, stolen my cheese?" I asked Roger. "Don't these people realize that I have come from a long ways away to help them and this is what they do to me?" Roger didn't know what to say at this point. So he said he was going home because he didn't want to be late to the dinner that was surely waiting for him. He invited me along and said that we probably weren't going to find my cheese anyway. Roger was always the pragmatist and I the eternal optimist, so I told him I was going to keeping on knocking on doors until I'd spoken to everyone in the clinic and found my cheese.

Roger gave me a look that said, "You're only going to frustrate yourself, but that's up to you." All I could think of was that this just couldn't be. My community wouldn't steal my cheese from me, right? I was a Peace Corps Volunteer after all. That would have been like stealing candy from a baby. Unthinkable! Unconscionable! But it was becoming more of a possibility in my mind.

As I went from one house to the next, I became hungrier and more worked up. My door knocking became louder and more vigorous as I continued my search. I also became more animated and less thoughtful as I spoke to each staff member and potential cheese thief. I knew someone was holding out on me. This cruel joke had gone on too long. It wasn't funny anymore.

After badmouthing the clinic staff, the town of Acoyapa, the people of Nicaragua and all of humanity I finally realized that I had been beaten. It was 8 P.M., the town was going to bed, the stores were all closed, and I was not going to be having cheese for dinner that night. I figured that going to the last house on my list just wasn't worth the effort. It was across town, and I was sure that Doña Lucrecia, the clinic janitor, wasn't going to tell me anything different than the last dozen people I had spoken to.

So I went home a broken-spirited and bitter man, grumbling to myself about the unfairness of life, the inconsideration of people for one another and the thoughtlessness of humanity. As I was stewing in my juices I heard a weak *knock, knock,*

knock at the door. I considered not answering the door because I didn't feel I could handle dealing with one more person that day, but I opened it anyway. Standing in the doorway was Doña Lucrecia, the only person from the clinic I hadn't spoken to. She was with her young son who was accompanying her in the darkness of the night. She looked cheerful, but a bit bashful. She immediately apologized for not being able to speak to me until now and said that she had been getting dinner on the table for her family and getting them ready for bed. It wasn't until now that she finally had the time to walk across town to see me. At this point she pulled out my neatly wrapped *quesillo* from her pocket and said that she had been keeping it safe for me since I had failed to return from my walk before the clinic had closed. She said that she had stopped by earlier in the evening to bring it to me, but that I had not been at home (obviously while I was out on my door-knocking campaign). This had been her next chance to come back and try again. She apologized profusely for being so late and said she hoped I wouldn't be too mad at her. I was speechless!

So here I was, the inconsiderate, short-sighted gringo that had made a fool of himself all evening long with his colleagues looking for a piece of cheese and bad-mouthing anyone and everyone he could along the way. I thanked Doña Lucrecia for her kindness and consideration, explained what a jerk I had been to our co-workers and asked her if she could ever forgive me for being such a fool and so disrespectful to our co-workers and her community. She said she understood that it must be hard to be so far away from family and friends and that she hoped that she and her community could help fill that void for me. I told her she already had.

I spent the rest of the evening retracing my steps going from house to house explaining that I'd found my cheese, that I was ashamed of my poor behavior and asking for forgiveness and understanding. In the end, we all had a good laugh and were able to see each other for who we really were: friends living and working together for better or for worse.

Matthew DuFresne was a Health Education Volunteer in Acoyapa, Nicaragua from 1994-97. He was also a Peace Corps Recruiter in Minnesota, Iowa, Wisconsin, North Dakota and South Dakota from 1998-2003. He recently finished his master's degree in Public Affairs at the Humphrey Institute. He currently works for the U.S. Department of Labor as an investigator in Minneapolis. He lives in Richfield, Minnesota, with his Nicaraguan wife, Mayra, and his three children, Danisbell, Laura Sofia, and Mateo Nicolas.

PART THREE

GETTING THROUGH THE DAYS

ALANNA RANDALL

✦
✦   ✦

The Scent of Iris

After only six weeks, disaster strikes this Volunteer's home.
Although she perseveres, she never really forgets.

THE SCENT OF IRIS STILL LINGERS ON MY SHIRT. IT'S A DISAGREEABLE odor: a mingling of dried up seawater, dirt, and soggy wood. Despite having been washed three times, the clothes I pulled from the rubble still reek.

Hurricane Iris passed through Placencia, Belize, on Monday, October 8, 2001, probably slamming my house apart sometime around 8 P.M. Two days later, pulling into Placencia, I barely recognized the village I called home. The damage grew increasingly worse the closer we got to the tip of the peninsula. Dense thickets of trees were cleared, with palms missing their fronds. Debris littered the road with pieces of zinc roof wrapped around power lines. Thatch buildings had completely disappeared. Beach cabanas had been picked up, skidded across the sidewalk and slammed apart or into other houses, leaving a trail of wood scraps, clothes, appliances, and other items of people's lives.

Many of the familiar landmarks were missing or had moved, and I almost didn't even recognize the place where my house once stood. I spotted the Beach Bazaar, a gift shop that once stood right next to my house. It was off its stilts, turned to its side and had traveled about fifteen feet from its original spot. Then it hit me.

"My house is gone!" I exclaimed, hopping out of the Peace Corps Land Cruiser.

Stepping carefully around scattered pieces of plywood, I spotted my fan lying near a gravesite. It still had my name blazoned across it in black Sharpie, a reminder that just six weeks before it had sat in the Peace Corps office waiting to hitch a ride down to me in my new home. I was numb. I didn't believe it, even as I sifted through the rubble. What could I find? Random items: a hiking boot that I wore once; black sandals that weren't comfortable; my med kit, useless; a shirt, still on its hanger.

I walked around Placencia's ruins, encountering my neighbors sifting through the wreckage, sorting their belongings and processing their emotions. They looked tired and told me stories of surviving Hurricane Iris.

"The wind pressure was so loud it was all I could hear," said Doyle. He watched the 150-mph winds pick up a house, spin it around, then fling it into another house.

"Thank God I'm still alive," he said with a smile.

I saw faces numb with disbelief and hopelessness, but I also saw smiles on their faces despite the debris piled high around them. Some claimed to be numb, but had already started the process of patching roofs and cleaning up. Sonny, the owner of the Beach Bazaar, was optimistic about the future and vowed he would "put that shit back up" and keep on living.

What about me? I had just moved to the little touristy fishing village at the end of the peninsula six weeks before. Now I found myself homeless and without a job. I bounced around, staying with the Country Director, my APCD, and other

Volunteers, until finally I moved into a wooden house up on a hillside, far away from the coast and the threat of another hurricane. I hung up my hammock, waved to my neighbors and settled into my life as a Peace Corps Volunteer in Belize.

Epilogue: Hurricane Iris was, in terms of wind speed, the strongest storm of the 2001 season and made landfall in Belize as a Category 4 hurricane; it caused $66.2 million in damage and killed at least 31 people. The name *Iris* was retired in the spring of 2002 by the World Meteorological Organization and will never again be used for an Atlantic hurricane.

Alanna Randall graduated from Western Michigan University with a BA in Tourism and in French in 2000. She then joined the Peace Corps and served in Belize from 2001-03 as an Environmental Education Coordinator and taught preschool classes for her secondary project. This experience led her to serve as an AmeriCorps member for two years in Tucson, Arizona and continue her new-found passion of working with youth. She lived in Tucson for another two years, working at nonprofit organizations serving youth before moving to Portland, Oregon. Alanna is currently working with the Girl Scouts of Oregon and Southwest Washington where she manages dedicated volunteers. She can often be found drawing with her Urban Sketchers Portland group, volunteering at House of Dreams cat shelter or editing monthly newsletters for the Columbia River Peace Corps Association.

MARY NOWEL QUIJANO

✳

4th of July

Provide a fiesta, and they will come.

A PEACE CORPS VOLUNTEER'S JOB IS WRITTEN BETWEEN THE LINES.
We worked hard and played hard as Volunteers. An unwritten job description was to be prepared for any opportunity to celebrate and share our culture with those around us. Furthermore, these opportunities to celebrate what we took for granted would become those memories we'd relish later in life. One such party unfolded and took place my first July in Honduras in 1975. The 4th of July would never be quite the same for me again.

I worked in Santa Rosa de Copan at the Escuela Experimental, a local elementary school. My counterpart was Profesor Bracamonte, the director of this school. He was a delightful person and very dedicated educator. We became friends immediately. On paper my responsibility in this cobblestone town set within the mountains was to train elementary school teachers in "modern" teaching techniques. When I read between the lines, I learned that wasn't my primary job.

I began my Peace Corps job as a second-grade teacher while the regular teacher was out sick until "*mañana*" arrived. On Saturdays I coached the kids' basketball team, and in the evenings I taught English to the high school students in Bracamonte's high school. Some ninety teenagers and young adults comprised my class. I remember before I convinced the director to cut the group in half, I stood on top of the teacher's desk so that I could project my voice to the students in the back of that long narrow classroom. In my spare time, I taught myself how to play the wooden recorder and then began a fifth-grade band, teaching the students the basics of music while I directed.

There was another job description lurking between the lines that designated me as the person in charge of arranging and presenting interesting assemblies for the school children. The 4th of July was a perfect opportunity to have some fun with a topic I knew quite a bit about. Lucky for me my friend Barbara, another PCV who worked in a nearby town, was in town for a month-long workshop. She welcomed the idea of helping me prepare a skit to share some basic ideas about the U.S. and its independence. Together we presented an entertaining and educational program to the students and, thanks to Barb's talent on the guitar, it was complete with music.

Our skit was a smash hit, and the students loved the music. Our closing song, "You're a Grand Old Flag" was received with such enthusiasm that we had to come up with more songs to satisfy our young screaming fans! We did what any good PCV of the '70s would do: we strummed out popular folk tunes and, in true Volunteer style, just sang our hearts out.

Curious reporters from the local radio station were there to see the program. They asked us for an interview afterwards that I thought went smoothly. I was curious to hear how my growing Spanish would sound on the radio.

The following day, the 4th of July, the interview aired, and I heard myself inviting the city to join us for the celebration. "Come and join the party at our house. We'll be singing and dancing in the streets and we'll top it off with fireworks!" We found out later that night that at least one hundred townspeople understood my Spanish and accepted the invitation. Of course, everyone in town knew where the gringos lived!

At that time in Honduras' history, there was strife between Honduras and the U.S. due to the exploitation of Honduran land by fruit companies. Relations were often strained between the Americans and Hondurans, and we sometimes walked a fine line as gringos in Honduras. But that 4th of July, with a cautious confidence, I found myself expressing my pride as an American and extending an invitation to my Honduran neighbors and townspeople to celebrate with me.

The mayor, who had married a woman from Texas, was flying the American flag outside his house that day. We felt that gave us license to do the same, plus we added the Honduran flag, a Scottish flag for Krysia—a Scottish Volunteer who lived in our house—and a Polish flag that Krysia, Barb, and I put up to celebrate our Polish heritage.

After putting out the four flags that we had made, we proceeded to sing the American, Honduran, Scottish, and Polish anthems. The neighbor kids solemnly joined in as we sang the Honduran anthem, and they respectfully listened as we sang the other anthems, and then for good measure we sang a rousing "You're a Grand Old Flag" as they cheered and clapped in rhythm. Before we cut a huge flag cake we had baked, we all sang "Happy Birthday," one song we could all sing in Spanish and English!

It was one of those moments of unexpected depth and meaning. We were showing concern and respect for each other irrespective of our origins or heritage. More importantly to us at the time, we were having a whole lot of fun! Later, a neighbor who watched from a distance told me she cried as she saw the sense of unity and caring that emanated from our little flag ceremony.

People came from all over the city! At least one hundred people (no kidding) showed up. They were in the patio, kitchen, dining room, living room, and in the street, and everyone was happily celebrating each other's culture that day! There was even musical entertainment provided by the neighbor kids playing a little marimba we had set up outside our house. We danced, sang, and enjoyed the fiesta into the night! Everyone cheered as the assorted bottle rockets and other fireworks lit up the sky. It seemed everyone danced more heartily when occasional misguided fireworks made their flight in a more horizontal pattern.

As we ended the celebration, we saluted our flags once more, Hondurans, Americans, standing together as one saluting each other's flags. Final fireworks, songs and goodwill ended the evening with smiles all around.

As we cleaned up, Krysia summed it up perfectly. "If all people could live like this, caring for one another, doing good things for one another and celebrating with one another like this, the world would have peace."

We hadn't planned a big party like this. It just happened, as so many things did during my days as a PCV. It left me with a feeling of fulfillment, contentment, and I must say, a bit of patriotism. I didn't have to read between the lines to see I had made a connection with my Honduran friends and that we all reaped the rewards of genuine respect and concern while we had a whole lot of fun.

Viva la independencia.

Mary Nowel Quijano spent fours years (1974-78) as a Peace Corps Volunteer in Honduras. All told, however, she was there for twelve years and really did come back with more than her luggage. She now teaches in San Antonio, Texas, and lives with her husband Jose whom she married as a PCV in her little town in the mountains, Santa Rosa de Capan. Their two daughters, who were born in Honduras, are in San Antonio and all grown up. She takes occasional trips back to Honduras to visit Jose's family and to reconnect to those wonderful Peace Corps days.

WALTER JAMES MURRAY

Dinner Pet

*The first Thanksgiving in a new, strange
place never fails to be memorable.*

IT WAS AT THE BEGINNING OF NOVEMBER 1962 THAT FOUR
other Peace Corps Volunteers and I arrived at Bom Jesus da
Lapa—Good Jesus of the Grotto—a town on the Sao Francisco
River in Bahia, Brazil, to reside for the next two years. The
other members of our Peace Corps group, designated Brazil II
with some ninety Volunteers in all, were scattered hither and
yon along the entire length of the 2,000-mile long river.

We in Lapa were to make use of our expertise, such as it was,
working with the Sao Francisco Valley Commission (CVSF),
a Brazilian government agency patterned after the Tennessee
Valley Authority (TVA) in America. We would work in a
variety of fields, including agriculture, health, and education.
Our contingent consisted of a married couple and three single
men, nearly complete strangers to one another (barring the
couple), thrown together into a three-bedroom tile-roofed
stucco house in a government compound. Electricity was supplied for only two hours in the evening. We had primitive
cooking facilities and as yet no cook, no refrigerator, furniture

that was mostly on order, and a bathroom that was frequently out of water. The list of shortcomings could be easily extended further. It would take weeks to get ourselves organized and until then, because of our dissimilar backgrounds and independent natures, we would have to get along with each other as best we could. One of our more immediate concerns was what to do about a dinner for the upcoming Thanksgiving Day. It would have to be a turkey.

Lapa, from an old Portuguese word meaning "cave" and the name by which the town was commonly known, was a river port serviced by paddle-wheel, wood-burning steamboats. It is located on a dry, dusty plain dominated by a three hundred-foot high limestone outcropping in the shape of a battleship. On top of the hill, a large cross had been erected, and within the hill were a number of caves, one of which held a Roman Catholic Church. Holy water dripped from the stalactites in the church. Off to one side was a room called the Sala das Milagres (room of the miracles) that held articles—*milagros*—many of wood, carved by hand in the shape of body parts. These were submitted by pilgrims and attested to their infirmities.

It was to the padres at the church we went to seek assistance on where we could find a turkey. The head priest (there were four, a Brazilian and three Dutchmen) was a Padre Victor, who offered to supply us a *peru* from their *fazenda* (farm) outside of town for three thousand cruzeiros (about four dollars). A *peru*, we learned, was the Portuguese word for turkey (in Turkey it's known as a "*hindu*"). We were told it would be delivered to our house a week before the holiday. We accepted the offer with alacrity.

A scragglier bird could not be imagined. Weighing no more than a couple of kilos (less than five pounds), it had few of the attributes of a North American butterball, and there was considerable doubt it could feed five hungry expatriates. We immediately decided that for the remaining days of the bird's life, it would be tethered in the backyard to fatten it up with as much food as we could coax the scrawny fowl to eat. As a consequence, there was no leftover the pampered pet didn't peck; no bird relished his or her situation as much as this one. Putting weight on the bird, however, was wishful thinking on our part as there was no observable increase in the bird's waistline.

On the given day, that is Thanksgiving Day, it was time to call an end to the bird's eating frenzy and partake in one of our own. It was taken for granted the married man, as the senior among us and the one with a background in agriculture, would be the executioner. Taking in hand a borrowed machete that Thanksgiving morning, he strode confidently out into the backyard while the rest of us made ourselves scarce. We wouldn't or, better, couldn't witness the end of what had become our feathered friend. We waited expectantly for him to accomplish his mission and before long he was back. But by the look on his face, we knew he hadn't been able to do it. The turkey continued to forage amid the scraps on the ground. Someone else would have to do the deed.

One of the single men, a geologist, stepped forward determinedly and grabbed the long knife and disappeared into the back yard. But in a short time he, too, was back, bowed and with no blood on his hands. He couldn't do it either. Our turkey had become a pet. It was Turkey 2, Volunteers 0.

Now it was the turn of the second of the three single men, the other geologist. No problem, he said, and set out resolutely for the backyard, the machete swinging lethally at his side. He was away longer than the other two but, alas, he came back having to acknowledge defeat as well. The score was now Turkey 3, Volunteers 0. The bird, in the meantime, kept pecking unconcernedly at the dwindling pile of scraps, serenely unaware of our desperate efforts to do it in.

As my compatriots turned their eyes toward me, I realized at once that I was the last hope for a turkey dinner. I knew what I had to do. A long-buried childhood memory of an uncle in Depression-era Peoria on Sunday mornings seizing a squawking chicken from its roost in a backyard coop and taking it to a weathered stump nearby to chop off its head filled my mind. Chicken in those bleak days was our usual Sunday dinner. My uncle had used a hatchet, but I figured a machete would work just as well. With a sigh of resignation I rose, took the still warm machete in hand and, in my turn, made for the backyard.

The bustling bird, accustomed to people by now, didn't even look up from its ceaseless pecking as I approached. Reaching down quickly and grabbing it by its legs, I upended it and maneuvered its elongated neck over a piece of a rotting branch fallen from a backyard tree. There was absolutely no resistance on the bird's part. Raising the machete over my head, I aimed, closed my eyes, and swung the blade down hard. When I opened my eyes I saw that the bloody neck still attached, albeit loosely, so I again brought the knife down, but this time I kept my eyes open. The suddenly disconnected head fell to the ground and its eyes, I noticed, were closed. I stood up still holding the decapitated remains by its legs and threw the bird off into a corner of the yard where it plopped onto the ground and flopped itself still. The score was now Volunteers 1, Turkey 0.

I picked up the lifeless bird and marched victoriously into the house to the plaudits of my peers. A pail of water was soon brought to a boil, and the carcass was immersed in it for what would be, we thought, a few minutes to facilitate the removal of the quills. While we stood around the pail waiting to take it out there was an unexpected sound of clapping hands signaling an arrival of a party at the door.

We saw it was a group of ladies from the neighborhood coming to pay a social call and led by the wife of the local *chefe*, or chief, of the government agency with whom we were employed. A period of awkwardness ensued while we introduced ourselves and tried to find a place to sit around a table in our bare-bones living room. Any sort of refreshments was out of the question because of a lack of resources. None of the ladies spoke English and our proficiency in Portuguese had yet to flower. While there was no want for words on both sides, the level of comprehension was abysmal. In the excitement and confusion of the meeting, the turkey—abandoned in the pail of boiling water—was temporarily forgotten.

Eventually the good ladies, obviously drained by the effort to communicate, arose and bid their good-byes. We were exhausted as well. As soon as they were out the gate we rushed to the kitchen to see how the bird had fared. It had not, we discovered, fared well at all. A leg came off when it was pulled out from the still steaming water and when we were able to see the whole carcass it looked positively revolting. What a mess! Cleaning it up as best we could, we readied a makeshift oven and stuck the remains in and hoped for the best.

Somehow we managed the meal with each one of us having at least a taste of our erstwhile pet. With other provender we'd scrounged at the local market and with what we had brought in our luggage, we were able to have a reasonably good holiday dinner. Most important, though, none of us went hungry.

Walter James Murray served in Brazil 2 from 1962-64, one of five volunteers sent to Bom Jesus da Lapa. Since then, he has taught in India, Laos, Saudi Arabia, Columbia, Japan, China, S. Korea, and Turkey.

KYLE FREUND

Viva la Revolución Telefónica

Cell phones, the law of unintended consequences, and
nostalgia for a world that has irrevocably changed.

IT BEGAN IN JANUARY 2005. IN THE DISTANCE I SAW IT. A CELL phone tower was being constructed within viewing distance of my very home.

Times were about to change in the little village of Chiábal, Guatemala. Many people had phones, but they were bulky handsets wired to large antennas that sprouted from the tin roofs of the village. The phones could be rented out to neighbors, and the service was sketchy at best.

As for cell phones, throughout the first year of my service, only when I climbed the hill behind my house could I get both a signal and a stunning view of the Huehuetenango Valley and various volcanoes in the distance. But the signal was a little tough to catch, and I spent extensive time and effort doing the high-mountain two-step trying to find the perfect position for talking. At times, standing on this rock would work, but then other days I would have to move over by the bush. Some days I would have to climb a tree.

As a result, the best signal and where it could be found was a frequent topic of conversation between me and Lucas, the other Volunteer in Chiábal.

But I enjoyed my sketchy service. It was almost like having my own personal assistant to take my calls. I would go up the hill and have four messages. Well, I can call Jesus later, but I better call the family. This other call can wait and so on. Plus a Sunday afternoon nap could never be interrupted by incoming calls.

At times, though, it would get frustrating, especially when you had important things to talk about and your minutes would run out and there was no way to get more. Other times it was frightening, like the time I was talking to my family when the thunderclouds rolled in and lightning was flashing all around. But for the most part it worked O.K., and it was all quite quaint. I could talk about how I had to climb a mountain to find a signal.

But that new cell phone tower looming in the distance changed it all. From the moment construction began, rumors circulated about the start date. Guadelupe had a second cousin who knew a guy working on the tower, and he said it would be running in March. I usually trusted the information of Doña Lety, who ran a nearby restaurant where the tower workers would take their lunch.

After several false dates and setbacks, service arrived on the mountain on May 28. Then the revolution began in earnest. Bulky handsets were quickly replaced by small cell phones, and a new class system formed.

The first rung consisted of those who had no phones. Next were those who had old phones, the only problem being that those phones didn't work with the new tower. Then there were those who had new phones that functioned with the tower, but who couldn't afford to buy minutes, so the phone was a status symbol that hung in a leather holster from the hip. Then there were the high-rollers who not only had a phone, but also could afford minutes to make calls and become a part of the wired world.

Nowhere was this hierarchy more evident than when I went with the students from the local high school on a trip to the ocean. It was just two weeks after the tower had been installed, and the new lineup had emerged among the students. During the entire trip those who had phones continuously played and plugged away on them. Those without phones tried to sleep or looked over the shoulder of their phone-enabled neighbors.

At the ocean, many of the students used a few minutes to call home to let their parents hear the ocean and let them know they were O.K.

And now the community was in touch. People walked across wide-open pasture land bordered by handmade, agave-crowned, stone fences made by their ancestors as they chatted away with grandma on the cell phone. I could stand in my kitchen talking with friends on my headset while cutting vegetables for dinner; and while life was still quite quaint, it wasn't quite the same.

Kyle Freund was a Marketing Volunteer in Guatemala from 2003-05. He is currently web editor at the Fairtrade Labelling Organization in Bonn, Germany. He continues to chronicle people, places, pulchritude and more at http://goodislove.wordpress.com.

PATRICIA EDMISTEN

✦

Christmas Eve, 1963

*Some Christmas Eves just stick with you even when
there's nothing romantic or nostalgic to remember.*

"*VETE DE AQUÍ CON ESE VESTIDO DE PLAYA,*" SAID THE HANDSOME
young priest. He left the confessional and entered the pew in
front of me. "Get out of here with that beach dress!" I glanced
at the woman on my right and at the one on my left. He
couldn't mean me. I wore a modest, powder blue dress with
cap sleeves, and a white lace *mantilla* covered my head and arms.

It was Christmas Eve, and the colonial church of Nuestro
Señor de Luren was packed. A small choir sang "*Noche de Paz,*"
and the gilded altar reflected light from blazing candles. Missing
my family, and still settling into Ica, a town in Peru's southern
coastal desert, I needed spiritual consolation. I had recently been
transferred from Arequipa, a much larger city in Peru's southern
Andes, to do relief work after the 1963 flood wiped away the
homes of the poor who lived in reed shacks along the banks of a
riverbed that was dry most of the year when it served as a latrine
and landfill. As Andean snows melted, a deluge headed for the
Pacific, roared over the banks and tossed the shanties like pick-
up-sticks, spitting out the *damnificados* like rockets.

143

"Get out of here with that beach dress!" he repeated, this time more forcefully. Standing straight, as my mother always reminded me to do in Milwaukee, I apologized to the people in my pew as I negotiated my way to the aisle to exit the church. Running home, I bumped into an elderly priest headed toward the church. I told him what had happened, and he begged me to return with him, apologizing for his fervent, young assistant. "No thank you, Father," I said, wiping away tears. "*Feliz Navidad.*"

Just as I entered the hallway leading to the modest house I shared with a girl from Delaware, I heard a man call to me in a sing-song voice. "*Señorita,* do you like this?" I turned around. Oh, my God. "*This?*" I hadn't seen "*this*" since my baby brother was in diapers, and I didn't want to see any more of "*this*" on Christmas Eve. I tore after him, chasing him down the block, using the foulest Spanish I could think of, which, given my Catholic girlhood, didn't surpass, "*hijo de puta!*"

He was half my five feet-ten inches, and I would have beat the shit out of him had I caught him. Instead, I bought a bottle of red Copa de Oro wine at the corner bodega, and once home, slumped into a torn green canvas lawn chair, swigged from the bottle and fell asleep, listening to Ella Fitzgerald sing "Don't Fence Me In" on my battery-operated Phillips portable phonograph.

Patricia (Silke) Edmisten served in Peru from 1962-64. She lives in Pensacola, Florida and Montezuma, North Carolina. The Peace Corps (and the Catholic Church) turned her into a royal pain-in-the-ass. She is the author of Nicaragua Divided: La Prensa and the Chamorro Legacy, *about the origins of the Nicaraguan Revolution, and* The Mourning of Angels, *an autobiographical novel inspired by her two Peace Corps years in Peru. Her book of poetry,* Wild Women with Tender Hearts, *won the 2007 Peace Corps Writers Award.*

RAFAELA CASTRO

Letters From the Prettiest Girl

*Writing home can be a way to measure success, failure, alienation,
maturity, and loneliness. When read years later,
they are a time machine.*

AS I'VE READ AND RE-READ THE LETTERS I WROTE MY FAMILY, IT
has dawned on me that I matured through my writing during the years I was away with the Peace Corps. I grew up as I
wrote and received letters from friends and family while I lived
in Brazil. I learned to concentrate and focus, to describe my
experiences, to express opinions about my experiences, and to
share those thoughts with my parents. I received many letters
from relatives, friends, and friends of friends, asking me questions about my work and life. I became a reporter, sending
news back to the homeland about my adventures and escapades.

Today I have in my possession only those letters I wrote to
my sisters and mother and father. They not only chronicle my
adventures in Brazil, but the actual writing, the taking of pen
to paper, the mental exertion of constructing descriptive sentences, and the unveiling of my most private thoughts, brought
about a coming-of-age enlightenment. My letters were
like writing assignments, my homework and my education.
Living in Brazil was definitely an education, but that was an

145

anticipated cultural growth, while writing was like a qualifying exam. I explored my inner world and developed the means to articulate what I found within myself. It was an unexpected reward while in pursuit of my *gran provocación*.

My first letters from Albuquerque and Peace Corps training were purely descriptive, informing my parents of my busy life and schedule. By including my mother and father in my daily activities, like hiking, horseback riding, and the practical training, I thought they'd feel safe and secure about my well-being. My letters had a light tone and I tried to make funny observations for their entertainment. They didn't ask questions nor make comments about my experiences, but I was informed that they enjoyed my letters. For instance, my father got a big kick out of the fact that I had to buy boots for the overnight treks into the Sandia Mountains. He loved that I was in possession of a pair of high-top boots. I wrote hastily, not taking time to express self-doubts, serious thoughts or provide fine details.

June 12, 1964
My roommate's name is Carolyn. She's from Atlanta, Georgia, and just graduated from college. She's real nice and talks with a Southern drawl, so I'll probably be talking like a Southerner when I come home.

July 8, 1964
We had lots of fun last weekend on our hike. The bus took us to the foot of the mountains, and at 3:30 P.M. we started walking up. Each of us had a pack that weighed between thirty and forty pounds. That was the hardest part, carrying that pack. We were in small groups and camped out in different places. My group camped out the highest, it was about 2 1/2 miles up and it took us almost two hours to walk up. We camped in a beautiful spot and could see all of

Albuquerque from it. But that walk up was hard. It was hot and carrying all that weight and walking almost straight up! For a while I was afraid I couldn't make it, but I surprised myself and was one of the first ones up there. (I was third.) The next day we had to rappel again, this time from a real high steep mountain. Then we walked back down the mountain and had a steak fry and watermelon at the bottom. We got home at 8:00. I was so tired and my face was all burned, but I had a good time.

Of course I didn't go to church that Sunday, but at the Newman Center they distribute Communion every day at 5:45 P.M. for the Peace Corps trainees. I've been going to Communion every day. There isn't time for Mass because we get out of class at 5:20 and they stop serving dinner at 6:15 and we usually have a class at 7:00. But it's nice to receive Communion every day. About six or eight of us go. We say one decade of the rosary together, for everybody in the Peace Corps. There are quite a few Catholics here.

July 26, 1964

We got two more shots last week, which makes eleven shots that we've gotten so far. We all have scars. Somebody said we were getting fifteen, but I think we're going to get more. They don't seem to want to stop giving them to us. Every Tuesday, Bang! Bang! two shots just like that!

The Selection Board meets Tuesday, and we should know by that night who is selected out. So think of me that night.

August 13, 1964

You were right, in my last letter I was tired, but not unhappy. Well, you can imagine how I felt after getting up at 5:15 all week. This week we went to a different place every day. Yesterday we made home visits with a Visiting Nurse. My nurse had mostly old patients. She had to give bed baths and shots to two old ladies. Most of the homes we went to were Mexican homes. I really enjoyed that. Tomorrow we go to Santa Fe again to a Catholic Maternity Institute.

Ma, the selection board meets in about two weeks, and I don't know what's going to happen. Since the last de-selection, two more girls have left to get married. Anyway, if I get selected out I'll be home a week early, if I make it, I'll be home September 5th. No matter when it is, it'll be soon.

August 31, 1964
Well, now I'm so excited I don't know what I'm doing! We're going to leave for Brazil from New York on September 17th at 9:00 P.M. But I'd like to arrive in New York on the 16th to visit a girl that was selected out.

My mother wrote back that she'd shared my letters with high school friends that visited her. That pleased me since I was having fun and wanted everyone to know about my bold adventures. I was caught up in a formidable exercise and didn't question anything, not even the de-selection process.

I loved Brazil and the Brazilians from the very first day I stepped off the plane in Recife. Feeling exhausted from the long plane ride, I remember also feeling apprehensive and overwhelmed. I looked at everything through the eyes of a dazed child wandering in a candy store. Yet I approached my new life with an open mind and an open heart. Like a sponge, I absorbed the exciting colorful sights, boisterous sounds, tropical aromas and the graciously friendly people. It was a challenge to convey my complex emotions to my family.

September 18, 1964
I don't know how to describe Recife. It's a very old city, and it has two canals that run right through the center. It's fun

to walk across the bridges. The streets are very narrow and there are people everywhere. It's like Mexico, you know, everybody likes to sell things, stands and open shops everywhere. Some of the buildings look like they need a paint job. They're yellow and the paint is peeling. But they're building new modern buildings everywhere. You can see a nice new building going up between two old rusty ones.

The strangest thing about being here is that nobody around can speak English! It seems so funny that everyone speaks Portuguese, and a lot of the people look like average Americans. I think I'm really going to like it here. I can't believe how lucky I am.

Gradually my perceptions of what I was observing and experiencing became discriminating, and I had to express my opinions in writing. Since we were trained to be health workers, to assist in public health posts, and visit homes as *visitadoras,* we were immediately conscious of the sanitation and nutritional conditions of the women and children. Culture shock set in very quickly once we witnessed the horrendous poverty of the rural communities of northeast Brazil. For weeks I was in a joyful state of titillation, fluctuating between shock at the impoverishment, and the excitement of accepting my new country and my home for the next year and nine months. My initial flush of euphoric adoration melted into realism, and I started looking at everything—including my PC colleagues' conduct—with a critical eye.

September 22, 1964
Tonight I'm in João Pessoa, the capital of the state Paraíba. You wouldn't believe how different this city is from Recife, it has some nice and pretty areas but most of it is bad. The poor areas are really bad. No paved roads, they're all muddy and full of holes and little, tiny houses. Little kids running

around with no clothes on and big full stomachs, which is a sign of malnutrition. It's really sad, but I hope I can live in an area like this. I've liked everyone that I've met.

September 24, 1964
Here in João Pessoa we've been visiting hospitals and clinics. I can understand quite a bit now, but when a doctor starts talking about diseases and medicine it's pretty hard. I am disappointed that I don't understand more than I do.

Some kids are having trouble with the discomforts. There is so much complaining. The bathrooms are bad and dirty. In fact I would prefer an outdoor bathroom. The showers aren't too bad, the water barely makes a dribble, and of course there is no hot water. Some of the girls have already been sick with diarrhea. But nothing has bothered me, I've been fine. I know I'll get sick, everybody always does. All they serve us is beans, rice, and bread. Sometimes meat, and always coffee. The coffee is good. For breakfast, we always have café, and different kinds of bread and biscuits, sometimes fruit. I love the café. In the morning we have café with hot milk, but only in the morning do you have milk with your coffee. After dinner you have a tiny cup of a very very strong coffee, called cafézinho, and you put a lot of sugar in it. It's great.

The Brazilians are wonderful warm people. They love to look at us. They come in our room and stand around, and we can't get rid of them. But when they start to speak, I can't understand them. It's frustrating. All the babies I've seen are just beautiful. And it's funny how many people mistake me for a Brazilian, that is until I speak. They say I have the features of a Brazilian, not of a Mexican, but I think a lot of the people here look like Mexicans

I haven't yet asked myself "What am I doing here?" And I'm hoping I never do, but I'm really disappointed in the way our girls are acting. They're complaining about *everything, and it's just the way they told us it would be. But don't worry about me because so far I like it.*

As I progressed and adapted to the Brazilian culture and made friends, I narrated my daily exploits in my letters home. Following the example of the other Volunteers, I also wrote in a journal. Between my letters and the journal I judiciously wrote down all the meticulous details of my daily routine. We completed six weeks of in-country service training, where we lived with other PC Volunteers, so it was a comfortable, gradual immersion into the language and culture of the country. We were in temporary living quarters, dependent on each other, and at first held back from making close friends with community people; however, it was a period of rapid learning and tremendous growth.

September 28, 1964

Today was our first day of training at the hospital. We had a few lectures, of course in Portuguese. I understand much better now. We saw two deliveries, too. The people around here are so poor. You wouldn't believe the houses or shacks that surround this town. A lot of women have their babies at home, but the doctors try to make them come to the hospital for their first baby. One lady walked into the hospital with her baby hanging halfway out! The baby was not upside down, with the head coming first, instead the feet were out and the head was stuck inside. The woman had a midwife with her, but the midwife didn't know what to do since the baby was like that (breech). Anyway, when the nurse had the baby out I thought it was dead. It was all purple and it wasn't breathing. She massaged it for a while and finally it started to breathe. It was so exciting to hear it cry. We saw another woman have her twelfth child. The people here are so poor!

It was mid-November before we were finally sent to our permanent sites. Now, I thought, my true Peace Corps experience will begin. But, I was mistaken. I was assigned to a large city, Campina Grande, and invited by a middle-class doctor to live with him, his wife, and their five children. They lived in a large house almost in the center of the city. Another PC Volunteer assigned to the city lived nearby, also with a family. I was disappointed because I had wanted to live in the *sertão*, the dry desolate backlands, in a small interior village. Yet, Dr. Mello welcomed me warmly, treated me like a daughter, and I soon learned to love him and his family.

Because it was a large city, it was difficult for Judy, the other Volunteer, and me to penetrate the bureaucracy of the complex health department. In frustration, we'd frequently end our days by visiting an American missionary family that lived in the city. There were two wonderful and friendly families that took us in and often fed us delicious American home-cooked meals, but their presence spoiled my image of a true, rough-and-vigorous Peace Corps adventure.

Campina Grande was a transportation hub, where all the buses from the interior and the coast connected. Consequently, we were constantly entertaining PC visitors from all over the state. I had envisioned myself isolated, deep in the interior, away from urban culture and American influences. It didn't occur to me to ask for a transfer, but unexpectedly I was urged by another Volunteer, who was stationed alone, to join him in a small town in the interior of Paraíba. After weeks of waiting for approval from our regional director, I was finally allowed to go to Catolé do Rocha, ten to twelve bus hours away. Immediately I fell in love with the *sertão*, the town, the people, and the convent where I lived for over a year.

February 1, 1965

I've finally arrived here in my little town, Catolé do Rocha. I'm pretty far from the coast, but I love it. This is a real pretty town. It's starting to rain now, so everything in the sertão *is turning green. I love the* colégio, *the nuns are just wonderful.*

I went to the health post today and boy, is it in bad condition! We have lots of work to do. Catolé has a population of about 5,000. But the health post is hidden and far from the poor areas. We're going to try and move it to an empty building in the center of town. Ma, the post is absolutely empty. It has one chair and a table. The people go there and the doctor (if he's there) writes out a prescription, and the people go home. They haven't got any money for medicine, so they throw the prescription away, and the child gets well or dies; most die. There is no place where the poor people can get help. I want to start a young mothers club there. I'm so excited because I have so much I can do, and I have such a good working partner.

March 9, 1965

The other day, a woman came with a little girl, and she got to the post after the doctor had left, and she started crying. Ma, if you could see this poverty, you wouldn't believe it. I visit the houses every morning; these people are poorer than poor. But the doctors and the people from the town don't care too much. You should be grateful for all the benefits you have in the States. Social Security and you have a hospital plan. These people live from day to day and they barely make it. Little kids die by the tens, of dysentery. The people from one bairro *are beginning to know me. I'm going to start holding health classes for young girls in a lady's* sala.

Now, I thought, my real Peace Corps work is really starting, and I immersed myself in the health and medical services of the community. My PC partner Terry was a great guy and we worked well together on some programs, but he traveled frequently so mostly I worked alone. My idealism was quickly shattered because nothing was easy and no one cared if I taught just one English class once a week, sat in a vacant health post reading magazines, or lounged in a hammock all day. I thought up various ideas, all related to health, nutrition, sanitation, and I started project after project. Eventually I developed a loose program that worked for me and for the neighborhoods, *bairros.*

I started clubs for young women, the non-educated washerwomen of Catolé who spent their days at the creek. I gave talks on sanitation, personal hygiene, prenatal information, and general women's health. I translated English materials into Portuguese and had prepared lectures on various topics related to bacterial diseases, sanitation, and the causes of the high infant mortality rate in the region. Families had ten and twelve children, expecting that half would die of *doença de infância.* I would travel to small rural settlements, sharecroppers' homes called *sitios,* and give talks on safe water and the importance of constructing toilets. Periodically, we'd dispense medication we received from the state health department for worms and dysentery. We would also give vaccinations for polio and typhoid fever.

March 26, 1965
I got pretty discouraged this week. Two of the babies I was visiting died of diarrhea. Everybody has diarrhea here. Tomorrow I'm going to a school that's nearby, to give a class on safe water. I met the director when I was in Souza and he wants me to come out every Saturday. It's a school for boys out in the country, so I'm looking forward to it. Monday,

I'm going to give the same talk to some women in the bairro. *Everybody here gets sick from the water.*

I made dear friends with many young women in town and felt totally at home in mud shacks and in the convent with the nuns and novices. I shared a bedroom with a lay schoolteacher from the convent. Every night she wrote her lessons while I wrote hundreds of letters, on onion-skin paper, to my mother, sisters, friends, and other PC Volunteers in Paraíba, Brazil and even Colombia. I wrote my mother about my double life, stating "I have two worlds almost. My social world of the town itself, which is one group, and my working and social relations with the poor people of the *bairros*, that is an entirely different group."

I led an external social life with my Brazilian girlfriends, my ongoing projects and in my relationships with some older adults in the community. But I also had a blossoming interior life, a life of the mind. The Peace Corps provided each site with a book locker containing a couple hundred paperback classics, and I had one in my bedroom. It must have been the first time in my life that I was conscious of developing my mind, so to speak, by reading and writing. My outer world, full of laughter, sharing food, singing, and passing on essential health information was in Portuguese while my inner world carried on in an English monologue with my mother and grappled with the disgrace of my disintegrating family in California.

I loved my Brazilian life even though I never became fully integrated into the upper echelons of Catolé's society. My work with the poor people stigmatized me as an agitator and possibly a communist. Even so, gradually I became happier and felt more secure in Brazil than in the previous life I'd led in the U.S. As the months speedily melted away, I worried that I wasn't fully contributing to the mission of the Peace

Corps and wondered if I would actually accomplish my goals and fulfill my pristine dreams.

> *September 16, 1965*
> *I don't know if you remembered, but it was a year ago today, that I left home. It doesn't seem possible. And Saturday it'll be one year since I arrived in Brazil. I still don't know the language very well, I still don't know the people very well, I still don't know the customs or ideas of this country. Our time here is so short, what can we possibly give these people? They have given me so much in one year, much more than I could possibly give them in two. God has been good to me, I am exactly the same now, as when I left home, physically anyway. I hope I've matured a little, and I think some of my ideas and impressions have changed. I've come into contact with so many beautiful things and people that they must have left an imprint on me. But don't worry Ma, I hope (and should) be a much better person when I come home, than I was when I left. The Peace Corps did you a favor.*

I met many amazing and memorable people who have stayed with me through the years but a few became more than memories, they've become long distance permanent friends. One such person was the priest from Catolé do Rocha, Frei Marcelino. A Capuchin, he was an extraordinary character, short and skinny, fair skinned, with blue eyes closely set in a large head. When I met him, I thought he looked much older than his thirty-six years. But growing up in an impoverished northeast Brazilian household had given him a gaunt appearance. He was not handsome, but he had a wit and an infectious laugh. When he walked down the street a crowd of women, children, and dogs followed, appealing for his *benção*. With a huge ego, bordering on arrogance, he possessed a bottomless well of physical energy and incontestable determination. Nothing ever appeared impossible to him, as his mind only saw opportunities and the bright side of every situation. His brown wool cassock flapped rapidly behind him as he rushed to attack with equal fervor problems caused by destructive forces of nature or destructive politicians. He could have been a distant relative of Saul Alinsky. At first I felt intimidated by him, but eventually we became best of friends, and I often wrote about him in my letters home.

February 1, 1965
The padre here is Frei Marcelino, I haven't met him yet because he's in Recife right now. But he's a little bomb, he's flying around here doing everything. Guess why he's in Recife? Castello Branco, President of Brazil, was in Recife Saturday, for about four hours, and Frei Marcelino was there to talk to him about electricity for Catolé. And he talked to him too! Can you believe it? This little padre talked to the President of Brazil about getting lights for a town of 5,000!! That little Frei can do anything! Right now we have electricity from a generator from 5-11 P.M. But there's a huge waterfall in Pernambuco that supplies energy to most of the Northeast, so he's trying to get power from there.

March 9, 1965
Frei Marcelino is finding us a place to move the health post, and he has all kinds of American drugs that he got I don't know where. He built a school with money he got from Germany. He can do anything! Right now I'm writing by candlelight, we haven't had electricity for three nights.

May 30, 1965
We're starting a big polio vaccination campaign June 1st. The vaccine had to be kept on ice so it was flown in by plane.

I had to stick around the colegio all day waiting for the man that was bringing it. At 12:30 P.M., I heard the plane fly overhead, so I hurried and put on my clothes, and two minutes later Frei Marcelino was here for me. And off we flew to the field where the plane landed. Me and the Boy Scouts!! Frei M. likes to do everything big, the Scouts played their drums and we made a lot of racket coming into town. We're going to vaccinate for two days, and have enough for 6,000 kids. There are at least ten cases of polio in Catolé already. We need the vaccine!

September 16, 1965
Tonight we have real light! Finally the electricity was hooked up.

Everyone went wild, and Monday we're going to have a big inauguration festa. It's real bright and it's full time, twenty-four hours a day, instead of five!! The whole town has to thank Frei Marcelino for this.

The many times when I doubted myself and wondered if I was succeeding or accomplishing anything, I'd unburden myself in the letters I wrote my mother. I don't quite understand it, but I expressed feelings to her that I couldn't express to anyone else. Even though I frequently shared my escapades with other PC Volunteers, and we joked about our successes and failures, I can't remember confiding my insecurities and doubts to anyone. Yet with my mother it was as if I were confessing to her, possibly awaiting an absolution, so I could feel cleansed of my dark shadows and uncertainties. Fearful of feeling alone in the world, I could always connect and feel close to her through letters across the thousands of miles.

Sept. 9, 1965

Today, everything is settling back to normal, after a week of festas. *Yesterday was the end of the eight-day* festa *for Catolé's patron saint. For eight days there has been a sort of bazaar down by the church. Also the day before yesterday, was Brazil's Independence Day, so that day was full of bands playing, kids singing, reciting poems, and everybody marching. We had two holidays in a row, this week is going to have three weekends! Things are almost normal, but we still have campaigning for the gubernatorial elections. And campaigning in Brazil is one big party! Every night there are bands playing, girls dancing Carnival in the streets, and lots of speech making. This is going on until October 3!!*

Because of all these festas, *my work has been a little slow. I'm working at the health post every morning, but my afternoons have been pretty free. My first English class is tomorrow night; Saturday I start the Health class at the Escola Agricola; next week I start teaching a first-aid class at Frei Marcelino's school. My club had a meeting today, we didn't get much done, but we decided to have hot dogs at our next meeting! It was their idea, not mine.*

I think we're going to have electricity full time by September 15. There was a big party for all the workers today, at the school. It's going to be great. Poor Frei Marcelino worked so hard for that. He is really a good guy, and I like him a lot, but we argue and fight like cats and dogs. But I know he likes it, and you know I like it too.

November 6, 1965

This week I finished my first-aid classes, and yesterday my students gave me a little festa. *They were so nice! They sang songs, and made speeches. One girl wrote a poem for me.*

They gave me a present, a beautiful sewing box, made from special wood, the kind I've sent home. I know that some people here like me, but I don't really know how they feel or think about me. These girls showed me that they accept me for what I am, and that they almost understand why I am here.

At times I feel like I am working so alone. I work because I push myself. Nobody really cares if I work or not, except myself. But these girls showed me that my work isn't unnoticed. They know what I'm doing and they almost understand why. That should leave an impression on them, when I leave.

At the end of two years, my transition back into family life was occupied with melancholic rituals. I was a witness to the dissolution of my parents' relationship. And it was a difficult time in America's social history; I struggled to behave consistently with my coming-of-age consciousness. After enrolling in a local community college, I transferred to UC Berkeley, graduating in the midst of tremendous campus turmoil.

As for Frei Marcelino, we remained friends. He was in his mid-sixties when he left the Capuchin order and married a woman who'd patiently been waiting for him for many years. Today he refers to himself as a "married priest" and not an "ex-priest" because he believes the Catholic Church will eventually change its position on this question, and because in his mind he can only think of himself as Frei Marcelino.

Rafaela Castro was born in Bakersfield, California but has lived most of her life in the San Francisco Bay Area. She was a PCV in Brazil from 1964-66, before receiving degrees in English Literature, Library Science, and Folklore from the University of California, Berkeley. She is the author of the Latino literature section in What Shall I Read Next?: Multicultural Literature; Chicano Folklore; *and* Provocaciones, Letters from the Prettiest Girl in Arvin.

KYLE FREUND

* ✦ *

Guatemalan Holiday

The author describes his five rules for how to properly
prepare for a holiday trip in Guatemala.

IT WAS SHAPING UP TO BE A GREAT COUPLE OF DAYS. AFTER A YEAR
and a half in Guatemala, I finally got invited to take part in a
real, true, honest-to-goodness Guatemalan holiday. The students of the institute where I taught English invited me on their
field trip to Puerto San Jose on the shores of the Pacific Ocean.
We were to leave on a Wednesday and return on a Thursday.

I looked forward to the trip as a way of ingratiating myself
with the students and exploring a bit more of the country—
and as a way of escaping the air of indolence surrounding the
cooperative.

But in order to be a true Guatemalan holiday, it is necessary
to follow a few rules.

Rule #1: Leave at the earliest possible moment of the new day

Warm and comfortable on my foam mattress, I was jolted awake
by my alarm: 2:45 A.M. Our bus was scheduled to leave at 3 A.M.,
and so I dragged myself out of bed, threw a couple handfuls of

161

Cheerios in my mouth, and stumbled into the deserted streets of Huehuetenango. (It is better to leave when the birds are dreaming and mother has yet to wake for the late night feeding.)

Upon arriving at the pre-selected meeting point at approximately 3:00:19 A.M. I saw the bus rounding the corner and heading out.

Note: As an addendum to Rule #1, *hora chapina* is suspended in the cases of vacations and holidays. *Hora Chapina* = Guatemalan Hours, if your meeting is at 9 A.M. you should arrive promptly at 9:37 A.M. or better yet, just don't show up.

I ran down a parallel block where I knew the bus would pass and managed to flag it down. The emergency exit popped open and four of my students called out my name. The students thought I had stood them up and were feeling a little let down; the teachers were nervous because they had no one who could play the role of lifeguard, which made me nervous given my lack of real swimming skills. But I suppose "in the land of the blind, the one-eyed man is king."

The bus barreled down the dark, empty highways as drowsy heads bobbed like sleepy parishoners during a bad homily. We were making good time, which seems to be the overarching goal of the first rule. But then Rule #2 took effect.

Rule #2: The vehicle in which you are riding should break down at least once, if not more

Once we were safely down the mountain and heading across the hot, sugar cane-crowded coastal plains, the brakes decided that they could take no more and politely declined to stop the bus. But the amount of worry this should cause was conspicuously absent. We charged up gentle hills and coasted down the other side honking to move cars out of the way.

Our journey continued like this for another hour before we stopped at a small village to check out the problem. The driver and his helper took out the repairman's most trusted tool, the hammer, and began to beat away on the brake drums hoping to jar something loose. When they were satisfied with the way things looked, we continued on our journey.

The heat on the coastal plain was a shock to the system for the students, and every time the bus slowed down and the breeze stopped blowing, beads of sweat immediately formed on every exposed piece of skin. And, given the situation with the brakes, stops became frequent (when we were able to stop).

Before reaching our destination, the bus broke down a total of four times, but spirits were high throughout. The journey alone was worth it for the students, who screamed as we passed through the tunnel under a mountain near Xela and looked with awe at an overpass we passed along the way.

"Wow, what's that?" Luciano asked as we passed under it. One of the students who had traveled a bit more informed him that cars could in fact cross over the bridge so that they didn't interfere with highway traffic. This explanation gave way to a dejected sigh when Luciano found out we wouldn't be passing over.

After all of the overpass heartbreak and breakdowns, we finally arrived at the beach, which brings us to Rule #3.

Rule #3: The time spent at the actual destination should be approximately a quarter of the travel time

We arrived at the shores of the Pacific at about 1:30 P.M., which brought us to a total of 10.5 hours of travel including the various stops for repairs. The beach was a protected port that lacked the waves and undertow that generally dominate the Pacific Coast of Guatemala.

Everyone trundled out of the bus, tiptoed across the hot, black, volcanic sand and jumped into the warm water. Eyes opened to saucer-like proportions as eyes that had never seen the ocean tried to comprehend the immeasurable expanse of water. The first time in the ocean is an exciting, scary prospect, and many of the students mercifully stayed close to shore. I worked on teaching the front crawl to a few, and the flailing arms and splashing legs quickly turned into a mess that moved neither forward nor backward. But the idea that they were learning gave them dignity, pride and, more importantly, something to show off.

Raul beckoned the girls who were giggling and basking in the water and demonstrated his swimming prowess. He fell face first into the salty water and began to thrash about for a bit. Then he stumbled to his feet, wiped the water from his eyes, spit out that which he had almost swallowed, and beamed a self-satisfied smile over at the girls who had lost interest in his showboating after a few seconds.

In total we spent about 3.5 hours cavorting before heading into town and to the "real" beach, which is lined with a variety of eating establishments and hotels of dubious quality.

Rule #4: The price of food at the restauants you visit should be inversely related to the quality and quantity of food

The beach at Puerto San Jose is crowded with ramshackle restaurants/hotels that face the ocean, and all visitors have to enter through the asshole of one of these hotels to reach the beach. Our bus driver took us to a restaurant/hotel that he swore was the best deal on the beach. We passed through a narrow, dimly-lit hallway filled with small, windowless rooms where weary vacationers spend their evenings on floppy, matted-down mattresses spotted with salty stains from sweaty bodies.

We sat down at plastic tables and waited for what would be a surprisingly underwhelming dinner after a trying day of travel and swimming. Our driver (without telling us) told the owners of the restaurant that our whole group would be eating at the restaurant, and so we were allowed to park for free. But then some students headed over to a competitor, and the owner came out howling of injustice.

In Puerto San Jose, the competition for weekday customers is a spectacle of unusual proportions. Normal, cordial relations are thrown out the window Monday through Thursday, and every hotel, restaurant, and vendor salivates over every potential customer. Two people arrived on ATVs offering rides along the beach, ice cream vendors sauntered over struggling to push their wooden-wheeled carts through the sand, and various people with boxes full of gum, knock-off Lance Armstrong bracelets and other assorted knick-knackery hawked their wares. There were almost more vendors than tourists.

As we watched the vendors prey upon the students from the safety of the restaurant, the teachers and I ordered the grilled fish with french fries. And then we waited. And waited. And waited for over an hour. It seemed that the owner was unhappy with the curt reply to his screams of injustice and was taking his dandy old time. When it finally arrived, the plate was accompanied with a small handful of french fries, a salad and a skinny fish, which, while having good flavor, lacked the bounty of flesh we had hoped for. We paid about $5 for the meal, which would normally cost $2.

After dinner, it was off to the school where we would hit the floor for some quick shut-eye before our big journey back the next morning.

Rule #5: Have a good time
All right, that's a hokey, dorky rule, but it's true. Granted we left early, we were pressed for time at the beach, and we were left wanting in the restaurant, but no one complained

and everyone was downright giddy at the prospect of going someplace new.

Even when we left for home at 7 A.M. Thursday morning and the brakes went out after an hour of driving, everyone was having a good time. And when we got stuck in the town of Siquinala for four hours to repair our crippled vehicle, we found a pool and a way to have fun.

And when we finally arrived in Huehuetenango at 7 P.M., everyone was ready to go again. Except for me. I was getting sick of my official Guatemalan holiday and was looking forward to getting off the bus, provided it was able to stop.

Kyle Freund also contributed "Viva la Revolución Telefónica" to this volume.

ALAN YOUNT

Over the Mountain

*The Volunteer went over the mountain, the Volunteer
went over the mountain, the Volunteer went over the
mountain and what do you think he saw?*

LIKE SO MANY PLANS MADE DURING PEACE CORPS SERVICE, IT
sounded like a good idea when it was proposed: "Let's walk
over the mountain from here to Olopa. We can visit Sara
during Olopa's fiesta." The plan was hatched during one of
those late-night beer-drinking sessions that occur when several
Volunteers happen to be in the same town at the same time.
"From here to Olopa" meant going from Quetzaltepeque, my
service site in the eastern department of Chiquimula, to Olopa,
another town in the same department. "Over the mountain"
was the part that should have given me pause. Olopa was served
by perfectly good chicken buses—so named for the baskets of
chickens often found amongst the luggage—that could make
the trip in three or four hours hours. Instead, I enthusiastically
volunteered to hike over a mountain to get there. It sounded
like a great idea...during a late-night beer-drinking session.

The year was 1986 and it must have been around mid-May,
as Olopa's *fiesta patrona*—patron saint's day—is May 15. Every
town in Guatemala has a patron saint and every town has a

fiesta to celebrate its saint. Olopa honors La Divina Pastora, the Divine Shepherdess, an image of Saint Mary as a shepherdess that is common throughout Latin America.

These fiestas were great fun not only for Guatemalans, but also for the Volunteers. Celebrations usually lasted a week and included some type of carnival. They often included a rodeo and always included dances and drinking. The locals would pour in from the surrounding rural areas, and local Volunteers would host their own parties side-by-side with the fiestas, pulling in Volunteers from all over the country. It was a time for Volunteers to "go native" and dress as the locals dressed and try out our nascent Spanish-speaking skills. It always seemed that I spoke much more fluently after several Gallos, Guatemala's national beer!

Undoubtedly, I was speaking quite fluently the night we decided to hike over the mountain. Our pledge to make the trek was sealed with many bottles of Gallo, and I remember awakening the next morning with a mountain of a hangover. I hoped to beg out of the hike, especially after learning that several of my *compañeros* had already hightailed it back to the departmental capital of Chiquimula to catch the local chicken bus. I, however, had slept through that escape and was trapped by my promise to the two remaining PCVs, both of whom were much more rugged and (apparently) less hungover than I.

We packed our backpacks. I'm still amazed at how little I traveled with back then: one shirt to change into and a pounded-on-a-rock clean pair of underwear. I could always pound the pair I was wearing on another rock at my destination if the need arose. Water bottles were filled and maps consulted. My fellow travelers were both "fish-heads"—fisheries volunteers—who were more skilled at map-reading than I, a nursing volunteer. They were always going off on their own into the wild in search of good locations for building a pond. I usually went accompanied by someone from the local Puesto de Salud, health center. Gringos with vaccines and needles usually needed more of an introduction than gringos looking to dig a pond.

We set out in the morning, hoping to get a good deal of the way to Olopa before the noonday sun beat down. The department of Chiquimula is in the far southeastern corner of Guatemala, bordering both Honduras and El Salvador. It is located in one of the hottest and most arid parts of the country where local deforestation has taken a great toll. Another Peace Corps program in Guatemala was forestry, which was comprised of PCVs who were also more skilled at map-reading— or getting the lay of the land—than I was.

My Peace Corps program was a WHO-sponsored vaccination program. WHO, the World Health Organization, had a goal of vaccinating every child in the world by some ridiculous date. Nonetheless, in an effort to accomplish that goal, I would spend three days a week in remote *aldeas*, rural collections of thatched huts that were within a day's reach of my site. On the first day, I would set out with someone from the local Puesto de Salud to take a census of the *aldea*. Had I gone alone, I would have found no one at home. A gringo asking a lot of questions about your kids was seen as something of a threat.

After a day of counting the population, we would return the next day to some agreed upon location with a heavy thermal container of vaccines: polio and MMR (measles, mumps, and rubella). Since most of our "patients" didn't show up at the agreed-upon location, we would return a third day with a somewhat smaller thermal container, and go to the homes of every family with kids on our census that didn't show up the day before. The MMR requires three vaccinations to be effective. Most kids didn't get all three. It was a frustrating program. But, I did get used to hiking around in the middle of nowhere. Maybe *that's* why I agreed to the over-the-mountain-to-Olopa hike?

The day of our hike started well enough. We got off to a good pace, and the exercise seemed to be burning my hangover away. And we did see some pretty sights along the way: Alpine-like high meadows and picturesque herds of sheep and cows. But, as with all such spontaneous endeavors, we hit a few snags along the way. The first was a nasty rainstorm that drove us to seek shelter for some time. Hey, at least it cooled us off, right? After the rain slowed down (notice, I didn't say "stopped"), we resumed our forced march, arriving at our second snag: something of a cliff that we had to scale to get to Olopa.

We finally made it up the cliff and into Olopa. We even found Sara's house. It was well after sunset, and we arrived to find that our friends from the night before—the other Volunteers who had "promised" to hike with us—were already there and way ahead of us in the Gallo-drinking department. As a matter of fact, they had been drinking all the way there, while riding *on the top* of a local bus from Chiquimula. Bus surfing we called it back then. Crazy is what I would call it today.

Of course, the clothes I was wearing were soaked and muddy from the rain and the climb. And the clothes in my bag were soaked and muddy from the rain and climb. Sara loaned me a *juipil*—a colorful indigenous Guatemalan woman's blouse—to wear. It wasn't exactly the "go native" outfit that I had planned to wear to the fiesta, but after a few medicinal bottles of Gallo, it didn't matter to me anymore. I went to the dance: the *gringo loco* in a woman's blouse!

The next day I went home: inside a bus, wondering, *why* I ever agreed to hike over the mountain. I realize now that I hiked over the mountain for the sheer joy of it. I hiked over the mountain so that I could tell people that I hiked over the mountain. I hiked over the mountain so that I could see and experience something different. When I think about it, hiking over the mountain is a lot like joining the Peace Corps in the first place.

After serving in the Peace Corps from 1985-86 in Guatemala, Alan Yount looked for more mountains to go over, beginning with law school and a law firm. He soon realized that he really missed the personal connections that he had while a Peace Corps Volunteer. So, he packed up his law degree and his house in Washington, D.C., and moved to New York City to become a New York City Teaching Fellow. Every day is a new hike over a new mountain. And he still loves it.

WILLIAM M. EVENSEN

The Amazing Jungle Walking Tour

Dedicated to the memory of Peace Corps Volunteers Paul L. Bond and Gerald F. Flynn, stationed in Ecuador, and Troy M. Ross, stationed in Peru, who died in a 1966 plane crash in the Andes of Peru.

THE BEST THING ABOUT THE PEACE CORPS IS ITS GENEROUS vacation allowance: twenty-four days per annum, an inspired policy that allows Volunteers ample time to explore their host countries and to take a break from their primitive living conditions. You could even argue that it's the key to Peace Corps' enduring success. Here's my argument.

We all know there are a lot of strategies on how to spend those valuable vacation days. Some Volunteers use them up all at once; some let them dwindle away a few days at a time. My wife and I planned a series of week-long vacations. With twentieth-century living deeply imprinted in our circuitry, we knew we'd need several respites from our rural site, high up in the Central Andes of Peru, where the average adult annual income was a puny $400.

We were in the last six months of our twenty-four-month tour of duty, performing tedious community development work amongst impoverished Quechua-speaking *campesinos* who, like ourselves, only spoke Spanish as a second language. We were emotionally pooped, in need of a boost.

We knew we had to steel ourselves for our "home stretch" run and our final push to leave a humanitarian mark. Now was the perfect time to take our last time-out from the eighteenth-century culture we were living in and indulge ourselves with a modern twentieth-century fix of hamburgers, private hot showers, flush toilets, and first-run movie theaters.

Getting this fix meant traveling to the capitol and using up our last seven days of Peace Corps vacation. Since all roads in Peru lead to Lima—the capitol since the sixteenth-century Spanish Conquest—we decided for our last trip to go via the Amazon Jungle (which is way east of the Andes, while Lima lies west of the Andes on the edge of the Pacific Ocean). Admittedly, this looping itinerary was the long way around for scoring your twentieth-century "Jones," especially if you consider we were 200 miles east of Lima when we started our trek, albeit 11,000 feet higher. In Peru distances mean nothing because altitude is everything.

Besides the obvious R&R benefits of this, our last vacation, we felt a moral obligation to visit the Amazon Basin, which occupies 50 percent of Peru's land mass and is home to 1 percent of its population. You might ask, how much of the jungle can you see in a week? It turns out, you can see more than you could imagine, provided you don't stop or dilly-dally.

With little time and even less money, we crafted a ground/air itinerary for accomplishing this mad seven-day dash, going from the Andes to the jungle to modern Lima and back up into the Andes.

The trip would go like this: Start in the Central Andes traveling by bus to Cerro de Pasco, traversing down through *la montana* to Pucallpa. End of the road. Catch small plane to

Iquitos 300 miles northeast, where the Amazon River begins its 3,900 mile-long journey across the South American continent to the Atlantic Ocean. From Iquitos, former nineteenth-century rubber capitol of the world, fly cheapie (non-Peace Corps authorized) airline back 600 miles over the Andes to Lima, where modern amenities awaited. Return to the Central Andes via an eight-hour bus trip. It was a 1,600-mile counter-clockwise route designed to end up in Lima at the tail end of our last Peace Corps vacation.

We began this seven-day jaunt in Huancayo, elevation 10,700 feet, the commercial seat of the fertile Mantaro Valley, in which we lived, and home to the Silent Indian Fair, which every Sunday attracted thousands of Quechua Indians from surrounding highland communities. Early in the morning we boarded one of the many buses that journey north to Cerro de Pasco, a grimy American mining town located at 13,500 feet and whose deadly mines are located at even higher elevations.

The high-altitude journey across the freezing treeless *altiplano* in a small, twenty-five-passenger bus—built on an unforgiving two-ton truck bed and jammed beyond capacity with vomiting Indian babies and squawking chickens—was little preparation for the foreboding starkness of Cerro de Pasco. Seeing an American company town brazenly polluting the environment and its workers was a politically numbing experience, even more so at that un-oxygenated altitude.

After departing Cerro de Pasco, the cramped bus began its bumpy descent down the eastern slope of the Andes. Many hours later, the semi-tropical temperatures of Huanuco brought life back into our frozen, bundled bodies and marked the end to Day 1. As the air warmed, we changed modes of transport, moving out of the claustrophobic bus and hitching a ride on an empty ten-ton truck on its return trip into the heart of the jungle. We stood behind the cab with an unobstructed view.

By the time we reached Tingo Maria we were deep in *la montaña*. From our perch above the cab, we had a spectacular 360-degree view of lush canyons, roaring rivers, and the dense green jungle carpet that stretched out as far as the eye could see. The only interruption in this idyllic view was the thin brown line of the road to Pucallpa, a paved-lane cut into the jungle's cornucopia of natural resources. It was civilization's calling card, a stent into the heart of our planet.

Tingo Maria was a frontier town covered with tin roofs. Vultures sat on top of every building; hence, garbage was not a problem. Everything was eaten. It was a town of necessities only: no frills, lots of land, lots of growing going on.

After Tingo Maria, *la selva* flattened out like a verdant sea. No tree grew above another. The vegetation had a ceiling level of about thirty feet, and the resultant green wall looked like a tsunami caught in mid-curl. There were no signs. No technology. Pre-civilization. Speculation about Earth's survival began to percolate up from our subconscious as we viewed the Earth in its primordial splendor.

Thirty kilometers from Pucallpa we came upon an emergency roadblock, not the political kind, but the road construction variety: "*El camino esta cerrado.*" An American company, courtesy of a USAID project, was paving the road, and rain had made the section they were working on completely impassable.

The Guardia Civil (municipal police) said we might have to wait a day or two. With less than a week of vacation left, that was an impossible option. Besides, this particular spot was not anyone's idea of Vacation Land. There was nothing but a tiny *tienda* and a small screen-enclosed office with a wooden table and one chair.

And who knows what goes with the Peruvian bureaucracy? The road could be open for days before the word was passed on to this remote jungle roadblock.

With so little wiggle-room in our itinerary, it seemed foolish to wait in such a forlorn spot for who knows how long. With no place to sleep, we decided to walk the last thirty kilometers (eighteen miles) to Pucallpa, transporting our one rather large suitcase, dangling from a pole, carried over our shoulders. Why the big suitcase? We were passing through three of Peru's very distinct worlds: ice-cold Andes, sweltering Amazon, and sophisticated Lima. All three zones require at least different footwear. And who thought we'd be stuck walking?

A Peruvian woman of modest net worth joined us, figuring it was better to walk with the gringos than to stay and be entertainment for the waiting *cholo* truck drivers, cowboys of the Amazon Basin. She wore a simple Western-style cotton dress and carried her modest suitcase balanced on top of her head, jungle-style.

The road was bone dry and there was no sign of rain. We had several hours of daylight left and figured we could walk four miles an hour. In four to five hours we'd cover the eighteen miles to Pucallpa, a bustling jungle outpost.

Within five minutes we were drenched in tropical sweat. There were no mileposts; and as members of the go-with-the-flow crowd, we carried no wristwatch. To know how far we had gone, I started counting the steps. Multiplying each step by three feet, I knew that every 1,762 strides we were one mile closer to Pucallpa.

It was an idea that didn't last an hour. Daylight didn't last much longer. The sun dropped out of the sky like a rock into a pond, taking with it all the light of day. Suddenly, we were alone in the jungle, except for the chatter of trillions of crickets. Above us, stretching from treetop horizon to treetop horizon, was a blue-black carpet studded with twinkling celestial lights of every size and configuration. Below the horizon, there was total darkness. We walked for miles and miles with our eyes on high, dazzled by the illuminated sky.

Around nine at night we came to a wide spot in the road where a small settlement of people lived. We asked if anyone had a car. "Yes, there are some gringos who live down the road; they have one." So I borrowed a bike, leaving my wife and suitcase as collateral, and rode off into the night until I found the home of two elderly missionaries from Redlands, California.

They had a car, all right, but it had been up on blocks for years. The couple was more than happy to put us up for the night. The Peruvian lady, however, was a soul of another color. She didn't get to stay in the house with us. As missionaries, they were not interested in her physical well being as much as her spiritual salvation. We had no strength to protest. Emotionally, physically, we were a pair of soggy socks, too weak to stand up.

The couple said we were thirteen kilometers (7.8 miles) from Pucallpa. They seemed starved for conversation, and it wasn't long before the prattling evangelists talked us into a stupor. Like zombies of the Caribbean, we staggered off to bed. In their bathroom, seeking solace from one another, we were horrified to find a monstrously long stool coiled in the toilet bowl, apparently being saved for the next morning's flush. We vowed to leave first thing in the morning.

It was raining when we awoke. The sky was gray and gloomy. To stay, even with a roof over our heads, seemed insane considering we only had five days left. The missionary couple talked the entire time. Even as we walked out the door into the rain, they babbled away about their glorious mission of saving native souls.

It had rained all night and the road was as slippery as snail slime. We fell often and didn't bounce on ground that felt like solid concrete. Finally, we came upon the road construction project: a bulldozer and a road-grader guarded by a live-in *cuidador*. He told us a company man came every day at noon to bring him his food, and we could wait for him. The tiny cab of a Mitsubishi road-grader never felt more comfortable. Though we weren't moving forward, the prospect of being transported out of this morass had dramatically improved.

Our rescuer, a Peruvian employee of the Brownsville, Texas, construction company, drove a four-wheel drive jeep. For the first time our mode of travel was commodious. It wasn't long before we saw for ourselves why the road to Pucallpa was closed. There was no road, only a gigantic quagmire of jungle mud. Stuck up to their axles were five large trucks. Their drivers sat dejectedly in their cabs, waiting for the rain to end and for the tropical sun to bake the earth dry enough to let them escape. Until then, they were captives of the Amazon Mud Goddess.

Our driver, a young civil engineer, said that in the past, drivers waiting for the rain to end and for the mud to dry had died in their trucks from exposure and starvation. At which point our four-wheel jeep started slipping in the mud. As the rain fell and the wheels spun, I leapt out and got behind the jeep to push. Mud flew up into my face, covering me from head to foot with a thick coat of warm, caramel-brown colored mud. I pushed and pushed; I'd be damned if we were going to get stuck. We didn't have enough vacation days for any delays.

Somehow, we got traction and finally made it to the Texas company compound. Outfitted with numerous modern luxuries—hot showers, drinkable water—the compound was our reward for walking, instead of waiting. After showering and eating lunch, the Texans said that we could stay at the compound or they would drive us to Pucallpa. Naturally, we chose the latter.

Once settled in Pucallpa, we took a canoe-taxi down the Ucayali River to visit the Shipibo Indians in the neighboring village of San Francisco. Adventist missionaries had left their mark here, as they feverishly worked the Andean tributaries translating the Bible into native dialects. When we walked into the small village, the women greeted us with wide smiles, but immediately covered their bare breasts as they had been taught to do when in the company of gringos. They were natural beauties with gleaming white teeth who cut their jet-black bangs straight across. Coyly, they cocked their heads back and forth, grinning at us like hopeful young girls at a community dance.

The Shipibo People live on 20x20-foot bamboo decks built four feet off the ever-moist ground. Ten feet above the deck, a thatched roof provides the family with shade. Their thin pottery and delicate fabrics are decorated with the same maze-like designs. These were happy creatures from a tropical lagoon.

The tiny one-room Pucallpa Museum has an incredible taxidermy collection: penguins, monkeys, jaguars; even a thirty-foot anaconda wraps around the rafters. The Peruvian Army reported finding a ninety-foot anaconda. Basically, in the fecund jungle things grow exponentially, including the fungi between your toes.

Back in Pulcallpa, we discovered that the airport had a quaint pastoral quality to it. What we thought was grazing land turned out to be the airfield! The plane we were going to take circled above and couldn't land because cows were on the runway. Eventually, with a little Andean coaxing—throwing rocks and delivering swift kicks to the cows—our DC3 touched down.

The 300-mile flight to Iquitos was totally intimidating: streams and tributaries meandering through the endless green swamp, like silver ribbons blowing in the wind. The immensity of the Amazon Basin sent shivers through my duodenum. An aerial view is overwhelming, incomprehensible. The jungle is an ocean of green, as undulating as the sea. If our plane went down, even if we survived, we'd never get out alive.

The occasional flash of chrome light reflecting off a tin roof below made you wonder. Who lives out here, where the only means of transportation is by tiny boat? Were they all ex-Nazis or just headhunters who had made it big? Petrified with both fear and awe, I forgot to breathe for most of the hour-long flight.

The sight of Iquitos and landing on terra firma was a breathtaking experience. At the end of the nineteenth century, in the middle of nowhere, Iquitos was built to accommodate the emerging rubber industry and the whims of its rubber barons. The town became so prosperous that it had its own opera house. Exquisite Mediterranean tiles still adorn the buildings in Old Iquitos.

The biggest surprise, however, is that the Amazon River at its origin is two miles wide! It is not the popular jungle image of vines cascading across your face as you make your way down river. Far from it; you can't even see the other side of the river.

The Port of Iquitos was bustling with activity. Despite the ponderous heat, native workers unloaded boats and schlepped huge banana stalks on their backs to waiting trucks like one huge conveyor. Women carried boxes on their heads, babies on their breasts; windowless buses, packed to the gills, roared by. Fortunately, every hotel room had a ceiling fan to circulate the heavy, moist jungle air. We lay motionless on our bed, exhausted; my wife painstakingly medicated her swollen, insect-bitten legs, a grim testimony to our short walk through the jungle.

With the ambulatory segment of our jungle trip behind us, we rented a jeep to drive to a Paiche Fish Breeding Farm in nearby Quispe Coche. The Paiche, indigenous to the Amazon Basin, are huge tuna-like creatures—6x2 feet—that are being raised in 40x20-foot cement swimming pool-sized nurseries! This aquaculture was a new answer to the growing demand for protein in Peru, a country that imports most of its food. Efforts to tap into the jungle's food- producing potential have been modest and mainly ineffectual. And no wonder; it is a constant battle, beating back the jungle.

Our jeep, apparently suffering from heatstroke, couldn't be revived and was pronounced dead at the Paiche Farm parking lot, requiring us to walk back to Iquitos. The pervasive, ubiquitous jungle was constantly taking its toll on the invaders. Twice our quickie "vacation" through the Amazon jungle had been slowed to a walk.

We returned to the Hotel Iquitos sweating profusely and itching for Lima and its lap of luxury. On the door of our room we found a telegram from our airline—LANSA, a company so small its four planes were continually in the air. The telegram explained that their plane flying from Cuzco-to-Iquitos had crashed. Thus, we wouldn't be able to fly to Lima the next morning. We could, they suggested, wait two days for their next Lima flight to arrive.

After learning that no one survived, we happily paid the extra to fly on the Peace Corps-approved Fawcett Airlines' next flight to Lima. Although this extra expenditure zapped our Lima budget, it did allow us to keep on truckin'.

Boarding the plane to Lima we received shocking news. Even though we didn't know them, there were three PCVs lying dead in the jungle in the plane we had planned to fly on.

For the most part, we sat in silence, praying for a safe journey over the towering, glacier-covered Andes.

As it turns out, the airplane doesn't actually fly over the air-thin 23,000-foot Andean mountain range. Rather, it flies precariously in between and around jagged mountain peaks, angling down narrow, steeply-terraced valleys on its breathtaking 600-mile journey to the arid Pacific coast of Peru.

After safely touching down at the Hugo Chavez Airport in Lima, we took a cab directly to Sears and bought hamburgers and double-chocolate milkshakes. After a luxurious hot shower at the International Hotel, where PCVs received a steep discount, we went searching for a first-run movie. *The Sound of Music* had just opened, and we ran right in. We sat through the movie twice, completely mesmerized, only getting up for more transfusions of popcorn and Coke.

We were so stoked by our vacation that we couldn't wait to get back to our site. Instead of taking the low-budget eight-hour Peruvian bus trip, we paid extra and took an expensive *collectivo* (shared-taxi) to Huancayo. A harrowing high-octane journey—passing on curves, passing at the top of the hill, no guard rails—that roared from sea-level Lima to the cold 16,000-foot pass of Mt. Ticlio, down into the sunny 10,000-foot-high Mantaro Valley in only five ear-popping hours! We arrived at our site in Sicaya by nightfall, flush out of vacation days, high on being alive.

We were ecstatic to be back in our one-room adobe apartment that had no running water, no flush toilet, and no electricity, although it did have natural refrigeration. We were ready to get back to work in the community. I'm not exactly sure what caused our rejuvenation, whether it was Lima's modern-day addictions or surviving our Amazon jungle vacation. Either way, we were fortunate to have lived through the recharging of our batteries.

Without question the Peace Corps was the best job of our lives, thanks most to its sagacious vacation policy.

William M. Evensen, who served in Peru from 1964-66, is a self-described activist/writer/publisher/prankster. He was the Co-Founder of Young Professionals for Kennedy, has been involved in UCLA's first heroin treatment and research program, produced the KELP Radio Players and has published books, historical calendars, and print features about Venice, California. He is currently writing a memoir about his career of social activism and how it was shaped by his Peace Corps service.

PATRICK H. HARE

God and Motorcycles

As Howie demonstrates, there's more to being an
effective Volunteer than a good first impression.

"TEGUS"—TEGUCIGALPA—WAS BEAUTIFUL, AND OFTEN NAKED
when we didn't want her to be. Howie and I lived in Tegus
forty years ago, not far from a church featuring Christ's silver
heart with a knife in it. Sculpted into the Caribbean yellow
plaster over the main door, the silver heart dripped red blood.
Women in our neighborhood, Barrio El Chile, especially
young ones, still balanced loads on their pretty poised heads,
but often the loads were plastic handbags. Change rode everywhere, bareback and rubbing raw.

After a few beers, Honduran friends would often say we had
already changed their lives. Specifically, during the pause that
refreshes, they would say, "This is the first time I've ever seen
the penis of a gringo." Roads cracked jeep frames; sports cars
were non-existent. The nightclub neighborhood was named
Belen, or in English, Bethlehem. Soccer was violent, not the
players, but the streets it was played on. Sharp volcano rock
jutted out of the sun-baked mud, tearing deep into falling

muscles. Dirt was a regular feature of faces, collars, and hands in the Barrio. Running water was an irregular feature.

Being clean almost had the status of being a gringo, which almost had the status of being God, particularly since God himself had forgotten Honduras. There were so few priests that almost no one poor got married, so the Pope once sent a mass marriage mission to save Hondurans from living in sin. A good horse was still something every man, even a city man, hoped for. But Honduran horses were rarely good, except at enduring suffering. In fact, enduring suffering was a Honduran national pastime, a one-word verb, to *aguantar*.

Tegus attracted urban immigrant smarts and drive. Then it cramped them against each other in dirty neighborhoods: tiny packed pastel ivy leagues of endless hope and no classes. We were supposed to help the hope. Manlio Martinez, a Honduran economist, liked the Peace Corps, but he called it "on the job training" for young Americans. He wanted to charge the U.S. for time spent on our training. One Volunteer introduced imported corn that grew skyscraper stalks. But the stalks never grew ears. Another Volunteer imported a stud pig for breeding, but it was too big to breed; the females were afraid of being crushed by the monster gringo pig. When we screwed up, Manilo called it, "The demolition derby of on the job training."

Howie's first project was a design for two-story rural affordable homes. We all, including some Honduran architects, thought the design was brilliant. But the homes were named the "Chicken Coops" by local *campesinos*, and people moved in very slowly. The two-story homes did look like oversized Honduran chicken coops. Poor rural Hondurans had never lived on two stories, or in chicken coops. Most did not want to do either, even the most *humilde campesinos*, the beaten wimp-dog humble. But Howie's project made no one, Honduran or Peace Corps, doubt Howie. I think, as Manlio Martinez understood, the drive to do things was one point of Peace Corps, and drive causes both hope and pain. Although successes came often, Peace Corps was the first real job for many of us, and often what we could add to the Honduran equation was mostly drive, even if it was just the drive to get to meetings on time. Howie's affluence in the drive department was why he was so watched by the rest of us.

In the middle of a soccer game between our neighborhood and Peace Corps Volunteers, played on an actual field, some players from our neighborhood took me aside. These were Hondurans I'd seen bounce small boulders off each other at a wedding gone bad, who drank themselves into senseless war-victim piles of the living dead, who ignored running falls on sharp volcanic rock, who were from a neighborhood that produced the country's top soccer player, who had fat-free muscles never softened by a French fry.

They took me aside and said, "Patricio, Patricio, stop Howie. He is running too hard. We know running and soccer. He is going to run himself to death." They were scared for him. Their voices were full of affection.

Forty years later, I remember how, when Howie got like he was in that game, when he made some internal decision to push himself, it seemed you could physically see his thoughts sink back behind, lower than his eyes. The cheek muscles right under his eyes flattened. His jaw relaxed in resolution, and his eyes went listless. Something, maybe his almost religious acceptance of some challenges as his simple fate, made him able to reach very deep into the force we use to push ourselves. Sometimes I felt liked I lived with a wolf.

Howie was into the seemingly high-tech hope of management theory applied to third-world development. When an

English-speaking Swedish U.N. management expert came to town on a flying visit, Howie set up a meeting with the expert for some of the Volunteers. The guy's schedule meant the meeting had to be painfully early. Howie wasn't there when we started, so I sat next to the expert. We were in another Volunteer's pink house that stood almost alone, set into a vacant, dirty, bare urban hillside, just being turned into building lots. The house was near Bethlehem, the nightclub district. Howie showed up a little late, looking like a Honduran mason. Honduran masons worked in business suits covered with white-gray dirt and cement. The suits showed that they were professionals. After the expert's talk, in English, Howie asked a question filled with intent. His forehead muscled down, and his eyes and cheeks muscled up and out a little over his dirty clothes and face, the way they always did when he asked an "intent" question. The need to push himself very hard was in his murky hoarse voice. The question tripped over itself, and nearly fell on the hard tiled floor. It was a knot of hunger, hangover, bad pronunciation, and worse logic before he managed to end it.

That day wasn't Howie's day. The night before hadn't been his night either, and neither was it Christmas Eve, but Howie, being a wise man, had still gone to Bethlehem, to the nightclub district, just in case. He had drunk enough to be rolled, and then got rolled again, the second time, into a ditch. When the sun came up late over Tegucigalpa's seven hills, and hit the ditch, Howie woke up hungover, beat-up, dirty, and hungry. He also woke up remembering he was a wolf and that today was the wolf's chance to eat U.N. management theory.

The English-speaking Swedish U.N. expert listened to Howie's intent, convoluted question very carefully, and then seemed to eye Howie's Honduran mason appearance with the just the same kind of restrained careful quality he had used in listening to Howie. Then the expert paused, shifting his body in his seat a little to give himself time, a pause, a short "I am moving very carefully here because I don't want to give offence" pause. And then he leaned over to me and asked very very quietly in his Swedish accent, "Do I need a translator? Is English this man's native language?"

When Howie left Honduras to go home, north, he went south. To Panama. To the Canal Zone. To buy a Norton motorcycle. To go north on. He drove it back to Honduras up the Pan American highway, which at that time was fenceless and featured horses and cows wandering on the road, or sometimes not wandering, because they were dead. Howie drove this huge Norton back to Honduras, back to our neighborhood, in which there were still a few horses and burros. The Norton was bigger than many of the burros, and seemed bigger than the horses, and in the eyes of many of our Honduran neighbors, seemed bigger than God, or at least faster. They called the Norton, "*la maquina*," the machine. "*La maquina de Howie.*"

Howie kept the Norton very clean. That fascinated people. One feature of Howie's drive was that he focused relentlessly on a single objective at a time, like the clean Norton, and forgot others, like the fact that being clean was a very important symbol to poor Hondurans of being a Peace Corps Volunteer, and more importantly a gringo, and therefore somehow via cleanliness, the next thing to God. The powerful Norton, being horse-like and more real than God, especially for Hondurans who saw many horses but almost never a priest, mostly made up in their eyes for Howie's confusing distance from both God and most gringos in terms of cleanliness. His personal drive and the Norton's power merged in their minds, but couldn't erase the neighborhood's long-held concern about Howie's obviously huge distance from the shiny-alumi-num-airplane clean of the God of Uncle Sam.

They could see that the big Norton, "*La maquina*," was the right horse for Howie, but they couldn't see why he didn't do the gringo super-clean-like-a-shiny-aluminum-airplane thing at all, except for the Norton. When he left, they incorporated his clean machine and personal dirt, and their admiration for him, into a neighborhood news story. It was about him and the horse he rode out on. They repeated this news story to each other like endless reruns of an astonishing home video on the TV news. "*Se fue Howie en la maquina*," it started, "*y con la mitad de Honduras*."

In full, the news on Howie's exit went like this: "Howie left. On the *maquina*, the Norton. And do you know what he carried on him as a souvenir? Half the dirt in Honduras. On his body. But, *fijate*! (But, get this!), that damn dirty Howie made sure that big steel bastard of a *maquina* was spotless."

Epilogue: Howie Knox, a father and husband, and an architect, lobsterman, and yacht racer, was from Stonington. He died in January 2005.

Patrick H. Hare was a Volunteer in Honduras from 1966-69. He is now an urban planner who specializes in forms of affordable housing that require no subsidy, such as accessory apartments and one-car and no-car mortgages. He lives in Connecticut where he is chair of the Planning and Zoning Commission, and also has a home in Washington, D.C.

KATHERINE JAMIESON

*

Balata

Just because something's foreign made doesn't
necessarily mean it works any better.

ABOUT A YEAR INTO OUR RELATIONSHIP, ARDIS WENT TO SEE A
doctor, an Arkansan woman on a month-long Christian
mission at the hospital. Though she hadn't seen a doctor in
years, and never a gynecologist, everything checked out fine.
However, the doctor was concerned that Ardis couldn't use
tampons because she froze up at the slightest penetration.
Unwittingly, she had recommended a dildo to loosen the
muscles and retrain her body.

"Do they even have dildos in Guyana?" I asked when she
told me, laughing. A dildo seemed an outrageous luxury item
in a country where you couldn't easily find paper clips.

Ardis fixed her soft brown eyes on me, amused by my
amusement. "Yes, monkey, they do," she said, and gave me a
short history of the evolution of the Guyanese sex toy.

Amerindians, the indigenous peoples of Guyana, lived
nearest to the country's massive rainforests and had made the
first dildos from the sap of a jungle tree. When formed and
dried, the sap looked like rubber and was solid, yet flexible.

Though it could be used to make many things, the name for the sap became synonymous with its most infamous creation. In Guyana, a dildo is a *balata*. The traditional version was now being outmoded by the American import, available only recently. Guyana had only had television for the past ten years. Cars hadn't been common until the late '80s. Now dildos.

Ardis told me that the best place to find a dildo was on Avenue of the Republic, one of the busiest streets in Georgetown, Guyana. It was right next to the car park where minibuses left for destinations all over the country; the area swarmed with Guyanese commuters and shoppers.

"Do you want me to get it for you?" I asked her, though I was just as nervous. Neither of us had used a dildo before, and weren't sure if we wanted to introduce this foreign element into our sex life.

"I don't know. Do you want to?" she asked.

"Well," I said carefully, "we could just get one and see how it works for us. It's not like we'd have to use it all the time."

She considered what I was saying, her beautiful brown face tightened in concentration, twisted black locks bouncing lightly around her head. Though she was confident in every other area of her life, this was a source of frustration. Ardis had less sexual experience than I did, and I knew she was curious what all the heterosexual fuss was about. In the end, I don't think she liked the idea of being shown up by a plastic gadget.

"O.K.," she said, "let's get one, let's see how it goes." She cuddled up to me, "Could be fun, nah?" she said softly.

Flour and other basic foreign goods had been banned in Ardis' childhood, and she had mastered the workings of the black market at a young age. Whether or not it had passed through customs, she knew how to get it. In the market, she led me to the stalls with the juiciest mangos, the longest *bourra*, the firmest paw paw, and with a few phone calls, she located and ordered Guyana's premier dildo for us. Since Ardis had a high profile job and sex toys were still firmly in the category of "wickedness" in Guyana, it was decided that I would make the dicey purchase. Though more of a standout, I had no reputation to protect: Guyanese expect white people to be "*wicke.*" Plus the item had originated in my dissolute country, after manufacture in China, so buying it was sort of an act of repatriation.

On the Friday I was slated to make the big purchase, my student Annameika, a plump first-year at the vocational high school where I taught, met me at the back door of the school building. She held something in her hand, wrapped in multiple plastic bags.

"Hello, Miss, good mawrning, Miss! Miss, my uncle catch dis yesterday an' he said give it to yuh nice white lady teachah! Miss I told him how you teach me fuh swim and so!" Annameika beamed at me, her clear brown skin reflecting the high morning sun.

"Look, Miss," she said, holding up the gift, and unwrapping a few layers of the bags. The head of a white, glassy-eyed fish peeked over the plastic wrapping.

"It's Banga Mary, Miss, ya must cook it up with seasoning, tomatoes, *bourra*, peppers and *wiri-wiri* peppers."

My students knew I was no cook. I had once given leftovers to a poor woman who wandered through the school begging. After tasting my offering she declined the rest. Not enough salt, she said.

"O.K., Annameika, thank you. This looks delicious. But, I can't take it home with me today because I'm going out after…"

"No, Miss, you must carry it and cook it tonight, Miss! The fish is more nice fresh, Miss!" The girl was animated now, pushing the fish into my hand.

I looked at the fish's head again, small beads of condensation on its flesh, dripping onto the plastic bags. Annameika looked at me expectantly. She would be standing there again on Monday waiting for a report of how I cooked the fish, how it tasted, who I shared it with, gathering details to report back to her uncle and the rest of her family.

"O.K., Annameika, I'll take it today and cook it tonight," I said. She smiled, showing a gold tooth with a Nike swoosh cutout on her third molar.

"Good Miss, yuh gon' like it nuff, nuff!" and she hurried up the stairs for the beginning of classes.

At 3:00, I said goodbye to my students, co-teachers and other staff with a large fish zipped into the outside pocket of my bag and thousands of multi-colored Guyana dollars in an inside compartment. After taking a minibus downtown, I found myself in the Friday afternoon melee of Avenue of the Republic. It was a common area to get "picked," or pickpocketed, so I had identified a roadside vendor who I always stopped to speak with in case anyone was looking to rob me. My Rasta friend had a small card table where he sold sticks of gum, candies, and *pholouri*, fried balls of cooked lentils. He had short, tight dreads and large, liquidy eyes.

"Good afternoon, sistah," he said, nodding languidly as I approached.

"Good afternoon, brothah," I replied, tapping his shoulder with my hand. We talked about the weather, the new reggae tape I had just bought, and the public murder of a woman on the dance floor of a local club by her ex-boyfriend. No one had stepped forward to testify, though there had been hundreds of witnesses. I bought a pack of *pholouri* with mango sour and shared it with him. Then we discussed the safest buses to ride out to Rose Hall, and where I was taking my family on their upcoming trip at Christmas. I was stalling.

Finally, I bought a pack of gum, wished my friend a good day and continued down the Avenue to a small storefront crammed between identical drug stores. The Guyanese courts were directly across the street, their imposing stone structures the oldest and most historic in the country. Queen Victoria stood guard in front, her nose broken off in riots during the anti-colonial period of the last dictatorship. I looked at her massive, queenly robes—so incongruous with the palm trees waving overhead—and her disfigured, but still stern face. She looked unforgiving in a uniquely British way, and I couldn't help imagining her utter disapproval of the modern-day daughters of her colonies.

The store was cool inside, and I inhaled the rare air-conditioned oxygen, turning my face to the vent on the high wall. It was one room, lined with high shelves up to the ceiling. Every shelf was crammed with merchandise: tiny bottles of brownish perfume, lipsticks, Baygon to kill bugs, Limacol for fainting spells, Gentian Violet for cuts, yellow, red, and pink paint to throw on Phagwah, the Hindu festival of spring. Then there were the bigger ticket items: shortwave radios, plastic wall clocks with inspirational Biblical quotes, *taw's* for cooking roti, *karahis* for cooking stew. On the very top shelves, farthest away from thieving hands, were the expensive, electronic items, CD players and cameras, and somewhere out of sight, I knew, dildos.

Guyanese shop differently than Americans. They tend to save for months to buy one specific item, case out all the stores that carry it to compare prices, then return to test its functionality, to whatever degree possible, in the store. Finally, they barter a good price, present the cash and return home as quickly as possible so that whatever they have bought doesn't get stolen. They expect their purchases to last for years, if not decades. Some of my friends still had full wardrobes from the '60s, pots and pans that had been passed down from their grandparents.

I looked about casually for a few moments, dazed by the surplus of material objects. I was out of touch with store shopping, having spent the last year trundling through the outdoor markets, asking advice from country women in aprons and hair ties about how to find the best *geera* for curry, which sorrel sepals to pick for making drinks. My biggest purchase in the past month was a turquoise plastic tub for hand-washing laundry.

"Miss, can I help you?" a young, thin Indian man asked, as I examined the gold earrings in the shape of Guyana under the glass counter. He wore a collared white shirt, stiff with starch, and a striped, polyester tie. Pomade stuck the jet-black strands of his hair together in little tufts. Looking around, I saw that all the salesmen were young, thin Indian men.

"I, well, a friend of mine ordered something," I began. I glanced around the small store to make sure I didn't know the other two people there. They were oblivious, both of them enraptured with their own potential purchases: an Indian woman tapping the bottom of a pressure cooker; an African-Guyanese man fiddling with the dials of several different alarm clocks. My co-shoppers were so deliberate in their purchases I was tempted to ask them for help with mine.

"Yes, of course, what's your friend's name," the man asked. He looked at me expectantly.

"Karen," I said. We had used Ardis' cousin's name, since, as far as we knew, there was only one Ardis in Guyana.

The young man went over to the counter near the cash register. My fellow shoppers were still doing final reviews of the products, shaking them, turning them upside down, asking detailed questions about their manufacture, warranty. A young Indian couple wandered in and asked to see a CD player. Through the glass front door, I could see hundreds of Guyanese streaming by. I imagined one of my students catching a glimpse of white skin through the glass, pushing open the door: *Miss, hello Miss! Whatcha shopping, Miss? Ya buy nice jewelry for me?* My stuttered, ridiculous excuse they wouldn't believe, like the time I had come in with a hickey on my neck and tried to pretend it was a mosquito bite I had scratched too much. Later Ardis had shamed me, *White gyal, you think they don't know what a hickey looks like?*

I watched my salesman next to the cash register, running his eyes down the handwritten page until he found "Karen's" order. He paused for a moment, blinked, then called over another salesman and whispered something to him. They both looked over at me, as I pretended to compare the quality of the flowered plastic mugs on the shelf. The second salesman went into the back, while the original one returned to the counter with a glint in his eye.

"Yes, we have the order for your friend. My colleague is going to fetch it." He smiled broadly. "My name is Ryan," he added, his small pointy teeth visible to the back rows.

"Thank you," I replied, for no reason. I hoped the dildo would come in a discreet package so the other customers wouldn't feel obliged to pray for my soul that weekend at church.

"And you are?" he asked, tilting his head coyly.

"Julie," I replied.

"O.K., Julie," he said, his tone dropping. He leaned closer to me across the glass case. "The item your friend has ordered can be a bit complicated to use. You will find instructions in the box."

"O.K., great, thank you," I said. I looked behind him for the other salesman.

"However," he continued, looking me in the eye, "if the instructions are not clear enough, I would be happy to show you how to use it."

I paused for a moment, then realized he was serious. "No, no, I don't think that will be necessary," I said quickly. The second salesman had returned now with a long box in a black, plastic bag. He handed it to Ryan and then stared at me as he skulked toward the other end of the counter. The black bag was a standard, like hundreds of anonymous black bags that everything purchased in Guyana came in, black bags that got washed out with the hose, clipped onto clotheslines to dry in the sun, then reused to store rice, hide money. The rapidly melting fish in my bag was also wrapped in a black bag. As I reached for it, Ryan put his hand on top of the package.

"Not here, of course," he said, lowering his voice. Again, he leaned forward like a conspirator, our chests tented over the bag, "but I'd be happy to come by you tonight." His eyes sparkled. I felt a rush of heat cut the air-conditioning, as the doorbells pealed, signaling another customer coming to see the goods.

"Oh, thank you, Ryan, but really," I said, "I think we can figure it out."

"All right," he said, narrowing his eyes as he pushed the black bag toward me. I slid the Guyana dollars into his hand. He reached into his shirt pocket for a card, jotted down a number on the back and wrote, "Ryan" in capital letters next to it. "In case you change your mind, you could call me at home, any time."

"O.K., thanks," I said. I could feel the other salesmen looking at me now, glancing up surreptitiously as they assisted other customers. It was time to leave.

I unzipped the front pocket of my bag and was greeted by the fish head peeking from the plastic wrapping. I stared at the fish for a moment, then calculated that the front pocket would fit, just barely, both the dildo and the fish. The bag had a back pocket, but I knew the box would get crushed bouncing against my hip as I walked the rest of the way to Ardis' house. I wanted her to see the whole thing intact before we opened it. The dildo joined the fish, and I emerged back into the afternoon swelter.

Ardis' brother Hilrod was staying with her, and because neither of us could cook, he cleaned and gutted the fish, stewing it with all the seasonings and vegetables my student had recommended. After we'd gone to bed and were nestled under the mosquito net, I recounted the story of my afternoon adventures.

"Guyanese men, I tell you!" Ardis said, laughing.

It was time for the unveiling. As we slid the box from its plastic bag, the full size of the device became evident. It was about eight inches long with pinkish-white coloring and a little battery pack on the bottom with two switches that controlled the speed. It looked cheap, and when we took it from its box it felt cheap, harder and bigger than we'd imagined. I was wishing we'd gone with the rubber Amerindian model.

"Wow, it's so big," I said as I touched it, "and so...white." I had never thought about what color it would be.

"Yeah," Ardis nodded as she reached to pick it up herself, "that thing white, white, white like a chicken." It was true: in the moonlight it almost glowed.

"I feel like he needs a name," I said.

"Ryan," she said, laughing and jabbing me in the arm with the dildo. And so it was.

I would like to say that Ryan served his purpose, releasing the grip of Ardis' pelvic muscles, and expanding our sex life dramatically. But he was so unrelenting in his hardness, and so artless in his buzzing vibrations that his presence in no way inspired us to the erotic. And his color, or lack thereof, never failed to shock. Every time we used him I was reminded of the few albinos I had seen on the streets, their skin damaged from years of sun exposure. Guyanese believed them cursed, called them "devil-whipped." Ryan, I thought, was an albino dildo.

In the end, Ryan was just too white and too foreign. Watching Ardis wield him, I sympathized with black parents who seek out dark-skinned dolls for their children. His flawless, pigment-less rubber was an affront, the white appendage glaring rudely against her lovely brown skin. He always seemed like an add-on, an afterthought, threatening to upset the balance of what we had invented for ourselves. Perhaps we were a bit afraid of him. In any case, after a few weeks, Ryan lay fallow in Ardis' drawer, nestled back in his plastic mold, his cardboard box. Over time he became just one more thing we had to hide.

Katherine Jamieson was an Urban Youth Development Volunteer in Guyana from 1996-98. A poet and creative nonfiction writer, her essays and articles have appeared in The New York Times, Newsday, Ms. Magazine, Washingtonian, The Writer's Chronicle, Bust, Narrative, Terrain, Brevity, *and* Meridian. *Her work was also anthologized in Lonely Planet's* Rite of Passage *and* Fearless Confessions: A Writer's Guide to Memoir, *and she has won fellowships and awards from Peace Corps Writers, the Virginia Center for the Creative Arts, Lantern Books, and* The Atlantic Monthly.

MARY NOWEL QUIJANO

✦
✦ ✦

Christmas in July

*The same Honduran town certainly knows how to
celebrate Christmas, whether in December or July.*

"YOU'LL COME BACK WITH MORE THAN YOUR LUGGAGE."

That's a catchy phrase on a poster that hangs on my wall
now. While in Peace Corps, I thought it was a directive.

Sometimes I almost felt like I wasn't doing enough for
my host country nationals because it seemed I was reap-
ing many more benefits from my time and effort as a Peace
Corps Volunteer than my Honduran counterparts. Peace
Corps always offered me opportunities to grow through
unique situations and events that just seemed to unfold as if
they were destined to be keepsakes that I'd be including in
my luggage back home someday. One such experience was
Christmas in July.

A month after I arrived in Honduras, I was faced with my
first Christmas away from home as a wide-eyed Peace Corps
trainee. December 1974 was the date. I can still remember
how empty and alone I felt, despite the tremendous partying
and celebrations going on around me. I can remember Mark, a
fellow trainee, and I questioning our decision to leave home as

we witnessed the strange behavior of our host country families that Christmas Eve night.

It was truly an unusual ritual. Something out of a Dr. Seuss book, but staged in a language we didn't quite understand. Our Honduran families danced around a piece of silver tree branch, flung firecrackers at each other while their feet never stopped moving to loud beating music, fueled themselves with a firewater called "*guaro*," and stopped to eat some food wrapped in a banana leaf. Christmas Day, they all slept it off, and never stepped outside to avoid the noxious smell of sulfur heavy in the air from all the fireworks the night before. Oh, where was my white Christmas, and peaceful dinner of turkey and dressing with pumpkin pie and whipped cream?

I survived—like we all did—but felt I had never had a true Christmas. Until July 2nd a half year later.

After training, I settled into a house in Santa Rosa de Copan with Burt, another Volunteer from my group and Krysia, a Volunteer from Scotland. Barbara, another PCV who worked in a nearby town, was in town for a month-long workshop. As is typical in most Peace Corps houses, there was always an assortment of visitors and travelers residing and sleeping on couches or floors for a day or a month.

We also had some volunteers from the Amigos of the Americas group visiting and staying for a short while. That summer we had all begun to bond: Volunteers, Amigos, and our Honduran friends and neighbors. At the beginning of July, a feeling of unity had begun to grow within the house, and we all enjoyed sharing our typical tasks in a home where all foods were prepared from scratch and our laundry was beaten clean on the scrub board at the outside *pila*. Dinnertime usually found us sitting together talking with each other, as there was no TV, no phone, and no email. I dare say we had begun to feel like a family, and it was great fun to sit around at dinner and share our stories.

It all began on July 1st when one of the Amigos of the Americas started humming a Christmas song as he was helping me bake some cookies for that night's dessert. There was a feeling of Christmas that this Amigo had brought out with his subconscious humming that prompted us to decide to celebrate Christmas.

Preparations were spontaneous and exciting. Some of our Honduran friends visited us that evening and picked up the spirit. One found a pine tree for the star we had made, while another drew a huge picture of Santa Claus for the neighbor kids who frequented our house. I pulled out my cards from last December to decorate the house, Barb practiced her Christmas songs on the guitar, and we wrapped goodies for Santa to deliver to the children in the evening. Then we scurried away to the market to fetch the plumpest chicken we could find, feet and all, and we prepared the house for a Christmas celebration that would continue to ring years afterwards!

Everyone who stepped in the house felt the Christmas spirit. It was complete: cards, mistletoe, Christmas flowers, candles, a pine tree with a star on top, roast (almost turkey) chicken, holiday cookies, muffins, presents, caroling, a feast. A silence came over the room as we read the Christmas Story in three languages before we ate, each person reading a line or two in their own language. The dinner was complete when Burt dressed as Santa came down the stairs yelling "Ho. Ho. Ho…!" with a sack of gifts for the *niños* as they squealed with delight.

At dinner that evening all of us, PCVs, Amigos, and Honduran friends and neighbors made an agreement. We promised to remember the group of twenty or so people, regardless of their reasons for being here, regardless of their country of origin, and say a little prayer for each one, wherever they might be every year in July.

Later, in the "after Christmas hush" that evening, I had a chance to reflect on what had transpired that day. I had found a community, a family, a group of people, from three different countries, all with different reasons for being there, and we had spent a day together as one united group filled with unique individuals all celebrating an event that transcended its traditional counterpart reserved for December. It fortified me: it filled the void I had felt seven months prior. We made history. Why, even the stores hadn't thought of Christmas in July yet! It was one of those defining moments when I knew that this experience was one that would continue to shape and define my future life, one that I would continue to reap the rewards from far into the future.

Yes, we did affect the lives of many host country nationals, but some of the true gems were those moments that were defined by how our lives had been affected. I still carry that day with me. If someone had told me that Krysia, Barb, and I would be emailing each other thirty years later on July 2nd to wish each other a Merry Christmas, I would have said, "What's email?" But you know, that's what we do. And we still remember the group with a smile and a little prayer of thanks for all the gifts that we received as we filled our bags that we'd carry back to our futures. More than our luggage? That was an understatement.

In closing, I'd like to wish my friends of long ago a Merry Christmas this next July 2nd. More than thirty years later, I still treasure the magic of that time and remember those who shared with us and made that event just one of the many things I brought back with my luggage.

Merry Christmas. *Feliz Navidad.* I remember.

Mary Nowel Quijano also contributed the previous story "4ᵗʰ of July" to this collection.

Giving

To give may be divine but it can also be very complicated.

MY MOTHER INSISTED ON VISITING ME IN GUATEMALA, WHERE I was working as a Peace Corps Volunteer, despite my exaggerated warnings about how difficult—how incommodious, how dangerous even—my life was. I knew my scare tactics would fail; had I been a soldier in a war, my mother would have parachuted into my foxhole.

In Guatemala, I was always conscious of being a privileged North American with access to material goods few people in Santa Cruz Verapaz, the small mountain town where I was living, could even imagine. So instead of flaunting my relative wealth, or even purchasing an occasional luxury item I might have found in the capital, I strove to live with what I saw as the same dignified simplicity as my friends and neighbors. I wasn't sure my mother, who hadn't had the same cultural awareness training I'd received in the Peace Corps—who had never lived anywhere outside of the eastern United States—would understand the life I'd embraced.

I'd told my mother about the eight girls and three boys who lived next door to me. I told her how they examined every object in my house and everything I wore; how they watched my every move and could tell me, weeks later, what time I had come home from working in the fields on a particular day or what hour I'd turned the light off in my courtyard on a certain night.

After announcing her intention to visit, my mother said, "I'll bring the children a present or two."

"Don't," I said.

"How can I come with nothing? I have to bring them something."

My mother was a former junior high school math teacher who had become, in her late thirties, the editor and publisher of a trade magazine for the automotive collision repair industry. As one of the few women in the business, she learned how to be tough, even confrontational. She was also a former marathon runner. Because of a bad knee, she didn't run marathons anymore, but she had a long distance runner's determination and stubbornness. If she had her heart set on bringing gifts, she would bring them, no matter my objections.

"O.K," I said. "But bring them something small. Very small."

"O.K," she agreed. "Something small."

"Please," I added.

"All right," she said.

From the balcony above the customs area at the Guatemala City airport, I spotted my mother immediately: the gray-haired woman straining to pull the two suitcases she'd brought. When I met her outside, I asked, "What have you got in there?"

"A few things," she said. "A few small things."

I lifted the suitcases. "These are heavy," I said, "for only a few small things."

"Don't forget I brought my clothes, too," she said.

"Have you started wearing bricks?" I asked.

I'd told the children next door about my mother's visit, and they were waiting for us on my front stoop when we arrived. They were curious about my mother's suitcases.

"What's inside?" asked Olga, who at age five was the youngest of the girls.

"Clothes," I said. "My mother's clothes."

"She has a lot of clothes," she said.

I asked the children to come back in half an hour. After they left, I could hear them in their courtyard, counting down the minutes.

"O.K," I told my mother, "let me assess the damage."

She'd brought Play-Doh, Lincoln Logs, and a dozen sets of scented markers. She'd brought coloring books and construction paper and candy. ("The gum is *sugarless*," she said in response to my protest.) She'd brought three recorders (the instrument) and a battery-powered keyboard. Worst of all, in my view, she'd brought eight Barbie dolls, glaring symbols of North American excess and cultural imperialism.

"Mom," I said, "you'll have to take it back."

"Take what back?"

"All of it."

"I can't take it back," she said. "I don't even remember where I bought everything. I had to go to six or seven stores to find it all."

"This," I said, gesturing toward her gifts, "will ruin me."

"You can give them whatever you want," she said. "We'll take the rest to an orphanage."

I realized the children expected some gift, and I didn't want to disappoint them. I also didn't want to disappoint my mother. "We'll give them the coloring books, the markers and the sugarless gum," I said. "The rest will have to go somewhere else."

When the countdown in the yard next door had reached zero, the children raced back to my house, banging on the door as if they intended to knock it down. My mother spread the coloring books, markers, and gum on the dining room table, and the children dove in.

They spent a long time coloring in the books and chewing the gum. When I announced it was time for them to go home, Elvira, the second oldest of the children, sidled up to me and asked if this was all my mother had brought.

"I think so," I said.

"Hmm," Elvira said, looking at me skeptically.

The children lined up to say good night to my mother, each one hugging her before they left. Receiving their hugs, my mother beamed.

Later, from my courtyard, I could hear them talking next door, repeating my mother's name like a password, the secret to unlock rooms full of treasures.

"I had a great time tonight," my mother told me before going to sleep.

"Same here," I said, which was only partly true. I was worried about how the children next door now saw me and her and the United States, even if they'd only received markers, coloring books, and gum. At the same time, I knew how pleased my mother was, and I couldn't help feeling happy about that.

My mother had always been a big gift giver. Every Christmas, the bottom of our tree would be piled high with presents. Sometimes there would be too many to fit. My father used to label this "wretched excess," and over the years he became an increasingly reluctant participant in the gift giving. For one thing, he could never compete with my mother: whatever he bought, she bought five of it, or bought the better brand or the newer model. He also believed in the "less is more" philosophy of gift giving. For him, one small gift, carefully chosen, was worth more than twenty gifts bought to fill the space beneath the tree. Their differing approaches to gift giving were undoubtedly one of the many reasons their marriage fell apart when I was fourteen.

My mother often said she didn't want my sister and me to have the deprived childhood she'd endured. When she was a teenager, her father had put her to work helping her brother with his newspaper route, sweeping stalls at a horse stable, and bussing tables. She'd even had to buy her own prom dress. Giving to us, she acknowledged, was her way of compensating for what she'd lacked growing up. But she never saw it as *over*-compensation.

As children, my sister and I loved presents—the more, the better. We used to compete to see who got the most gifts. As we grew older, however, we became worn down by our mother's generosity. She gave us so much that it was difficult, if not impossible, to reciprocate. Whatever we bought her looked minuscule and cheap by comparison. We also began to see our mother's generosity as not entirely selfless. This was especially true the year after the divorce, when, at Christmas and on our birthdays, we received more gifts than ever before. In giving to us, we suspected, she wanted something back: loyalty, emotional support and, when she introduced her boyfriend to us, acceptance.

The next morning I awoke to the sound of an electric keyboard in the dining room. My mother was entertaining the children from next door, whose knock I hadn't heard.

"We've run out of coloring books," my mother explained.

My mother didn't speak Spanish, and the children spoke no English, but the language barrier didn't seem to hinder their play. Everyone was taking a turn banging on the keyboard.

"You didn't give them the keyboard, did you?" I asked her.

"I don't think so," she said.

"Good."

"But I'm afraid they know about the Barbie dolls."

"What?" I flushed with anger. "How?"

"They looked through the bedroom window," my mother said, "and saw them beside the bed."

A few moments later, after finishing her turn on the keyboard, Elvira came up to me. "Marcos," she said, "are the dolls for us?"

I knew I would have a hard time explaining whom the dolls were for, if not for them. Besides, I saw something plaintive and yearning in Elvira's face, and I knew how quickly and easily I could turn her expression into joy. At that moment, I felt the power of the gift giver, and it was irresistible.

"Yes," I said, "they're yours."

I immediately regretted it.

Barbie dolls were not unknown in Guatemala, but were sold only in the capital and at more expensive prices than in the United States. The dolls, I knew, would mark me as someone of great wealth. In addition, buxom, long-legged, blonde Barbie dolls represented a stereotype of North American women that did nothing to encourage pride in dark-skinned children.

As my mother handed out the Barbie dolls to the girls (she gave the boys the recorders, Play-Doh and Lincoln Logs), I wondered about the consequences of her gifts. My mother would be gone in a week, but I had ten months left in my Peace Corps tour. Yet, even as I fretted over the message my mother was sending, I couldn't help but feel touched by the scene. My mother smiled as she handed the dolls to the girls, and they giggled with pleasure at receiving them. And when, one by one, they stepped up to hug her in thanks, I saw again the joy in my mother's face.

That evening, the children returned to my house with their mothers. I'd never met the three women, only seen them washing clothes. Although they'd probably been curious to see the inside of my house and to meet me, it would have been unseemly for them to have entered the home of a single man. My mother's presence now made it permissible.

Conversation between my mother and the children's mothers was slow because of the language barrier. Olivia, the oldest girl, had to translate from Pokomchí into Spanish and I from Spanish into English. Three languages played in the air above my dining room table like a trio of instruments.

The women's questions to my mother were simple and polite. "How is your trip to Guatemala so far?" "What do you think of Santa Cruz?" My mother's questions to them were equally restrained. Nevertheless, it was a real conversation.

Trying to be hospitable in the best Guatemalan fashion, I prepared lemonade for everyone. During my work in the villages around Santa Cruz, I'd often been given such drinks by my hosts. Worried about drinking impure water, I frequently looked for an opportunity to pour them into bushes. There was no danger of my lemonade containing impure water, as the mothers knew, but the taste was another story: I noticed Olivia slipping under my dining room table to consume both her mother's and her aunts' drinks in quick, sacrificial gulps. Not all gifts went over as well as my mother's.

I was awakened the following morning by loud banging on my front door. Outside, a dozen neighborhood children were standing in the sunlight, looking hopeful.

"We heard your mother came," one said.

"We heard she had presents," said another.

By this time, my mother was standing behind me, rubbing the sleep from her eyes. "What did they say?" she asked.

I told her.

"Oh, God," she said. "I think I've run out of presents."

When I gave her an angry look, she said, "We'll have to buy more."

"We can't buy more," I said. "If we buy presents for these kids, more kids will come. Don't you see?"

I turned to the children. "Sorry," I said, "there are no more presents."

"Why did your mother give presents to them?" a boy asked, pointing next door. His question bore no anger or resentment, only a sad curiosity.

"Because," I said, "they're my neighbors."

And the boy asked, "Aren't we also your neighbors?"

At the airport, as my mother was about to board her plane back to the States, she said, "I'm sorry about the presents. Did I make it hard on you?"

"No," I said, lying to protect her. "It's no problem."

We had spent a pleasant week together. After a few days in Santa Cruz, we'd traveled to Antigua, where we met up with Grace, a fellow Volunteer, and walked around the ruins of sixteenth-century churches. We'd stayed up late and my mother entertained—or bored—Grace with stories from my childhood. Although a part of me still resented what my mother had done, another part of me was glad she'd come. This, I supposed, would always be my paradox: even as I felt embarrassed by my mother—or overwhelmed by her, or misunderstood by her—I wanted her with me.

When I returned to Santa Cruz, the children from next door were waiting for me on my front stoop. "Is your mother gone?" Olga asked, and when I nodded, they all sighed with disappointment.

"When," Elvira asked, "is she coming back?"

"I don't know," I said.

"Next week?" Olga asked hopefully.

"No."

"In two weeks?" she tried again.

"No."

"Three?"

I laughed. "Probably not even in three."

In the evening, we played Red Light, Green Light in the street. When it was nearly dark, I said I had to go home.

"One more game!" the children cried, but I told them I was tired. "Besides," I said, "you can play with the toys my mother gave you."

"Oh, yes," Olivia said, "except our mothers sold four of the dolls."

A woman from one of the town's wealthiest families, Olivia explained, had heard about the Barbie dolls and had come to each mother with a purse full of quetzales.

"Why didn't they sell her all the dolls?" I asked.

"Olga pulled the heads off two," Olivia said, sighing, "and Elvira dropped one in the outhouse."

Olivia's mother had put the last Barbie doll in a glass case next to a statue of the Virgin Mary. "It is something only to look at," Olivia said, "not to touch."

A week after my mother left, I tried to make up for her inappropriate generosity by giving the eight girls what I considered to be culturally suitable gifts: new *cortes*. I didn't know if the girls needed new *cortes*; the ones they had, while not new, looked fine, and *cortes*, which are made of durable fabric, tend to last for years. But determined to right a wrong—the thought of a Barbie doll sitting like an icon in their house was especially disturbing—I piled them onto a bus to Cobán and escorted them into a store.

The girls looked hesitant and ill at ease, but I pressed on, encouraging them to select whatever they liked. The salesman, a small, mustachioed man, dumped *corte* material on a table and said to each of them in turn, "You like this one, don't you?" Only Olivia refused to be swayed by the salesman, considering a few patterns before deciding on one; the rest chose the first material he showed them, even though I'd tried to prod them to be more choosy.

When I'd imagined this moment, I'd pictured the girls being satisfied and proud, grateful that I'd shown respect for their culture and traditions. But when we left the store, they seemed only relieved.

Six months after her first visit, my mother returned to Guatemala. This time, she brought no gifts. I'd wanted it this way. When I met her at the airport, I congratulated her on her restraint. "I'm just following your orders," she said. Looking at me critically, she added, "You know, I only wanted to make them happy."

"I know."

I pretended to be understanding, but secretly I gloated. I had blunted my mother's excess. I had gotten her to act the way I wanted.

When we arrived at my house, however, we found the children waiting for us. I began to worry that once they saw that my mother had come with nothing, they would go home disappointed. I was afraid my mother would feel rejected. Suddenly, I wanted her to have gifts—a suitcase full of them. I didn't want her to feel unloved.

As I lifted my mother's single suitcase into my house, the children followed us. "What's inside?" Olga asked, and when I said, "Clothes," she didn't challenge me with a doubtful smile or an incredulous look.

I wished my mother's clothes would turn into teddy bears.

I looked to see if I my mother's face showed any concern or anxiety. She seemed content, although I couldn't be sure: she was good at disguising her feelings. She sat at my dining-room table, and the children gathered around, gazing at her, waiting. There was a long silence, and I wondered when, bored and discouraged, the children would file out the door. I wondered what words I would use to console my mother. Sitting at my table, she looked old and vulnerable. I realized how selfish I'd been to deny her the chance to give.

At last, breaking the silence, my mother said to me, "Ask them what they're studying in school."

I asked, and Olga replied, "I'm learning to write the alphabet."

My mother turned to me and said, "I remember teaching you to write the alphabet. I used a baking pan and cornmeal. Do you remember?"

"No," I said, "but I remember you telling me about it."

"Do you have a pan and cornmeal?"

I had a pan, but no cornmeal. My mother said flour would do. She poured a covering of flour into the pan and asked Olga to come sit with her. Olga climbed into her lap.

"We're going to learn how to write letters," my mother said, and she placed her hand over Olga's. Then, gently, my mother guided Olga's finger to form the letter O.

Seeing her creation, Olga laughed with pleasure. "Look!" she said to the others. "Look!"

I let out a breath—of relief, of pleasure—as the children formed a line. Giggling with excitement, they waited to be the next to sit in my mother's lap and trace the alphabet with her in a flour-coated pan.

Mark Brazaitis is the author of three books of fiction, including The River of Lost Voices: Stories from Guatemala, *winner of the 1998 Iowa Short Fiction Award, and a book of poems,* The Other Language, *winner of the 2008 ABZ Poetry Prize. A Peace Corps Volunteer in Guatemala from 1990-93, he is an associate professor of English and the director of the Creative Writing Program at West Virginia University.*

PART FOUR

CLOSE ENCOUNTERS

ELLEN URBANI

Our Samuel

The author discovers that trickery, misdirection and
obfuscation cut across cultures and often save lives.

THE POSTMAN SUFFERED THE UNCERTAINTY MANY LONG MONTHS until finally he broke.

"Miss Elena," he said, standing beside his bicycle, fingering the nailed-on wooden seat in anxious anticipation of my maybe-really-bad-news response, "what has happened to our Samuel?"

I had no idea to whom he referred, but this is not unusual. "Our Samuel?" I repeated, a question, as in, "You and I, who see each other so rarely, only when you bring me my opened and peered through letters, we have a mutual Samuel, whomever this Samuel is?"

"Yes," he said, and leaned against the stone-wall casing of my door, which might hold him up when the horror of the truth swept out of my mouth and erupted all over him. He wore a woolen tam, which he took off, and put the edge in his mouth and bit it like a man preparing to be hurt grievously without the blessing of anesthesia. His old wrinkled face wrinkled worse, for clearly the fate of Samuel tormented him. "Frst hgt schtik," he groaned, but I had to coax him—

"Come now, take the hat out of your mouth, I can't understand these things you are saying,"—before he pulled the soiled fabric from his lips and said emphatically, "First Samuel got sick, then he got sicker, then he went to the hospital…"

But still I did not follow him or understand anything of which he spoke. I geared up to give him the Scarlet O'Hara stare, the right brow furrowed, the left arched, the look I practiced for months in the bathroom mirror after seeing *Gone With the Wind* for the first time in the sixth grade, but ultimately the postman said, "…then Samuel had surgery, and then the telegrams stopped!"

Oh, yes. I finally caught on.

Samuel is code.

Poor old man, fretting all this time. I didn't get it either at first, but at least I only suffered a short time before I figured out the Samuel gig, the pall of his sickness hanging on me just a few days; whereas it had been with the postman for months and looked to have spread. Too much vicarious agony can torture a soul and wreck the complexion.

Samuel is a ruse.

The Samuel telegrams all arrived within two weeks of each other, toward the end of May or the beginning of June, and because the postman had opened and read them all before resealing them with unsticky tape and delivering them to me, he remembered the contents well. First the note that Samuel was sick, and me wracking my brain wondering, "Do I know a Samuel?" and rifling mentally through the endless retinue of extended friends and family, and the friends and family of my extended friends and family, finding no Samuel among them. Then I felt worse, because clearly this Samuel wanted me to be aware of his illness, and yet I could not even think whom he might be. The anxiety built through the week with each new post, for Samuel deteriorated quickly, got rushed to the hospital, underwent emergency surgery, hung tenuously to life in intensive care.

Samuel is not a real person.

This maybe should have occurred to me at the beginning, but I suffered too much with the mystery of his identity to notice—until I lined up the telegrams all together in a row on the kitchen table to divine their purpose—that each was sent by a different person, people whose names, like Samuel's, I did not recognize. Important-sounding people, with government-issue names (sometimes it takes surprises like this to remind me that I work for the government, that I am not my own independent entity in Zataquepeque). I got out my embassy notebook and there, after some searching, found all the names in the section on "Internal Threat," meaning attack from within, which coups count as. We had three coups at the beginning of the summer, three in two weeks, and the lady's name on the first telegram—the message itself being absolutely irrelevant—meant evacuate the capital (which I had done, all on my own, without needing to be directed by a surreptitious signature on a coded document). The subsequent signatures meant not to leave my site, to check in by telegraph or telephone to verify my safety, to prepare to flee under cover of night, and finally to ignore all previous telegrams for everything turned out fine and reverted to normal.

It had all ended before I figured out what any of it meant.

I burned the telegrams in the trash the next day, stenographic testaments to a non-event that had not touched my life in any lingering way. The coups passed; their only measurable impact came these months later in the form of this profound and lingering dread, which the invented Samuel had inspired in the postman.

"Samuel is fine," I said at length, and because it seemed both accurate and honest within the confines of this make-believe situation, where the truth got danced around as if it barely existed, I added, "Samuel recovered fully, with no visible scars, and in fact hardly remembers anything about what happened."

The postman let loose with a long breath of air, as if he'd been holding it these many months, waiting to exhale.

"Oh, thank goodness," he groaned, exhausted with relief. "Walk with me, we must let people know—we have all been so worried!"

He held my hand in one of his, pushed his bike with the other. We first strolled past the tavern where he spent his weekends, then to the *comedor* where he took his breakfast. We went to all the places where for many months the post-man had tormented the assembled townsfolk's ragged nerves with unceasing, climaxing worry for the health of my imaginary friend. At each door we now paused; the postman raised our clasped fists high in a victory salute, and shouted through the open doorways, "Elena's friend Samuel is recovered!" to which, to a man, the people gathered inside would lift a hand either to heaven or to their hearts and with a collective sigh of pure joy and the sign of the cross, shout to me their encouragement and glee:

"What a blessed relief!!"

"Hurray for Samuel; praised be his doctors!"

"Ay, *dios bendiga*, it is a miracle from God!"

"Long live our friend and *compadre*, the estimable Samuel!"

As the day wore on, in the Latin way, their relief became more palpable, their exuberance more boundless, their gestures more effusive and their emotions more taxed. By that evening, grown men cried. Chests got pounded and bottles got raised and dogs howled and children quieted before the profound spell of collective rejoicing. Long into the night, and for many nights thereafter, from the off-canter barroom tables and the dirty ditches, from the unlit street corners and from the faces pressed, regrettably, against the opposite side of my bedroom wall, a lone or accompanied voice would arise in toast: "To Samuel!"

Samuel never went away, as imaginary friends are supposed to do with the passage of time. Samuel stayed with me and consumed the rest. They asked about him always, and guarded his tenuous return to health as if his recovery signified a chance for us all. Do not be fooled into thinking the villagers had no more realistic things on which to hang their worries. Calamity surrounded us: Breast milk dried up and crops withered. It did not rain enough, or it rained so much that houses and bloated beings floated past. Men went to work in the morning and never returned. Lookouts hid in the hills and watched for guerrillas, armies, police, shouting their warnings to an unprepared town. Governments changed hands three times in two weeks. Satraps ruled. Women got violated. Children got taken.

I heard stories of the sweeps. With the civil war over, all should have changed, the massacres should have stopped and the kidnappings ended. Guatemala wanted its aid back from the rest of the world, and its media blitz made everyone else (who did not live there) believe in reform and in newly enacted social justice. They plastered the world and their own people, too, with propaganda. I have one of the flyers, pressed on me by a camouflaged man with an Uzi, and it reads verbatim, in faltering English:

Do you know that in Guatemala there are places where you are discover new and unforgettable experiences, miscelanous corner of natural atractives, santuary of the mayan breed, where popullation and army work for the defence of the peace. Our compromise, to guarantee the peace and to protectits confort. Guatemala's Army...Basic recommendations follow when you are visiting Guatemala.

1. Have an English-Spanish dictionary.
2. Obtain a tourist guide booklet of the country (it can be adquired the Guatemala's institute of tourism—INGUAT).
3. Carry the necessary items for the type of region to visit (according to weather).
4. In case of emergency approach the detachment of army commands. They will be willing to serve you.
5. In case you need any monetary transaction address to Guatemala's bank, 7th Avenue 22-01 Zone 1 or to banks system.
6. In case of robbery, accident or if you need transportation information approach the national police that will be located in different places of the country.
7. In case of accident communicate to the fire department, phone 122.
8. If you wish to communicate to the United States dial 190 direct USA.
9. For information services communicate to phone 124.

Each phone call is free of change.

Everything here is free of change. We know better than to expect otherwise, which is why what happened scared but did not surprise me.

"Elena!" Lucinda screamed, and though I could not see her yet, for I toiled out back, I recognized her voice even at this unaccustomed pitch. She beat upon my door.

"They are coming!" she yelled and lunged at me as I stepped into the street. I must have looked as if I would question her, but time ran short so she anticipated me: "The army," she said. "They are coming to recruit boys."

They are coming, she meant, in their trucks to steal away the sons ages twelve and up, whom mothers might never again behold. People darted frantically around us, but Lucinda held my gaze and stared at me deeply. It is an historic look that has repeated itself too often, passed from woman to woman, from one who must plead to one who has privilege; it is the look of a mother begging, expecting, that her fellow female will behave as one.

"Take my children," Lucinda pleaded, pressing her two boys into my arms. She turned then and fled without pause for she trusted me and knew my heart. She had nothing and therefore no place to hide her children. I would hide them for her.

The army men swept through quickly, one into each home, taking the boys. I stepped back as the stout man in the shiny boots clicked across my stone floor. He went right to the altar room, the room I kept padlocked due to the spooky sensation the relics and artifacts and statues within inspired in me. "That room is hexed," I said. "You should not enter."

"Open this door," he said, and though I had the key hidden in my hand—the men came upon us so quickly, I had not had time to replace it yet—I acted as if it still hung in the kitchen basket, as if it had been so long since I used it that I had forgotten the key's precise place.

I pretended to fumble around, looking first in one basket and then the other; when he cleared his throat impatiently I said, pertly, "Here is the key," and extended it to him, not wanting to make the situation worse.

"Open this door," he repeated, but I responded:

"Oh no! I will not open that door, I will not go near that room!" I made myself animated—"Act!" I willed myself. "Act well!"—and let my very real fear creep into my voice. "I have been told that the last person to enter that room choked to death on a chicken bone that very night," I lied, "and before that the mistress, having looked through the open doorway, died in childbirth with her baby stillborn the very next day. The shamans now say that anyone who opens that door will look upon the very face of death, and death itself will haunt him and come for him within that very same week."

His look says he does not believe in shamans, but I suspect this is a false front; he must be a superstitious man. Superstition is the religion every Guatemalan is born to. I press on in my scary voice.

"So open the door yourself," I say, "for you are far braver than I!" Backing up against the wall, covering my eyes with my hands, I say: "I cannot even look, but tell me, sir, if it is true, if you see death's face when you open the door."

Even now, I feel a sense of community, and horror, at how close we came to getting caught.

He turned the key, pushed on the door, and though I expected the crash, it terrified me just the same. I jumped; the soldier jumped. I felt all the blood in my body pound at once on the walls of my heart so hard it caused me actual pain, but the boys did not scream, bless them, and the soldier ran so fast from my house he didn't even bother to re-lock the door (which to me would be a dumb thing, you know, not even trying to lock death back in, leaving it free to tear after you).

I didn't wait too long, but only long enough, before going inside the altar room, winding through the statues to the back, helping the boys down from their perch on a gilded edifice. I had lifted them up there, had said, "Trust me, and be quiet, I will keep you safe." On my way back out I had grabbed the life-sized plaster Lucifer statue that had at one time likely been part of some religious depiction of the great heated battle for a tormented soul. The archrival, Michael, is in the room too. But it is Lucifer I tugged with all my might, propping him finally beside the door. After exiting I wedged my arm back in and dragged the very edge of the statue into the path of the opening door, so that when pushed against this devil might totter, off balance, and topple (fly, if you will, with his frightening face) toward any person daring to enter. And finally, just as I heard the voice from beyond and the hard rapping that said, "Open up! This house is to be searched," I winked at the boys, a playful, whimsical gesture, so that they might think we were engaged in a game and not a war.

Lucinda's boys hid in my house once more, and with them many other boys, too. I could have hidden a whole village worth of teenagers in my altar room from then on, for the unsettling story—which by now must have become old army lore!—kept all subsequent marauders from setting so much as a foot over my threshold. Clearly the mothers knew, that is why they sent their boys to me, but they never spoke to me of these incidents. No lament, no thank you, no acknowledgement of a kind that anyone else might have recognized, for as I said, this is a place where the truth is danced around, where enough is bad that the bad stuff does not get discussed.

Instead, the mothers, and the fathers, too, they ask me about Samuel; more so, I noticed, after these misadventures. Samuel is still code, and we all learned to readily decipher his missives.

"I have been thinking about your friend Samuel," someone would say as she passed in the street, and I knew this to mean, "You are in my thoughts and in my prayers, Elena."

"Give my regards to Samuel," meant, "Thank you, Elena, for this thing you have done for my family, this thing of which I am too frightened to speak."

And, "How is Samuel doing?" meant, "What do you think? Are we safe? Will all turn out well?"

I had no choice. Hope required I create a good, safe life for Samuel, for us all.

So it is that not only did Samuel recover, he fell in love and married. Moved to Miami. Everyone begged then for a photo, and at first I did not know what to do, but eventually I passed around a picture from a distant cousin's wedding that I had recently received in the mail. The postman brought it to me. It is a happy picture.

Who is to say the beaming bridegroom is not our Samuel? Who is to say what is truly real? I say, thank God for the subterfuge of our Samuel. He gave to us a good and sheltered subject on which to rest our troubled thoughts.

Ellen Urbani is a Yankee by birth who ventured west to Oregon via Alabama (college) and then served in the Peace Corps in Guatemala from 1991-93. Judging by her accent (a Southern drawl over a Spanish trill with a Phili edge) she admits she doesn't fit in any-where. Having grown up in a family of Irish/Italian immigrants who all speak loudly, at once, never on coordinating subjects, she subsequently talks fast and has to work hard not to interrupt. But Ellen can also whip up a mean tomato sauce from scratch and tell a damn good story. "Our Samuel" is excerpted from her first book, When I Was Elena, *a memoir about the years she lived in post-civil war Guatemala. It was published in March 2006 as a Book Sense Notable selection. For more info, check out www.ellenurbani.com. At present she is working on a novel set in the South in the wake of Hurricane Katrina.*

✳

What They Don't Teach You...

This encounter with breast milk on a bus in Bolivia
demonstrates that there are some things that even
Peace Corps training can't prepare you for.

WE WERE GROOMED, PSYCHED, AND FIRED UP "TO GET THIS SHIP on the high sea, sailor" with just a tinge of underlying apprehension. We had been equipped with survival Spanish language skills, some knowledge of the history and culture of our assigned country, and an entire international vaccination card with stamps for shots against all sorts of exotic sounding ailments, like yellow fever, cholera, and the plague.

We had been driven around *al fresco* in the back of trucks, farmed out to Mormon families for Sunday night dinner, and spent a whole Saturday on an Indian reservation to hone our cross-cultural communication skills. We had even slaughtered chickens with our bare hands because we might just have to do so someday. Our ragtag bunch of recent college graduates from across the country was about as ready for engagement as any contingent of fresh troops bound for the front lines.

So at midnight on that long-awaited and fateful date, we all piled onto the plane in Miami bound for La Paz with scheduled stopovers in Puerto Rico and Peru. Our adventure had

227

really begun. We had stepped across the threshold. Our young and tender lives would never be the same again.

Most of us still harbored a slight hangover from one too many celebratory "last drinks in the good old US of A" and toasts to our upcoming adventure while waiting for the flight in the airport bar. Like blood brothers or Marines before landing on the beachhead, three of us made an oath that we would return to that very table in that dimly lit bar in two years for one final round of drinks together before returning to civilian life. Of course, life can never be that orchestrated. I re-entered the U.S. by land through Nogales, Arizona, not the scrubbed clean Miami Airport, and Bill and Steve marched to their own drummers, but at the time, the bravado of that gesture filled us with courage and soothed our growing anxieties.

Two years—although less than 10 percent of our lives to that point in time—carried all the weight and mystery of a century, a vast cavern of time and space to be filled, people yet to be met, personal challenges beyond our imagination, and places whose names can't be pronounced properly in English. Looking down the barrel of two years overseas was daunting.

You could have heard a pin drop when the plane finally descended into Bolivian airspace with vast dust-colored panoramas of seemingly empty, semi-desert *altiplano* stretching from horizon to horizon. Our faces were pasted to the windows, and we were all absorbed in our own first impressions of what had previously only been photographs and stories. Then, as the plane's tires screeched and spun on the tarmac and we coasted slowly to a stop, the tension was finally broken by someone near the back of plane saying: "Gawd, it's amazing what Walt Disney can do."

From that moment onward, my experience and memories became less group-oriented and more personal. When the shells start falling, it's every man for himself. I do remember being short of breath with a pounding head because of the 11,000-foot altitude, especially when vaulting up stairs in youthful exuberance, but in my case the adjustment was compounded in short order by falling prey to the mother of all head colds.

It was just my luck to have been vaccinated against the Black Death only to be laid low by a common, garden-variety virus. As a result, my first impression of the country was an abstract blur of meetings, orientations, feverish sleepless nights, and general malaise. But time heals all wounds, and with the regenerative power of youth and antibiotics, I recovered and gradually moved deeper upcountry.

Soon I was in my assigned site, and working as hard as I could to adapt and live up to the self-imposed standards of a "good" Peace Corps Volunteer that I had fabricated from all the media hype and war stories recited in boot camp. I studied Spanish grammar late into the night by candlelight. I stuffed myself into crowded buses and played *cacho* with dice and a leather cup while swigging beer, like I had done those things all my life. I smiled at everyone, desperate to be accepted as an easy-going, amiable "gringo," the exception to the "ugly American" standard. I almost hurt myself I smiled so much.

But when I tossed my backpack up into the back of a flat-bed truck that was already well populated by Quechua-speaking *campesinos*, sitting around on mounds of sacks and heaps of boxes, I had an experience for which I was not adequately prepared, in spite of all the good intentions of the well-meaning and dedicated Peace Corps trainers.

I had been in the back of many trucks with strangers, so I was accustomed to the blank stares of disbelief at my sudden appearance. Since I only knew a few greetings in Quechua and figured that my broken Spanish was not going to get me very far with this crowd, I just nodded and smiled broadly into all the dark shining faces.

Eventually I snuggled amongst the other passengers into my own personal niche that was just big enough for my backpack and puny gringo ass. Off we went, lurching and swaying from side to side, bouncing off each other, holding onto moving objects for balance and dear life. Everyone more or less just settled in for a good long shake up. In times like that, I learned to go into a rather dazed state of suspended animation. Being numb and mindless helped the time pass and softened the jolts and harsh bumps that punctuate a backroads journey anywhere in the third world.

As I settled in, I sized up my companions, noticing several complete families. Back-country kids, although not aggressive, are always the last ones to stop staring. In fact, some never stop, because mine were probably the first blue eyes they had ever looked into and seldom do such entertaining beings suddenly appear in the midst of their daily routines. Like all PCVs, at first I was very self-conscious, but you get used to it after awhile. The constant sharp jolts and pounding of the truck over the rutted roads were a good distraction, too, for both me and the kids. Occasionally one would be so engrossed in staring at me that he would topple over in a heap of embarrassment and parental barks when the truck lurched violently, only to scramble back atop the burlap sack from which he had so unceremoniously fallen to commence staring sheepishly again at me.

The men slowly removed coca leaves and lime from colorful pouches on their belts and inserted the mixture into their mouths to deaden the trip's unpleasant sensations without mind control. Their slow steady chewing reminded me of llamas ruminating peacefully, but I tried not to stare, especially when a young *chola* removed a breast from her *aguayo* and began nursing her baby right next to my face. Instead, I diverted my eyes and searched for some misplaced item in my backpack on the truck bed, as we all rocked and reeled, occasionally groaning in unison at some particularly painful and pronounced jolt.

Then it happened, a deep rut, a sharp swerve by the driver, and the large black nipple of that round plump breast suddenly popped out of the mouth of the infant and sent a stream of warm mother's milk across my face from just above my right ear, clear across both lenses of my eyeglasses, and down my left cheek in a jaunty angle. My world turned a creamy white.

I suppose at some point in my early life I had had breast milk splashed on my face, but it had been during my pre-history and certainly didn't occur when I was doing my best to be invisible or elevate my mental consciousness to another and much different realm of existence than my immediate surroundings. Anyway, its warmth and sticky smell seemed familiar at some distant level of recollection, which caused me to sit in a stupor for a few seconds to ponder that sensation before reacting.

My audience was amused, to say the least. A little ripple of surprised laughter went through the crowd like "the wave" going around a baseball stadium. This was the stuff of great comical performances. Not only later that evening could they tell their friends and family that they shared the journey with an alien, who didn't speak their language, dressed oddly, and smiled constantly, but they also learned that these pale sickly creatures blush bright red when hosed with a little body fluid, which is probably incomprehensible to someone whose skin does not turn red.

Actually, it wasn't little. Although it gets larger each time I tell the story, from what I could tell from my discreet glances, it was truly a very full and amazingly firm breast, and after weeks of dining in the back of bouncing flat bed trucks that kid had the sucking power of an octopus. In fact, he was in the middle of a long draw that would have made a bong master proud when that big slippery thing just gained a life of its own.

It all happened so fast that he didn't even have time to protest, much less hold on. All was right with the world. Then suddenly he was sucking air. It was in. It was out. The gringo got doused. It was back in. The gringo turned red. His mom smiled. He giggled as the truck continued to rock and sway.

Naturally, my first reaction was to restore my vision. After cleaning my glasses on my shirt and returning them to the bridge of my nose, I mopped up the rivulets of warm sustenance on my cheek, shirt, backpack, and elsewhere in my immediate surroundings with my shirtsleeve, which was growing increasingly damp and smelly.

Then I slowly glanced up into a sea of expectant faces, frozen in wonder. Would the gringo be angry and bellow curses in some foreign tongue? Would he strike out at the offender or demand compensation for the indignity? Would he die right there and then of the redness disease?

All eyes were on me as I frantically searched my brain for the appropriate cross-cultural response from my Peace Corps training. Surely "how to recover from major embarrassments" had been covered in some lecture or movie. Hours of lectures and handouts flashed before my eyes, but there was nothing, zilch, nada that I could recite that would turn off the stares and comfort me in my time of need. The spotlight shone brightly. I was on center stage.

Seconds ticked by. No words of comfort or apology were forthcoming from the dark brown faces. Nobody reached out a hand to help me tidy up. There were no apparent signals or body language suggestions of what the appropriate cultural response should be on my part, so I reacted like every blue-blooded Yankee would under those circumstances. I cleaned myself up, shrugged my "*asi es la vida*" shrug, and grinned ever wider, wondering silently if the bush telegraph would reach all the way to my village and flavor my identity to legendary proportions in whispers and stifled laughter ever after. For the remainder of that bone-jarring, smelly trip, I also wondered if I had the *cojones* at that particular juncture of my life to include a description of the incident in my next letter home to Mom.

I didn't. What was I going to say: "Hey Mom, the next time breastfeeding comes up in conversation at the dinner table, here's a story for you." Truth be told, my letters home could never fully convey in any meaningful way the spectrum of sights, sounds, tastes, jolts, loneliness, elation, surprise, frustration, longing, foreboding, and the sheer adrenalin rush of immersion in a totally alien environment. You just had to be there. People with different life experiences could never understand. Letters are better left for topics like passing head colds, to which the recipient can relate.

After many launderings, I finally did manage to get that lingering odor out of my shirtsleeve, but I was not able to wash out the memory so easily. That's probably what returning Peace Corps Volunteers and Marine Corps veterans have in common. Earthy, down and dirty war stories, tucked away in memory, hoping that someday an opportunity will come along when conditions and blood alcohol levels are just right to free them from their cage and let them finally take wing.

But I can tell you one thing. I've never been able to look at a *Playboy* centerfold in the same way again; so in hindsight, it's probably a very good thing that they don't mention stories like mine during Peace Corps training, at least to the guys. After all, when you're twenty-two years old, idealism has its limits.

Bob Hudgens was a Peace Corps Volunteer in Bolivia from 1967-70. When he graduated from the University of California at Davis in 1967, he applied to graduate school, to Officer Candidate School at Travis Air Force Base (the Vietnam War was raging) and to the Peace Corps. The Peace Corps road, though less traveled, made all the difference. After two graduate degrees, one marriage, and a total of twenty years overseas on four continents, he is presently the Director of International Programs at California State University, Fresno; from California to California in a rather circuitous fashion, bringing the world back home and passing the baton.

MARK BRAZAITIS

First Words

We have met the neighbors and they are us.

1.

At seven Edna is already half a woman,
her wrists aching from hours sorting cardamom
beans.
Her cousins are going to school this year,
and they return in the afternoon
with snippets of Spanish
to mix with their Pokomchí.
Edna follows them to my house,
where they drop notebooks on my table
to show me the vowels they've scratched in
pencil
a dozen times below the *maestra's* neat example.
Edna displays her own recent learning,
the first words of Spanish I've heard her speak:
"Mi papá está bolo."

The phrase follows me
as I walk the streets of Santa Cruz

passing drunks in doorways, mouths crowded
with flies.
I have never spoken with Edna's father,
only seen him framed in the front window of the
house next door,
staring out with small, pitiless eyes.

2.

My father ate half gallons of ice cream at one
sitting,
and kept a scoop in the silverware drawer.
One afternoon, when I'd done something wrong
(I was four, and don't remember what),
he curled his fingers around the yellow handle
and slapped the head across my back.
My mother found me in the stairwell
and wiped my tears with the ends
of her violet dress.
Later he told her: "I don't know what I'm doing."
He built an office in the attic,
where he could watch my sister and me
play in the fenced-in yard.

3.

Before long, Edna has a new brother.
When he is able to walk,
Hugo stands outside his front door,
watching what passes
with the mute serenity of a Buddha.
Whenever I see him, I call "Hugo!"
and he looks up with his round face
and startling, large eyes.

4.

There is a story my mother told me
when she was in a forgiving mood
and wanted to explain my father
so I might understand.
When my father was eight,
his father invited him and a friend to a baseball
game.
Weeks of anticipation,
imitations of home run swings,
boasts about who would catch a foul ball.
When the day arrived,
my father waited past dark,
waited until the bottom half of the fifth inning,
before his father came home,
fell onto the couch
and pissed his pants.

5.

I walk by their house, shout: "Hugo!"
Barefoot, he wears overalls too large,
the straps curling from his body like
parentheses.
A Sphinx, he stands silent guard.

At night, I hear his father's shouts,
loud enough to silence the street dogs.
I listen for crying.
I hear only the angry wind.

6.

I have been in Guatemala for two years,
and one morning in a corn field
I decide I've reinvented myself,
cleaned my soul with rays of a new sun,

the sweat and passion of new work,
rhythms of a new language.
But the next time I see this tiny Buddha, this
Sphinx,
he points a small, plump finger at my heart:
"Hugo!" he says. "Hugo!"

Mark Brazaitis also contributed "Giving" to this volume.

REBECCA MARTIN

✦

The Birth

In one small village, a girl is born, a daughter educated,
and some women stand up for what is right.

PART I

"Meliti, voy a visitar una meri que está dando la luz. Brün. (Meliti,
I'm going to visit a woman who's giving birth. Let's go)," said
Sra. Carmen, my favorite person and first adult friend in the
village. She never asks me if I want to do anything, just informs
me what she's doing and then waits for me to follow.

We made our way down the slick clay mountainside. I
try to keep my steps slower so that she can keep up with me.
They laugh at how I always seem to be running places, while
they walk slowly from one point to another. As we came to
a clearing, I saw the birthing woman's house. It was on stilts
and made of wood planks. A small square of a house filled
with bamboo beds and old *naguas* for bedding. The two small
windows let in little air and light. The whole house was thick
with dust and sweat.

Through the planks on the floor, I could see the dirt of the
ground beneath where another baby sat, quietly swatting bugs

and chickens. I stood, wondering how this woman could lie on this hard wood floor with a few palm fronds under her and an old *nagwa* for her head. Occasionally a tear would come to her eye, but she never cried out. Just clenched and unclenched her hands. Hands made rough from a life of work, brown and wrinkled, barely the sign of a fingernail. Clench, unclench.

I watched the woman giving birth. I watched the other women watching the one on the floor, talking quietly as she clenched and unclenched. A lost chicken woke up and ran across her swollen, spasmodic belly. She lifted a thin hand to shoo the chicken and wipe a hair from off her streaked forehead. And for a brief moment I could see the origins of all mankind—pouring out onto a hard, crude floor, from a woman with her eyes squeezed shut, animals all around her swollen, silent body

The women around her continued to talk about small, daily things as I watched the woman and her belly. Thinking like a person from *afuera*, I did my best to time contractions by the emotion on her face. The others thought I was crazy watching the woman and my watch with equal intensity, a growing look of panic on my face. After a day of watching and waiting, I walked slowly back to my house. Through a village full of *chakaras* filled with crying babies and many more running around their houses. With one more entering the world that night. Clench, unclench.

And so I sit in my little cement room, eating my first meal today, jellybeans from an Easter care-package. More than a month has passed since Easter came and went unnoticed. I say out loud to no one, "I should probably cook something." No one answers. So I don't.

I sit and wait in the quiet, listening to the voices of my neighbors, talking, laughing, yelling. And I wait for a cry. The *gente* come and tell me the woman finally gave birth to *familia mia*. A little girl. A baby girl whose birth makes five. But only four are living they tell me. And so I sit and wonder what her life will be. Will she grow up strong and healthy with a mind that thinks outside this tiny mountain village? Will she have her first baby at fourteen and be married at sixteen? Will another Peace Corps Volunteer find her here many years from now on the floor birthing a fifth girl of her own? Ancient by the time she reaches the age I am now. I wonder if she has a choice and if she will know there was a choice.

Part II

As I come out of the clearing, the grandma bursts into a big toothless grin, so happy to have me stop by their house. She stops washing and gives me a big hug. I treasure her brief moment of emotion and affection and hug her back. The baby is now six months old. Her dark hair a faded yellow. The color of the vitamin-deprived. Her big belly sticks out over her skinny little legs as she just sits there. Dried yellow pus fills the corner of her eyes. She looks at me with watery big dark eyes.

I look away.

We talk about her other granddaughter, the sixth grader. She'll be graduating soon, I say. I think I can get her a *beca*, a scholarship, to go to seventh grade in the large town at the bottom of the mountain. Katarine, a girl with big hands and shy eyes, gets good grades and tells me she wants to be a teacher someday. Her eyes spark as she talks about it. I tell her I hope she can be, how quick she is, how great it would be to have Ngöbe teachers in Ngöbe schools, how she can do good work, study and *salir adelante*.

I come back later to tell her she's won the scholarship. I measure her feet and we go shopping for a uniform, *cuadernos*, pencils, socks. She's so happy and proud. Her mom thanks me for giving her daughter this opportunity. She wishes her older daughter had finished school. Instead she is sitting on a rock with her baby boy and watching her green bananas boil. Sweat rolling down her face matching the snot running down her son's.

Sra. Carmen comes to get me. Katarine has been raped they say. Such calmness in their voices. "Will she still be able to go to school?" they ask me. I say, "of course" and ask if the girl is O.K. Clench, unclench. They tell me she's at her aunt's, and I can go talk to her if I want.

So now I sit in a stifling little room looking at this girl, hot tears and vomit rising in the back of my throat. I ask her if she's gotten her period yet. So calm. I ask if she still wants go to school or go back home. She says she still wants to study. I tell her how great that is and that I will help her. She says she's doing well. She tells me "It was harder at first, but now I know better what I have to do and I'm going to do even better next quarter." Such a grown-up, abstract thought, rare for her. And I remember my freshman year of college and thinking the same thing.

I go back to tell her mother that I talked with Katarine. She and Sra. Carmen and her other neighbors sit with me and tell me that the family of the man who raped her came to the village. They brought several pounds of rice and offered to marry the girl or give them the rice. They told them not to go to the police.

I imagine shooting this man and his family, cutting them to pieces with a machete. Perhaps I'm not a pacifist. But what am I to do with all my rage in this world where justice doesn't live. I scream inside my head. I think of what rice means to this family and the starved-blond babies. She still doesn't crawl. She just stares at me. Her ten months on this planet, what does she see? But I think of all the other little girls and the world they will grow up in if we do nothing. Clench, unclench.

I calmly say to the women looking at me so intently. Such a weight on me. "Well, I know the rice would help you. But what this man did is wrong. If we don't stand up and say we don't want this happening here, what will happen when the baby is all grown up? I can't tell you what to do, because I know this is hard. But your daughter is worth more than that I think."

They say, "That's what we thought, too." They tell me they just wanted to know what I thought they should do. They feel better they say, knowing that as an educated person I would know what to do.

I can't breathe.

I smile at them, reassure them. I tell them I'm proud of them. "You are smart women," I say. "You knew the right thing to do. You just have to be strong together," I tell them. My motivational speaker takes over, and I try to rally them. My emotionless women. I sometimes feel like they think I'm nearly all crazy.

I picture Chris Farley's *Saturday Night Live* motivational speeches. I laugh to myself as I hike back down the mountain, the hot sun beating down on my back. Maybe I am nearly all crazy. I carry my *chakara* with trembling hands and wonder if my strength will ever come back. Can you use it all up? Maybe I'm becoming an emotionless woman, too. Too many births, too many sick babies, too many eyes and hands reaching for me. Too much emotion.

Katarine asks me to help her with her homework. Her Aunt Olivia smiles at me and pets my head. She says how grateful she is that I help her family. She does what she can to help her sister and her children, but it's good to know that other people are also looking out for them. I smile at her and tell Katarine good luck in her class. She smiles softly and looks back at her book, already starting her next chapter. As I walk away, I picture the words leaving the page, bursting inside her mind. The endless possibilities in the birth of knowledge.

Rebecca Martin earned her BS from UW-Madison in 2000 and her MPH from UW-La Crosse in 2007. After serving in Comarca Ngöbe-Buglé, Panama from 2001-03, she went to work in health education and health promotion focusing on maternal/child and sexual/reproductive health. And like a good Panamanian and Ngöbe woman, she continues to point with her lips, lets out the occasional salomar, craves anything made with fried corn, and freely admits to still hoarding water. This story is the winner of The Jason and Lucy Greer Foundation for the Arts prize.

JOHN   KOTULA

Guillermo's Lion

An artist's life no matter how short or obscure can leave a
legacy through his paintings and the people who knew him.

ONE OF THE FIRST THINGS I DID WHEN I ARRIVED IN SONAGUERA, Honduras, as a Peace Corps Volunteer was help out with the vaccination campaign. I went around to the villages with a team from the Health Center. We set up mainly in schools. In the village of Cuyulapa, we had had a busy morning, but by afternoon things had slowed down. I took a break to look around the school, introduce myself to the teachers, and try out my Spanish on the kids.

The school had a large assembly room and looking through the windows, I saw some pretty good murals painted on the walls: portraits of historical figures, the national flower and national tree, the Honduran flag and the official seal, probably all copied from a civics textbook. I asked the director who had done them, and she said a man named Guillermo from Arenas, the next village over. I said I'd like to meet him, and so the director grabbed a passing kid and sent him off on a bike to find Guillermo. When I got to the Health Center the next morning, he was waiting for me, having ridden his bike forty minutes from Arenas. He was a small, thin, handsome man, wearing a green long-sleeved shirt, way too big for him, buttoned up to the throat.

We went across the street for a soda and what passed for a conversation given my level of Spanish. I managed to tell him that I was an artist and wanted to meet artists in the area. I hoped in the future we could work together to present information about health issues such as HIV/AIDS. He was quiet and deferential, but clearly interested in what I was saying. He told me that his usual work was cutting oranges, but that whenever he had the chance he painted. He had some drawings with him that he unrolled one at a time to show me. Among others, there was a lion laying on the bank of a river, a dove spreading its wings above a bible, and an unfinished, imaginary city of domes, arches and towers.

My two favorites were portraits: one of a man in profile wearing a cowboy hat, and the other a delicately drawn frontal view of a young man with his collar buttoned up just like Guillermo's. They weren't good drawings in any technical sense, but like the paintings in the school, they were sweet and endearing, and I liked them a lot. We agreed to meet every couple of weeks to look at each other's drawings and to talk. He showed up two weeks later. I showed him my sketchbook and took a photo of him that I later used as a source to do a portrait. He didn't make our third meeting, but I wasn't worried because I figured he'd be easy enough to find if I could develop the opportunity to work together.

About three weeks later, my wife Deb and I were walking toward the Health Center in the early evening. A man came up behind us, touched my arm and said, "Excuse me. The boy in the car wants to talk to you." He pointed to a pickup parked a few yards behind us. Guillermo was sitting in the passenger seat. I knew it was him right away, but I was confused because the change in his appearance was so dramatic. My first reaction was that he looked much younger, like he must have looked as a boy. Then I realized that he was very sick and had lost so much weight it was as if he had shrunk to a smaller version of himself. It was also disorienting to shake hands with him because his touch felt so much hotter than you expect a human touch to feel.

"Guillermo," I said. "You're sick."

"Yes," he said. "My problem is AIDS."

He told me that he had been to a doctor in Tacoa. I couldn't understand what the doctor had said or what the plan was. I think I asked if he was going to the hospital and he said, "Not yet." He was having trouble holding his head up and talking. I tried talking to the other men, his older brother, Eulalio, and his neighbor, Jose, about the hospital and about medicine, and I think I kept getting "not yet" as an answer. Finally, I made arrangements to visit him at his home on Monday. They told me to stop at Jose's house, across from the Catholic Church and he'd show me the way.

Three days later, I found the neighbor's house easily. While I was waiting for him to rouse a teenage son to show me the way to Guillermo's, I noticed a large painting on the kitchen wall: an elegant and peaceful lion walking through a lush jungle. I knew right away it was Guillermo's. It had the same sweet and endearing qualities as his other pictures, but this was also a good painting, large, vivid, well rendered and personal. I was willing to bet that it wasn't a generic lion, but was in some way meaningful to Guillermo. It was my hope to get the chance to ask him about it.

I walked a half-mile or so up the road with the neighbor's son, sharing the road with cows, horses, pigs, and bicycles over a skinny log spanning a small stream, the only way across with dry feet if you were walking. We walked through orange groves for ten minutes and then turned up a path leading into a packed dirt yard where a family was cooking and washing in front of a small cinder-block house.

I talked for a while with a man who turned out to be Guillermo's younger brother visiting with his family from Tacoa. He told me Guillermo was worse, that he couldn't talk, that he was confused, but that he wanted to see me. We walked up a pretty path, further back into the orange grove, to another small house. Guillermo lived here with his mother and two of her grandchildren, the teenage son and daughter of a sister of Guillermo's who had died. It was clear that the life of the family took place in the yard where there was a wood-burning mud stove, a table, a *pila* (all-purpose sink) and shade. The house was just for sleeping. It had two rooms with two beds in each room. In the back room the diminutive Guillermo was sleeping. I knew he was thirty-one, but he looked twelve. How could it be that just a month ago he road his bike forty minutes each way to visit me in Sonaguera?

He woke up, sat up, gestured to his mouth, his right arm, his right leg. His brother told me his right side was sleeping. I held his hand, and it was still feverish. I gave him the photograph and the portrait I had drawn from it. His mother came in to look at them, too. I thought, "She has lost one child I know of, the dead daughter, now her son is dying. She is probably younger than I am."

I told the brother I'd just met that Guillermo had to go to the hospital. He said I had to wait and talk to his older brother. Just a couple of minutes later, Eulalio came in. He had a form, a paper from the Health Center in Tocoa. It said that Guillermo had a positive HIV test two years ago. It was a referral to Hospital Atlantida in La Ceiba, three or four hours away by bus, the only place where retro-viral treatment was available.

The family was gentle and loving. They lived in the middle of a beautiful orange grove. They had no money, no car. Their brother weighed ninety pounds. His right side was sleeping. He needed to go to the hospital. He was too weak to change buses twice, to wait an hour in between in the sun on the highway. Besides, there was no money.

I asked about the neighbor and his truck. There was no money for gas. I offered to pay for the gas. Eulalio and I went to talk to the neighbor. It was possible. It was a long drive, but for 800 lempira it was possible. We made the deal. They would stop at my house at 5:30 the next morning on their way to the hospital with Guillermo.

When Eulalio and I got back to their house, Guillermo was sitting up in the yard. His younger brother was feeding him small bites of Cup-O-Noodle. I went home with a sack of oranges and two small paintings of Guillermo's: a portrait of Francisco Morazán, a Honduran hero who almost united Central America in the 1830s, and another of Francisco Ferrera, independent Honduras' first elected president.

Paying 800 lempira for gas was charity, not development. It was not what the Peace Corps is about. It was not sustainable. I couldn't personally fund the transportation of every AIDS patient in Honduras. At the time, it felt like the best fifty dollars I ever spent.

It may have been that since the night Guillermo's brother touched my arm in the street, the family was waiting for me to help. There is the possibility that they saw being acquainted with the gringo as their best resource. When I asked if they were going to the hospital and they said, "Not yet," that may have meant, "Not until you help us." They never asked, but should I have figured out sooner what was needed from me?

The next time I saw Guillermo, he was in the AIDS unit at Hospital Atlantida in La Ceiba. In a room full of men, maybe fifteen of them, who looked like they were dying, he looked the closest to death. Deb and I had introduced ourselves to Dr. Flores, the director of the AIDS treatment program. He was friendly and generous with his time. He talked to us in his office for a half hour answering all our questions. I felt, immediately, that given the limitations of the system, Guillermo was in good hands.

Dr. Flores accompanied us up to the ward to see Guillermo, whose hospital johnny had ridden up exposing his stick legs and underwear. His big brother tugged it back down covering him better. Dr. Flores said the paralysis and cognitive dysfunction were from toxoplasmosis. It was in his brain. If they could get it under control, he would be a good candidate for retro-viral therapy. More immediately he needed a CAT scan to see how much brain damage there had been. There were no funds for this scan. It cost 3,000 lempira. If we could give something, it would be a big help. Dr. Flores was very direct for a Honduran. Deb and I came back with 1,000 lempira from our account in the States.

That night in our hotel room, as I was falling asleep, I asked Deb what if the CAT scan showed so much brain damage that they decided he was not a good candidate for retro-viral treatment? What if my involvement helped keep him alive, but the paralysis was permanent and he couldn't cut oranges or paint? What if his mother and brother had to care for him as an invalid?

Guillermo died on June 29 at ten in the morning. He got well enough to leave the hospital and travel home, but quickly became very ill again. He died six days later. Eulalio sent word to us that he had died and the hour of his death. It was understood that he would be buried twenty-four hours later.

When Deb and I arrived at the Evangelical church in Arenas, only his mother, sister-in-law, and niece were there.

They had been with him all night. The inside of the church was dim and cool compared to the glare of the street. The casket seemed impossibly narrow. It was wood, painted gray and white. There was a rough handrail screwed to the side for lifting it. About a quarter of the top was hinged and opened to reveal a Plexiglas viewing plate. There was no pretense that the casket held anything other than a corpse. Guillermo's skull-like head was hooded by a white towel. There was cotton in his mouth and nose. His eyes and lips were slightly opened. I looked at him for a while and remembered other deaths: my mother, Deb's dad, Gerry MarAurelle, Francis Giambroni. There was a smell. Clearly, it was time to get him into the ground.

Right at 10:00 the church filled up, probably fifty people arrived within ten minutes, including Eulalio. He talked with us a while. It came up that he had been looking for a camera. I had put mine in my pocket that morning, thinking that if there was time, I would take pictures of the painting of the lion. I agreed to take pictures of the funeral including ones of Guillermo's corpse.

I helped carry the casket from the church to the back of a pickup. It was very light. There were two other pickups and the fifty or so people all piled in. That was the funeral procession: three pickups and a group of maybe fifteen people on bikes following behind.

The cemetery was just past the family's house, down a dirt path, through an orange grove. Guillermo's grave had been dug in the shade of a large tree, right next to where his father was buried. Four men carried the casket from the truck to the grave and put it down on the ground. Eulalio opened the lid so people could look through the Plexiglas again. He signalled me to take pictures. In these photos, Guillermo was visible, but there were also reflections of the trees and sky above him. In Spanish the word for sky and heaven is the same: *cielo*.

The minister arrived and stood on the mound of dirt that had come out of the grave. He said that there was no need to pray for Guillermo because he had gone to his real life, his eternal life. He was with Jesus in glory and would be forever. The minister had a kind voice. His young son stood just below him on the mound of dirt, tossing pebbles toward the grave.

The men worked out the logistics of the ropes and lowered the casket into the grave. It took some doing to get the ropes free and pull them back out. The children all came up to the edge of the grave and threw in handfuls of dirt from the pile. Then the men shovelled. There were three shovels and they relieved each other silently. It probably took twenty minutes to fill the grave.

After a time, I asked Eulalio if people knew his brother had died of AIDS. He said no. I asked him if the family knew. He said no. I knew that people knew, because when they learned that I knew Guillermo, they told me he died of AIDS. I knew the family knew because I had been part of conversations about his illness with everyone in the family present. I took Eulalio's answer to mean it was something we don't talk about. It was not acknowledged.

After Guillermo died, I sought out his artwork and photographed it. There was a surprising amount. The Catholic Church in Sonaguera had two beautiful easel paintings. There was a large mural in an Evangelical church in Barrio Veinticinco. Deb came across another painting of a lion in the house of a midwife she was interviewing. I heard of several others as far away as La Ceiba. Having these images was important to me.

Deb and I went back to see Dr. Flores, the director of the AIDS treatment program where Guillermo was hospitalized. I had printed out a photo of Guillermo's Lion for him. We waited to see him in the pharmacy at the hospital where he was giving out prescriptions. He was working in an office separated from the waiting room by a curtain. He noticed us and nodded, but finished with his patient. I said to Deb, half joking, "He thinks we came to ask for our money back." He did in fact explain to us that it had been too late to use the donation to get a CAT scan for Guillermo. He said we could either have the 1,000 lempira back or he would keep it and use it to help another patient. We said to keep it and I gave him the photo. He started crying quite hard. None of us could talk for a while. He must see so much death. I respect him greatly for doing the work he does and somehow managing to stay emotionally alive.

It seems to me, that as an artist, Guillermo had the ideal relationship to his community. He made it a more beautiful place, decorating homes, schools and churches. He helped people pay attention to things they might not otherwise have noticed. He was a man that the community couldn't afford to loose so young. It stuck with me that if my work in Honduras could in any small way prevent premature deaths it would be time well spent.

I never got to talk to him about his lion.

John Kotula is an artist and writer who lives in Rhode Island. When he was with Peace Corp in Honduras from 2005-07, he took pride in being the oldest volunteer in the country. He considers those two years to be among the best of his life.

JEANNETTE LEBOYER

The Underbelly

*Murder and revenge mark a Paraguayan town with more
than just two crosses by the side of a dirt road.*

THE SKIES IN PARAGUAY NEVER CEASED TO PROVIDE ME WITH A
sense of serenity at the end of the day. Whatever happened
during the day, whether I was busy or relaxed, the walk home
allowed me to take in the sights and sounds of my community
of Colonia Guarani in rural Paraguay. One day in particular
gave me a feeling of solemnity, more so than usual, as I looked
around at the gentle hills and bucolic landscapes surrounding
me while I was walking up the hill with my three young companions. Perhaps it was the circumstance; perhaps the skies felt
the gravity of the moment and wanted to echo it in the only
way it knew how—with a paintbrush of pale pinks, yellows,
and purples set against a backdrop of every shade of green.
When I walked back that afternoon, it was as if the light of the
skies knew that week would be one I would remember with
melancholy.

It was only three days before that I had arrived back to
Paraguay after a short hiatus in the States. In the twist of time

that only comes from traveling long distances, I was thrown back into the world of the unexpected. That afternoon, I was walking back from a *reza*, the prayers that are recited with friends and family of a deceased the week after somebody dies. This *reza* was especially bittersweet, as it was for a twenty-year-old man who took his own life with a rifle a few days prior. His name was Ever Paralta. He had an identical twin, Edgar, who would become a constant reminder of the brother lost. I had lived with the Paralta family when I first moved into my community of Colonia Guarani, just under two years before his death. And more intensely chilling was that he shot himself in the house I used to live in, in the house that the twins had taken over as their own.

Now, walking back, I was recalling the time I spent in that first house. Those first moments I spent on site, surrounded by this family filled with dark-eyed children that peered at me from doorsteps, from behind trees, from behind their mother. The entire family was shy and quiet at first, and while I thought they would come around to become more talkative and comfortable with me, they never really did. I ended up moving in permanently with another family, closer to the center of the community and with whom I felt a stronger connection. With time, I became distant from that first family, but during that afternoon *reza,* I closely felt the pain of the household and of the entire community to lose someone so young.

Little did I know that on the walk up the hill with Morena (my ten-year-old "sister") and two other girls, I would soon be faced with another tragic event. Just as we neared the top of the hill, still about 500 meters from our houses, we heard two shots in the distance. I thought almost nothing of them, because people use guns in Paraguay to scare away pigs and animals from their fields. Within minutes however, we crested the hill so we could see down the red dusty road, and people were running in the distance.

A neighbor shouted to us, "Come over here, come inside quick, Oscar has been shot! By Karai Ayala!" (Karai is the Guarani equivalent to Señor). It was in a blur of disbelief that we were ushered into my neighbor Ña Jacinta's house, (Ña is the Guarani equivalent for Señora) and the reality of the moment struck down hard.

Amidst people running in circles around me, with Ña Jacinta's fifteen-year-old son carrying a shotgun and asking his mother where the bullets were, I sat down to hear that Oscar was playing cards and drinking *caña* (sugar cane alcohol) with Karai Ayala. Seemingly without motive (playing cards and drinking is never a good enough motive), Karai Ayala shot young Oscar. Ayala was an old man, probably nearing eighty years old, thin and gray-haired. He had buried his wife just months before. Oscar couldn't have been more than twenty-five years old and helped run his father's farm with his two brothers. And now Oscar was shot, lying on the porch of the house, and Ayala had locked himself inside. One thing that was certain amidst the story that was emerging: Oscar's brothers were out for vengeance.

The next hours held my heart constricted and pounding. These were my neighbors and friends of the past two years, and, while I was a part of the community, I also still felt like someone looking in. In this surreal state of mind, I was moving in slow motion. I saw the scramble of men to Ayala's house and heard the cries of people, both in sadness and rage. The anger and tragedy hung thick in the air.

I also knew that I had to get home because I had three young girls with me, whose mothers would no doubt be worrying during the tumult. And yet, we had to pass Ayala's house to get to our houses, but no one would let us do that. There was a blockage of people in the middle of the road crying and watching on either side of his house, creating an invisible line on either side of Ayala's house that we weren't able to cross. So as the light from the purple skies dimmed to twilight, I took the girls through the fields of corn and *mandioca* in our bare and muddied feet to circumnavigate Ayala's hours as far away as possible.

We finally got back to my host family's house, where my host-mother, Ña Maximina, cried out when she saw us arrive. She quickly recapped what had happened and checked to make sure everyone arrived back in one piece. Oscar's sister had come inside our house to wait and cry on Ña Maximina's shoulders. Less than sixty meters away, Oscar's brothers were still standing outside Ayala's house, waiting for him to come out. Ayala was locked inside, and to this day, I wonder what was going through his mind as he sat alone and hunted inside his home of thirty years.

We used my cell phone (one of the only ones in the community) to call Oscar's sisters in Buenos Aires, to tell them to take the next bus home to bury their brother. We also tried to call the police. In true Paraguayan fashion, they didn't show up until after they were needed. While there was a small police outpost less than two kilometers away, they were not officially in Colonia Guarani's jurisdiction, so they didn't feel it necessary to come by. More likely, they had little desire to come between a gun and the brothers' need for vengeance.

And so, with nothing left to do but wait for the police or other divine intervention (neither of which arrived), we just sat in Ña Maximina's living room. My little *casita* (which was a glorified extension of the main house) was about twenty meters closer to Karai Ayala's house, and while my normal bedtime of 9:00 P.M. was nearing, there was no chance I would sit alone in my house, that much closer to guns and violence. I have never been so close to death as I was that night, even in Paraguay where death is common and entwined with everyday life. I didn't want to get any closer.

Sitting on a chair in a turquoise painted room listening to the quiet sobs of Oscar's sister, my mind zoomed out to the immensity of what had happened. In one day—in fact, in a matter of hours—I was confronted with two aspects of the underbelly of Paraguayan life. In the daylight hours on an average day here, drinking *terere* (a cold version of yerba mate tea) brings the sounds of laughter and conversation. People look toward the future and understand that they have numerous challenges to face living a subsistence lifestyle in a developing country. However, more often than not, they are surrounded by family, children, and neighbors that make their existence lighter and filled with daily joys.

And yet, in my quiet community of 150 families, there was no mistaking the undercurrents of depression and negativity. When teenagers or young adults grow into the harsh realities of subsistence lifestyles, but are bombarded by images on television or in bigger cities of the unattainable world, it is understandable that they would feel helpless in their circumstance. While the network of family is strong in Paraguay, communication about feelings of depression, frustration and unhappiness is not their forte; people do their best to hide their deeper emotions, perhaps as a defense mechanism against feelings getting out of their control. From my perspective, as a privileged girl from the land of opportunity, I realized I could never fully understand such deep feelings of hopelessness and despair. I was taught that there are always opportunities to take advantage of, that I can choose my destiny, that things will nearly always turn out all right. Paraguay's children cannot say the same things. In the months prior, I had heard about three other incidences where a fifteen or sixteen-year-old took his or her life, with a gun, with a noose, and worst of all, with the pesticides they have to apply to their own field.

And working parallel to depression are alcohol and violence. These two intertwine like the grapevines I grew in my front yard. This was not the first time I'd seen the two come together with a fury. Cheap alcohol is used as a means to get away from the hardships of daily life. Violence rides side by side with alcohol, as those repressed feelings come bubbling up with the lack of inhibition. While I felt safe and protected with my family and host-parents, who never touched a drop of alcohol save for Christmas and New Years, I saw its effects surrounding me.

In my time as a Volunteer, I saw someone's face cut open with a machete during a drunken argument; I went to a funeral of a man who was shot during a game of cards while drinking (to leave a young mother of three children to fend for herself); I saw young men of sixteen come home from parties with black eyes and cuts on their faces. The situations rarely improve because police enforcement is so weak and policemen rarely come to aid and protect, mainly because they know to stay out of the violence and protect their own lives first. They already have salaried jobs that they know better than to risk.

After what seemed like a stretch into eternity, but in reality was only hours after Oscar's shooting, we heard a scramble and shouts of men from the direction of Karai Ayala's house. I realized I was holding my breath and let it out slowly. I could hear in the silence of the night, they were climbing on the roof of Karai Ayala's house, pulling back the wooden shingles. Within moments, as we stared into the faces and eyes of our friends and family sitting together motionless, seven consecutive shots rang out. With that, we knew the standoff was over. Oscar's brothers had their revenge; Karai Ayala was dead.

I woke up the next morning to a stillness that quickly reminded me of the night before. It seemed as though even the roosters were honoring the tragedies with their silence. I lay in bed for longer than usual, postponing my morning yerba maté ritual. The same thoughts kept running through my head: I had been part of two tragic events in my community, both as senseless as the other and both equally baffling. As a Volunteer, I knew both these acts were out of my control. I was here to teach about agriculture and gardening and nutrition. They don't tell you how to teach nonviolence, sobriety, and support for depression. And on some level, I felt this was the kind of education that was needed more than anything. The only thing left for me to do was to be a friend to my neighbors, now more than any other time.

The community of Colonia Guarani became closer in the days and weeks following the events. That following week, I went to a funeral or *reza* every day, switching between the families of both Oscar and Ever. During the funeral of Oscar two days later, the neighbors walked in procession holding hands and crying together. Everyone realized these deaths were senseless, and yet the support for the families was overwhelming. Neighbors made sure no family member was alone and without a shoulder to lean on. Each *reza* was full of people every afternoon, in show of support that made me realize that with these two tragedies that happened within days of each other, there was hope that the community would learn and grow from them. With such community support, during the days following we were already being healed. To this day, the two crosses set next to the red dirt road remind Colonia Guarani not to repeat the events of that week.

Jeannette Leboyer served in Paraguay from 2002-04. She is a graduate student at the UW-Madison studying for a master's degree in Environment and Resources, and Energy Analysis and Policy. Her experiences as a PC Volunteer had a profound impact on her life. When she's not thinking about Paraguay or writing her thesis, you can find her riding her bike, hiking or playing Frisbee in the summer and skiing and ice skating in the winter.

WALTER JAMES MURRAY

✳

Obituary for Roberto

For this Volunteer, an infant's death leads to a completely unexpected and never-to-be-forgotten request.

WHILE PREPARING LESSON PLANS FOR THE FOLLOWING DAY IN MY house in Bom Jesus da Lapa, Bahia, three young women made their presence known at my door by the usual clapping of hands, as knocking on a door is not practicable in villages in Brazil. I got up from my table and invited them in, recognizing them as prostitutes who worked in the town. They joined me at the table.

They were three teenagers, most likely fifteen or sixteen years of age, illiterate, and surprisingly comfortable in my presence. Brazilian law states that for a woman to prostitute herself, she must be at least eighteen years of age, but in the small towns the law is oftentimes ignored and young girls can make a living there until they reach the legal age. Then they can migrate to the larger cities, like Sao Paulo, where they believe they can make a better living, such as it is.

The girls spoke only Portuguese. By that time my ability in the language had progressed to where I could communicate reasonably well, depending on the subject. In any event, I didn't have a problem understanding what they had come for and subsequently in doing what they needed done.

Getting down to business right away, they told me a child of one of them, a baby, had died earlier that day and they were in need of someone to write out an announcement they wanted broadcast live over the town's public address system that evening. The baby's name was Roberto; he had lived five months. They merely wanted me to be their scribe.

On a sheet of paper I drafted, in Portuguese, an announcement, just a couple of lines, telling of the death of the boy, that he would be taken to the cemetery in the morning, and that the townspeople were invited to attend. When it was done, they thanked me and went on their way. It was one of the most extraordinary and sorrowful things I have ever been asked to do, and I couldn't help but have a feeling of wonderment that they had come to me.

Walter James Murray was in Brazil 2, from 1962-64.

SHANE TOWNSEND

The Boy From "Kill the Cat"

A village's genuine concern for the author's family
crosses borders and language barriers.

NOT A SINGLE PIRANHA THAT DAY, NOT EVEN A BITE. SO I WAS happily distracted from my piscatorial misfortune by friends asking, "José, how's your family in Mississippi?" You see, despite the confusion about my name, everyone in this indigenous Chiquitano village in lowland Bolivia knew Mississippi was home.

"Shane" had immediately proven an impossible utterance. "*Scheit!*" That was as close as we came, and with each passing day the "e" lost a little of itself to the "i." Several weeks of smiling retreats to the safety of my mosquito net left my ego sullied, and I knew I had to change my name. But how? I certainly understood good intentions gone wild.

"Seat yourself," I once tried to say while offering a chair to a lady, but the all-too familiar cackles, hoots, and giggles betrayed the translation: "Feel yourself." Confusing *sentar* with *sentir*, I told her to feel herself; over a plate of guinea pig and rice, no less.

I abandoned "Shane" for "José" in honor of the legions of Bolivians named for Mary, Joseph, and others of that cohort. And later, proud of my developing linguistic wit, I began introducing myself as "José, *fin del pueblo*," convinced I had decoded "Townsend" into "at the end of town." After about a year of crinkle-eyed introductions, a friend explained that I was calling myself something akin to "Joseph, end of the people." I could just imagine the fun people had with that one: "That's Joseph who will bring the end of the people," or "That's Joseph whose family has brought the end to another people and that's why he's homeless and here with us, garbled Spanish and melanin-deficient glory shining in the moonlight."

"Mississippi" *is* a word in Quechua, that much was agreed. The exact translation, though, was difficult, as it always is when Spanish is the second language of all involved and you still don't speak well enough to ask for toilet paper without the insurance of a wiping gesture. "Kill the cat," some laughed. "Hang the cat," said others, chuckling a more specific interpretation. I was happy not to translate it.

Dead cat and all, folk in San Juancito welcomed me into their adobe and *motacú* palm homes. And they did so, I believe, because they appreciated my rural Mississippi roots: we used to gig flounder by lantern light in the backwaters of Krebs' Lake, sliding our feet to avoid the stingray's spine. Once, on a night-long coon hunt in the creek bottom, a mountain lion's scream had paralyzed everything, frogs, whippoorwills, us. And in the Pascagoula River swamp, we snatched water moccasins by day and alligators by night, their eyes shining red in the spotlight's beam.

So there was a familiarity in San Juancito, in Don José's good-natured, "Let me show you how to fish," and in the peace. There was peace. Some evenings we tossed hand-lines baited with meat to catch piranhas. At night with spears, waist deep in the same water, we gigged long-whiskered catfish and caiman so heavy that the bamboo spear sagged under their weight—well, maybe a little. But most often, nearing midnight on the darkest nights, we used machetes to cleave the dorsals of wary dorado, the freshwater barracuda. Easing side by side, we slid our feet through the clear waters of the Rio Paraguá, searching by the thin beam of one light for an errant shadow, taking careful aim and willing yet another fish.

"A country boy like us," they said. José, *fin del pueblo, el gringo campesino de mata el gato*: Joseph, the end of the people, the country boy from "kill the cat."

So that August evening, when the first of my friends asked, "José, how's your family in Mississippi?" I smiled, not hearing the concern that must have been there. But the newscaster's voice rang clear through that monofilament-entwined radio: "The biggest hurricane in history" was on its way to Mississippi. And in a village of forty families, tucked away in the forest near the Brazilian border, some wrung their hands and others prayed for "our family" there, and it did not matter that they didn't know my name.

Shane Townsend (or Mudcat as Hellfire Longmire and other Peace Corps friends call him) served as a micro-enterprise development Volunteer with the Peace Corps in and near San Ignacio de Velasco, Bolivia from 2003-05. A Mississippi native, he is a musician, a writer, and a fan of well-strung hammocks.

RICHARD R. SITLER

* * *

Bus Preacher

The author experiences a religious epiphany
on a public bus to Kingston.

ON A CITY BUS FROM SPANISH TOWN TO KINGSTON, A YOUNG
woman was preaching and testifying. She started shortly after
the bus passed the bypass roundabout, just before the Craven A
cigarette factory on the A1. Before then the riders were quiet.
It was a little after 7:00 A.M. With an abrupt interruption of the
silence, this young woman began loudly shouting about how
fortunate we all are to be able to ride a bus that morning.

She began talking about people not as fortunate. She said,
"There are people who cannot get out of bed. They are
hooked up to tubes to keep them alive. There are people who
have to have a tube and bag attached to them to allow them
to defecate." The young lady always used the most extreme
sensational examples. She was definitely going for the shock
value. She continued by talking about the poor souls who
would go to bed not knowing that they would not wake up
the next morning.

The young gal's voice was more of a cry, but husky
and very loud. She thundered her message. Her manner of

shouting was hurried, and she seemed to go on and on without having to stop to breathe. As she was talking about those poor souls who would die in their sleep, I was wishing I were one of them. Here I was barely awake, and I was trapped on a bus for the next two hours or so with this young evangelist shouting her sermon and giving me a headache. Most people ignored her and silently stared ahead. There were three or four women who encouraged the bus preacher with "Amen" and other religious rejoinders.

The woman continued her message by reminding everyone of the works of Satan in Jamaica.

"There are men abusing women in this country. There are men in this country raping children." Then she talked about men who performed such heinous acts as raping babies. Since Jamaicans often use the term baby for any child under the age of twelve, she made sure everyone knew she was talking about children under the age of one. I hadn't seen a lot of stories in *The Gleaner* or *Observer* about this, so I didn't know if there is such a problem or not.

The young lady continued to talk about the evil "*chi chi* men." In Jamaica homosexuals are called "*chi chi* men" or "batty men." The "*chi chi* man" is basically the scapegoat of Jamaica society. Some blame them for all of the social ills of the country. So a message such as the one given by the bus preacher would not be complete without a firm rebuke of the "*chi chi* men."

Once the bus preacher set the stage, she introduced herself into the message. She stated that she was a nineteen-year-old student at Campion College—a prep school in Kingston. She talked about the difficulties of being a student. She talked about how most schoolgirls are not serious about their studies. They play, flirt, and party. Because of her firm unwavering faith in God she was above all of that. "I am not like those other schoolgirls. God called me," she proclaimed.

So God called her to shout her message of self-righteousness. She was convinced that the Devil was in control of Jamaica. She did, however, go on to tell us that God forgives. "Yes, God forgives everyone. He will forgive the rapist, the murderer and everyone. He will even forgive the Rasta man." This last comment was directed at the kindly looking old dready standing right in front of me. (The preacher woman was standing directly behind me.) I scanned the beatific face of the follower of the Lion of Judah to see if there was any sign or expression to this retribution directed toward him. He did not acknowledge the statement at all, and he retained a kindly, content, and calm look on his dreadlock-framed face. Looking upon him I suddenly felt calmer.

I was thinking of things I wanted to say or things I would say if she drew me into her presentation, which I did not want to happen. If you show that you do not appreciate the preaching, everyone will look at you as a heathen. Then some will feel the need to try to save your soul. I also thought about standing up to give my own competing sermon with another theological viewpoint.

I thought about the religions I could profess: Hindu? No, I do not know enough about it. Muslim? They might think I was some kind of white Taliban terrorist. Jewish? That would make some accuse my people of killing their savior. I also thought about obscure religions as Zoroastrian or Taoism, but I figured that no one would recognize those religions. Anyway, what true Taoist would bother to proselytize upon a bus?

Finally, I realized that even if I wanted to hold a competing sermon—to battle like the famous Jamaican sound system battles—that I could never compete with this young preacher. For while I was thinking all of these thoughts, the young lady was still shouting out her points about the greatness of God while never stopping to inhale or exhale. Wow, talk about the power of the Holy Ghost! Personally, I would rather she use that talent to play a musical instrument. She could be like the saxophone player Kenny G who seems to be able to play long notes that go one forever without having to take a breathe. I am not really a big fan of Kenny G's style of easy listening jazz; however, I do admire his talents and especially his ability to hold long notes.

As we were entering Kingston, the young lady finally finished her sermon to my relief. I thought maybe the last few miles blessed silence would fill the bus.

In concluding her sermon, she offered to pray with anyone who wished to testify or who wanted to come to the Lord right there on the bus. She was confident that her inspirational words would cause many to want to get on their knees right there and give their lives to Christ or to reaffirm their faith and leave behind their previous lives of whoring, gang-banging and baby-raping. There did not seem to be any takers. After getting little response she said, "Oh, and if there are any back-sliders I will be glad to help bring you back to Christ."

This invitation caused the schoolgirl sitting by me to ask her classmate standing in the aisle, "What is a backslider?" She probably was thinking like me about the similarity of the word backslider to the Jamaican curse "backside." Backside is kind of the equivalent to the American word "asshole," or maybe it is a little closer to the British word "bugger." We both had giggled at the word backslider.

The bus evangelist sat down behind me and began talking to two school children she thought needed some personal salvation attention. From what I heard of the conversation, the schoolgirls did not seem to be too interested and were not ready to get on their knees on that bus to give their lives to Christ right then and there.

Well, my dream of at least fifteen minutes of silence was shattered when an older woman, maybe in her thirties, got up to add her two cents. "This young lady is to be commended for her faith and fervor," the woman praised. She went on to tell how fortunate we were to hear the word of God that morning on the bus.

As I exited the bus in Half Way Tree and walked toward New Kingston, I pondered why it was this bus sermonizing was making me have such negative thoughts instead of causing me to want to embrace God as the speaker intended. Maybe it was some of her nonintellectual, simplistic, almost ignorant ideas. While speaking about the greatness of God, she also talked about the complexity of the Earth. She talked about going up in an airplane and looking down and seeing how the ground and the sea met perfectly. She asked how could anyone but God create this and on seeing this how could you not believe in God? I was raised a Presbyterian where the sermons tend to be more like university lectures.

I realized it was more than her lack of serious theological inquiry that made me consider siding with the devil because I did find her explanation of Hell intriguing. She stated that "Hell is the most holy place." Without pausing to let that sink in or even taking a breath, she said it again, "Hell is the most Holy Place." She emphasized the statement even more as if when she said it the first time people had gasped, even though no one did. She obviously had practiced this part of her message and had prepared the repeating of this revolutionary thought because she just knew that it would astonish everyone. She went on to explain the concept. She said that all the gunmen, baby-rapers and backsliders go to Hell where they can no longer partake in their evil practices. In Hell, she told us, all they can do is burn and wish that they had accepted God when they had the opportunity. So, Hell is a very holy place because everyone there is praying that they could be in heaven instead. I think that was her point.

Not too long ago, there was a fad in the U.S. evangelical community to wear wrist bands with the letters WWJD which stands for "What Would Jesus Do?" I tried to imagine Jesus preaching on that bus. I couldn't. I think Jesus would not have stood up and harangued the poor haggard passengers about how lucky they were to not be in a hospital with tubes sticking out of them, or worse, waking up dead. I do not think that Jesus was much of a shouter.

Could this be a WWJD moment? When I first sat down, a primary schoolchild of about eight entered the bus with his mother and they stood in the aisle by me. The child tried to zip her book bag up, but the zipper came off track causing the bag not to close. Her books and school supplies were perilously about to drop out.

The mother exclaimed, "Cho, serves you right," as she sucked her teeth. The child frowned, but said nothing. The high school student sitting next to me offered to hold the book bag in her lap. She held it so the contents would not fall out. The whole time I imagined the little girl's problem of trying to carry the bag without losing the contents. I was sure the mother would give her the switch if she lost anything from the bag.

Finally, I decided to try to fix the zipper. I reached over and pulled the zipper that was off track up out of the way, so that I could try to pull the zipper on the other side that was still on track to close the bag. The zipper still on track was missing most of its pull-tab, so it made it difficult to pull. I got the zipper pulled half way around the bag and then the high school girl pulled it the rest of the way, closing the bag.

I realized that although I did it to help the little girl that actually it was about me doing something to make myself feel worthwhile. Maybe that is what the bus preacher girl needed as well. To feel important. To feel like she could save souls.

Richard R. Sitler served as a Peace Corps Volunteer in Jamaica from 2000-02. He worked at the Lluidas Vale All Age School in the community of Lluidas Vale in St. Catherine Parish. Sitler returned to Jamaica in 2006 as a Peace Corps Crisis Corps Volunteer and served the Warton Community Development Action Committee as a curriculum developer. He is a photojournalist by profession with over ten years of work for various newspapers in Ohio, Indiana, New Hampshire, and New Jersey. Sitler has specialized in covering the everyday lives of people in the communities his newspapers served. He has won several awards for this work.

KRISTA PERLEBERG

Pretty Woman

Happiness can be many things. For a hardware store
owner in Ecuador, it's a Lands' End Catalog.

I HAVE A RECURRING DREAM THAT I WILL SAVE $1,000 FOR A
clothes-shopping trip just for me, in a Midwestern town where
I figure I could find nice clothes reasonably priced. I would try
on any clothes that I wanted and model them in front of a three-
way dressing room mirror. I might go to the high-end stores or a
small fashion boutique or a plain ol' department store. I can shop
anywhere I wish, and I can buy one very expensive outfit or 100
different cheaper items. The choice is mine because this fantasy
is all for me. I'll stay at a fancy hotel with a bellhop who will
carry my packages to my room. After tipping and sending the
bellhop off, I will turn to my packages, smile and fall on to the
bed with an exhausted but glorious and satisfied smile. Sounds a
little like the movie *Pretty Woman?* So, it might be. I sure would
have fun. I enjoy imagining myself doing just such a thing.

   As I look around my surroundings, I come back to my
reality: the middle of the world where I am a Peace Corps
Volunteer in a hot and dry coastal town. The town has dirt
streets, dusty sidewalks, doorless stores, sidewalk stands offering

tropical fruit juices made with questionable water sources, and food vendors selling *choclo* with mayo and parmesan cheese. These unusually decorated corn-on-the-cob taste great. The local *tiendas* sell lots of plastic, especially cheap plastic bowls, usually called *tinas*, used for everything from a mixing bowl to the kitchen sink to a child's bathtub. Among other daily items, I can find single rolls of melt-a-way pink or purple toilet paper, single eggs, cans of tuna, ketchup and piles of coconuts. The one clothes *tienda* sells polyester slinky shirts, plastic gold jewelry, and fancy ball gowns for *quinceañeras*, girls' fifteenth birthday celebrations.

One evening I found myself on the equator in Pedernales, Ecuador, helping my counterpart and friend indulge in her own version of my fantasy. I helped her write a $1,000 order to Lands' End for shorts, shoes, shirts, and pants. My counterpart, Charito, is the president of the NGO I work with. She is also the owner of the most successful hardware store in all of northern Manabi province.

For months I have passed all my magazines on to Charito. I had bought some of the magazines at international hotels in the bigger cities of Ecuador or I found some in the giveaway box at the PC Volunteer lounge. I also found some magazines left by travelers who had stayed at a hostel I used while visiting PC headquarters.

One magazine I brought Charito happened to be a Lands' End catalog. I am not sure how I stumbled upon that one in Ecuador, but Charito found heaven when she saw the catalog. She fell in love with the clothes and told me she would need a thousand U.S. dollars to buy all that she wanted. Charito can't read English, but chose everything from the pictures alone. She put little dots by each item she wanted.

A month later, Charito told me she had the money and was ready to place an order. We bought a bottle of Chilean wine at the only wine *tienda* in town, ordered in chicken and rice and *platinos*, and began writing out Charito's fashion order. We started with page 1 and worked through the entire catalog. I clarified some points for her, such as if a sweater was wool or cotton or why was there a pair of pants that cost $98. (They were 100 percent wool.) Charito wanted to know what the differences between the three types of similar looking khaki pants. Basically, length and price were the differences.

At first, Charito began estimating her measurements. Because it was difficult for me to pick the correct size, I told Charito we really needed to measure her. We were placing an order to a company a continent away, and we had only one chance to get it right. I really wanted her to be happy with the results. Charito said she didn't have a measuring tape.

I said, "You own a hardware store, you sell measuring tapes."

With a chuckle we went downstairs into her store and found a carpenter's tape. Standing in the middle of the nails, screws, machetes, hammers, and pipe fittings, I measured Charito's bust, waist, hips, and inseam. It's a good thing we measured, we found out when we returned upstairs to our wine and the catalog. We had had only one bottle of wine, but she had some outlandish guesses.

Charito ordered different types and colors of pants, shorts, shirts, and sandals. I convinced her to get leggings instead of wool pants. I couldn't change her mind about a short-sleeved sweater. Personally, I think a coastal town on the equator of the world is way too hot for sweaters, but I have North American sweat glands. What do I know? Charito insisted on the plaid flannel-lined cotton pants. She thought the turned up plaid cuff looked real nice. The price (and temperature) women pay for beauty. Charito made sure to choose colors that could handle the Pedernales dust. She did get a few things in bright colors, and we both agreed khaki/tan colors are quite functional for the lower half.

Charito is thirty-seven years old. She has no husband, an important distinction here, or family. She calls my husband and me her children. She went to business school in Ecuador's capital, Quito, and now owns the successful hardware store. Not a stereotypical third-world woman, she also has an intense interest and concern for the coastal forest and has worked hard to help co-found an ecological foundation to preserve some of the last remaining forest in the area. We love her. She is so much more than a counterpart, she's our "Mama Gringa," which she loves to be called.

The following week, I was in Quito and placed her order at an internet café. We arranged for the whole process to be done before my family came to visit in a couple of months. They agreed to bring Charito's fashion frenzy down in their suitcases.

Charito justified this shopping trip saying she won't buy any more clothes for a whole year. We toasted our hard work that evening, and I saw an Ecuadorian "pretty woman" smile.

Krista Perleberg was an environmental educator with the Peace Corps in Ecuador from 1997-99. She is a forester, an environmental educator, a teacher, and now works full-time in her most cherished role: as a mom. Krista is also a volunteer Master Gardener with the WSU cooperative extension program, offering advice about pests and plants in the garden.

✦

I Am Rich

A Volunteer discovers that being rich is in the mind of her beholder.

I AM RICH. MAGDA TOLD ME SO. EVEN THOUGH MY HOUSE IS made out of adobe, my living room floods every time it rains, and I don't have indoor plumbing—I am rich. I laughed when Magda told me this. It was almost like an accusation. I had just hiked up the mountain from Tutule to Granadillo huffing and puffing all the way.

"If only I had a motorcycle," I thought as I trekked up the trail. But no, that wouldn't work. Besides being against Peace Corps policy, nobody in any of the *aldeas* had a *moto*, so I didn't either. I thought that people respected me for this. And I guess they did—to an extent. But that didn't stop Magda from singling me out. We were sitting on a log outside her two-room house made of mud and sticks that she shared with eight other people (her mother, sister-in-law, and six kids under the age of five).

"You are rich," she said.

I laughed. "What are you talking about?" I asked her.

"You have beautiful shoes," Magda stated matter-of-factly.

I looked down at my bright red Nike sneakers. I had gotten them off the clearance rack at an outlet store back in Georgia. My mother had called them gaudy. A fellow Volunteer laughed every time that she saw my "flashy shoes" as she referred to them. Magda, who owned only *chancletas*—and not very good ones at that—called them beautiful. I looked at her feet. Magda and I were roughly the same age—mid-twenties. But her feet were, well, different from mine. I doubt that she had ever had worn a pair of closed-toed shoes in her entire life.

Her feet, like those of most of the *catrachos* I worked with looked, um..."rugged" might be a good word. I knew for a fact that Magda's family didn't own a pair of nail clippers because Sarah Ruth, my former site-mate, used to take nail clippers with her every time that we visited. She would just "go to town," as my mamaw would say: all the kids lined up and nails flying everywhere. But Sarah Ruth was gone, and it was just me, and I was under fire.

"You wear glasses for the sun," Magda continued.

Again, I was guilty as charged. "I have sensitive eyes..." I started to explain, but Magda just looked at me, almost daring me to say that her eyes weren't sensitive, too. So I mumbled something about blue eyes being weaker than brown ones, although I had no I idea if it was true or not. Probably not. And at that moment, I realized that Magda was right—that I was, or rather, I AM, rich.

I am rich because I grew up with a myriad of opportunities that Magda could never imagine: a good public school education, two employed parents, hospitals, libraries. And those are just the basics. I was raised to think for myself and to believe that I have the ability to create my own destiny: all in an environment conducive to helping me reach my potential. When I take into account two-thirds of the world, I am rich with my tennis shoes and sunglasses. And when I take into account the other third, I am rich because I have been given the opportunity to realize my wealth. Thank you, Magda, for pointing this out to me.

Amber Davis Collins served as a Family Hillside Farming Volunteer in San Pedro de Tutule, La Paz, Honduras, from 2002-2004. She has a master's degree in Agricultural Education from the University of Georgia. In 2006 Amber was awarded a Presidential Volunteer Service Award from George W. Bush, and in 2007 she was awarded the U.S. Environmental Protection Agency's Environmental Justice Award for her work with Latino farm worker issues. Amber and her husband, Scott, live in Smyrna, Georgia with their two cats, Maya and Kuna.

DORIS RUBENSTEIN

✳

The Wandering Judia

Peace Corps Volunteers come in all sizes, shapes,
and colors. They come in all faiths as well.

As a religious Jew, I knew that my Peace Corps experience might be a bit different than the experience of, say, a Roman Catholic PCV as we rode out our service in Ecuador, a distinctly Catholic country. Indeed, my observance of Jewish dietary laws prevented me from so much as tasting the two "national dishes" of Ecuador: *fritada*, a pork dish, and *cebiche*, a seafood concoction. Despite my avoidance of such delicacies, I still managed, as did most female PCVs in Ecuador, to gain a good fifteen pounds over my two years of service.

There was but one other Jewish trainee in our group that started out at the training center in Ponce, Puerto Rico, in late August 1971. When we arrived in Ecuador, we found only three other active PCVs. It was not enough for a Peace Corps *minyan*, but it was enough for the seasoned Volunteers to tip us off to a few foibles that we might encounter as Jews after being in Ecuador for a while. Indeed, although my experience may have differed but slightly from those of my gentile associates,

I was amazed to find tremendous similarities between certain experiences I had and those of other Jewish Volunteers.

Having traveled the world since my two years in Ecuador, I know for certain that the humble *gentecita* are among the most polite people in the world. They are also among the most curious. The Ecuadorian *peon* has the most polite way, it turns out, of extracting the most intimate information from total strangers.

As do most PCVs, I traveled widely in Ecuador on buses. Although I have dark hair and olive skin, I still stood out as an American in such situations. Early in my service, I was on a bus, seated next to a small, poor Ecuadorian man. We hunkered together for a trip of several hours to a common destination.

My companion introduced himself and shook hands, as is the Ecuadorian custom. Of course, I offered my hand and my name in return.

"Ah, and is the *señorita* a visitor to Ecuador?" my companion asked.

"*Si*," I responded. "I'm an American."

"And are you a tourist in Ecuador?" he probed further.

"No," I replied, "I'm a Peace Corps Volunteer."

I was not surprised that the man knew what a Peace Corps Volunteer was. At that time, there were nearly two hundred PCVs in Ecuador, and there had been nearly that many in-country for quite a few years. Nearly every *campesino* had met a PCV or knew someone who had.

He inquired politely about my family and marital status. He asked if I was becoming accustomed to the life in Ecuador. And then, came the show stopper:

"And, of course, *señorita,* you are a Catholic?" he queried.

"No, *señor,*" I replied softly, but firmly. "I am a Jew."

"A Jew?" The man rolled the word around on his tongue. It tasted strange.

"And what is a Jew?" he continued, curiously but politely.

"Well, *señor,* we believe only in God the Father," I explained simply.

"Hmmm," he murmured, considering the idea. "I understand. So you do not believe in Jesus Christ?"

I was pleased that he got it. "No, *señor.* Only in God the Father."

But, suddenly, his face grew agitated and worried. He turned to me, and with a shaky voice, pleaded, "But, certainly, *señorita,* you must believe in the Virgin!"

It broke my heart to tell him no.

The Ecuadorian *peon* is hopelessly devoted to the Virgin. She is the source of all kindness and solace to a people so desperately downtrodden by poverty, disease, and ignorance. She may not hold open heaven's door, but she holds them in her comforting bosom in this life.

At this point, the conversation ended.

Doris Rubenstein was a Peace Corps Volunteer in Ecuador from 2002-03. She is the author and editor of four books including the best-selling The Good Corporate Citizen: A Practical Guide.

JESSI FLYNN

The Easter Bunny's
Culinary Skills

Communicating across cultures is never an easy or simple
proposition, whether it's about fishing or the Easter Bunny.

THE NAME OF THE RAINFOREST PART OF PANAMA WHERE I LIVED
was Ñö Kribo, meaning "Source of the Big Water" in Ngäbere,
the indigenous language. It was a land of wide, towering trees,
powerful rivers, monumental rainstorms, and humidity like a
warm, damp, blanket wrapped around my body. Growing up
in the suburbs of Boston, I had seen such sights only on the
pages of *National Geographic* magazines.

Within my first seven days in town, all 800 people in the
town of Norteño wanted to meet me, the new Peace Corps
Volunteer and the only white person in town. They helped
me carry my two heavy bags to my new house. Each of the
bags contained more stuff for just myself than most families in
the village owned. The house I moved into had been built by
the previous Peace Corps Volunteer. It was a raised wooden
15x15-foot box placed high up on six-foot stilts, with a corru-
gated tin roof and two rooms inside. Most of the other houses
were more traditional huts. They were just a raised platform
with two-foot-high walls around them to prevent children

from falling over the edge, with a giant brown roof made of layered palm leaves.

Toucans flew over looking like their huge rainbow beaks were defying gravity, and parrots squabbled incessantly. I kept hearing a sound like static electricity, which was out of place where there was no power. I later found it was the call of the "Chief" bird, a large black bird with a bright yellow tail that weaves basket nests hung from tree branches.

Norteño smelled alive. Steamy green growth, the dizzying perfume of coffee blossoms, and the smells of close-living humanity: wood smoke from cooking fires in every hut, an occasional waft of human waste or burning plastic trash.

Modern conveniences, such as electricity and running water, weren't included in the living conditions. I used a kerosene lantern or flashlight and had to haul my water in five-gallon buckets from a spigot at the bottom of the hill, a few minute's walk from my house. There was water tubing connected to my house; however, there was not always water, and when there was, "items," such as small fish, would appear in it. To filter out these items, the neighbors had tied an old piece of kids' purple underwear around the end of the spigot. Out of sight, out of mind.

In my first week there, I learned that visiting was an expected daily activity. My village, and the Ngäbe culture in general, took shooting the breeze to a whole new, official level. The word for visiting, *basare*, did not merely mean visiting. The word itself implies time. Idle, visiting, time. "*Ti niki basare*" (usually sung out, with the last word sounding more like 'basAAAArree!'), or "I'm going visiting" was the village's social network. Their personal Facebook. If you announced upon arrival at someone's house that you were *basare*, it meant the host provided at least coffee or hot chocolate, and often a plate of boiled green bananas, a boiled root crop, or another seasonal dish.

Sharing food and drink in this culture was of utmost importance. It is a very communal culture. Those who had, gave. Those who did not have, received. Sharing tested what you had and what you could, and would, give. Not sharing a lot, or not sharing the best of the food or drink, would earn you a title of *kubore* or "selfish." That was the worst title in the village, a big branded "K" on your forehead. It meant people you offended would never speak to you again, which was apparently possible even in a village as small as Norteño, as I personally found out.

As I walked through town, learning the faces and paths, people expected me to go *basare*. Everyone invited me up into their huts and gave me a cup of hot chocolate made from the chocolate beans they grew themselves. The chocolate, served in plastic pink or green cups that were rough and worn like they had been used as sandbox toys, tasted like watered down, lukewarm baker's chocolate.

As I responded to someone calling me to their hut and climbed up the notched log that served as front steps, a kid would hand me a beaten-up cup of chocolate. I would settle into a cross-legged seat on the creaky, flexible floor, made from a series of strips of palm tree bark, smoothed over time from feet, sleeping bodies, spills, and the humid climate. The women giggled behind their hands, chattering away in a language that sounded like they were swallowing their words while their tongue tried to escape.

"*He he....* Do you drive a car?" someone who spoke some Spanish would be ushered to speak to me, as the only word I had mastered in Ngäbere in the first week was "hello."

"Yes. I have a car."

They would all gasp, stare at each other, fall toward each other in shyness, and resume the giggles. I could have been naked, on stage, in the spotlight, in front of thousands of people for as much a part of the group as I felt.

"You HAVE a car? Or do you DRIVE a car?"

I had not yet learned the hierarchy of car ownership and drivers in Panama yet, and definitely not in this part of the country. Vehicles serve much more of a work function here. Oftentimes, one person owned a car, or bus, and hired people to drive it for profit as a cab or for transporting crops or wood. Only the more affluent people in the city owned vehicles for convenience or getting to work.

When I said, "I own and drive the car," they just stared at me.

"Is it hard to drive?"

"Well, you have to go to school to learn to drive, but after that, it's easy."

Again, I was met with blank stares of incredulity. The majority of people here wouldn't even make it to high school, never mind a school purely for driving a car. Great first impression.

My neighbors also came *basare* at my house, and they had a great sense of smell. As soon as I got coffee boiling in the morning, people appeared. I quickly learned to never prepare coffee or breakfast for one. They would simply show up, and say "*Ti tä basare.*"

One of my frequent *basare* guests from the day I arrived in town was the grandmother from two huts over. She was a rotund woman, with a broad, open face, coffee-colored skin, almond eyes, and thick dark hair streaked with grey reaching down to her mid-back. Her wide, calloused feet were barefoot, as most of the women's and children's were. Every day she wore a knee-length, short-sleeved, handmade dress of light cotton with a design of small flowers on a green or blue background. She spoke only Ngäbere.

Each morning, right as the coffee boiled, she would climb up my wooden stairs that were narrower than her waist singing, "*Ti niki basaaaare!*" She looked very approving when I asked, "Coffee?" as she sat on the wooden bench in my front room. She would glow if I asked if she wanted powdered milk or more sugar—both luxuries in the town—in her coffee. We would try every minute or so to talk, but we couldn't understand each other. So she would just sip her coffee, look at me with a crinkle in her eye, chuckle—which made her whole body and the bench, and sometimes the whole stilted house we sat in, shake—and pat me on my leg.

While the grandmother visited, grandchildren would tag along to color and be her translators, since many of them learned Spanish in school. In fact, my front room had become the unofficial town primary school as soon as the kids discovered I had paper, crayons, and books with pictures in them. The school didn't even have these. The kids would sprawl across the wooden floor and color, occasionally stopping to take two-handed sips from her blue plastic coffee cup, and translate from Ngäbere to Spanish and back. However, the long questions and answers between me and the grandmother would often be translated in a couple of words mumbled into the kids' drawings. I'd sit sipping my coffee, and wonder what they said that made her chuckle.

My first Saturday in my new village, I went fishing with my neighboring family, the Molinas. I was fascinated by a culture whose members still fished for their evening meal out of necessity and not for pleasure or income. They did not usually use, or have, cash. They grew, bartered, or worked for what they needed. The Molina kids ran along barefooted, wearing only blue shorts, completely sure of themselves as they crossed rivers, and periodically dove in and spearfished their own dinner. I, however, clumped along behind in boots, wearing a watch and glasses. I tripped, tried to brace myself, and ended up breaking the neighbor's fishing rod, made from a young piece of mangrove wood. The father, Claudio, had hiked twelve hours round trip to the coastal mangroves to make it.

I tried to hide the fact for a minute. They had heard me fall and turned to see if I was O.K. I tried to look like I hadn't fallen. My glasses were fogged up and slipping down my nose with sweat. I had blisters forming in my rubber boots. I apparently couldn't even walk, never mind spearfish to carry my own weight around here. I thought I was supposed to be here to help people, but instead, I was becoming a quick burden for them. And I had just broken Claudio's hard-earned fishing rod. I felt so inadequate.

I eventually fessed up. Claudio's and his wife Yolanda's faces looked disappointed at the reality of losing a fishing rod and all the potential fish that could come from it. But Claudio said, *"No te preocupes,"*—"Don't worry yourself. We'll make a new one some day." I had become the oldest child of the family.

Back at home in my "shower" after our fishing trip, I reached up to the overhead spigot with the underwear filter and felt something slick. I looked up to see a small green tree frog with huge eyes and long suction cup fingers peering back at me. Even the frogs stared at me.

The next day I woke up, not thinking of Norteño, but of home, where it was Easter Sunday, my grandmother's birthday, and tax day. My first thought was "It's Easter, and I'm awkward and alone in this strange place. What am I doing?"

The roosters had already quieted by the time I rolled out from under my scratchy green-checkered sheet, pushed aside my mosquito net, and swung my legs off the wooden table I slept on. I bucket bathed next to the table, water running down through the wooden floor slats. As I made a breakfast of saltine crackers with peanut butter and jelly, I was already sweating. I filled a metal pot with water I had hauled up to my house and put it on my gas camp stove. Right on time, the morning coffee and kid invasion showed up.

I eventually wandered down to the center of the village, just a couple minutes from my house. On the way I was called to the pay phone. A call for me? There was only one pay phone for miles around. It always looked funny to me. A regular blue plastic pay phone, standing all by itself in a village of wooden huts. It only worked about half the time, since it was solar powered, and located in a rainforest. A sunny day to charge it was hard to come by. It had been installed a few years before I arrived in 2001. It was the first phone many of the people in the village had seen. In Ngäbere, they called it *"Blite kugrote,"* meaning to speak through a tree vine.

It was Lena calling, one of my fellow Peace Corps Volunteers with whom I had flown to Panama and spent the first three months of training. She was assigned to a village about an hour bus ride away. Her voice was shaking. When I asked if she was O.K., she burst out crying and said she was coming to visit; she was already half way to Norteño, calling from a pay phone where the bus stopped. I met her halfway down the road to Norteño.

"I just don't know what to do!" she sobbed as we hugged.

We walked through the soccer field, up the muddy hill to my house, and she settled into the hammock I had strung up in the front room, the only furniture I had that wasn't hard wooden tables or benches.

"I don't know how to tell who's trying to help me, and who's trying to take advantage of me." It was like she was channeling my thoughts. "People keep giving me prices for building my house, or for cooking food for me, or coming over right when I cook, and they want food, and I don't know who's being honest, and who's not, and I don't know who I can ask."

As she spoke my same concerns aloud, I mixed up a pot of rice, and another of fried plantains. I warmed a can of sardines, which I hate, but which were one of the only portable protein sources I had, short of raising chickens (which I later did) or cooking beans for hours. I spooned the sardines over the rice, and served us an Easter feast on my two blue plastic plates. I kept my door shut, and tried to avoid looking at the rows of eyes of the children standing on my stairs, peering in at us through the gaps between the wooden planks that served as my walls.

"Someone pooped in my latrine the other day. But next to the seat, on the floor!" I exclaimed. I just didn't know how to deal with this stuff either. Not knowing how to deal with someone's excrement and how much it bothered me made us laugh hysterically, wiping away tears from laughter and frustration.

We shared a dessert of a Cadbury Crème Egg. Wow, it had only been seven days since we had gone to our villages. A week had never been so intense, or emotionally wracking. But it was so good to know someone else was going through it, too.

About an hour before dusk, I walked her back to the river. We paid Paulino ten cents each to pole us across the gentle river rapids in his dugout canoe. We hugged each other, not wanting it to be goodbye. It felt like when mom, the only person you know, left you at school with all the strangers on the first day of kindergarten.

On the way back to my house, I felt a deep pang of homesickness, knowing my whole family was at Easter dinner together. Their lives were happening without me, and I wouldn't be back with them for years. I called home collect from the pay phone, and got to talk to each family member in turn. It was so good to hear them so close, right there, next to

my ear. They were real. They were still there. I hid my face
in the pay phone as the tears ran down my cheeks, avoiding
the stares of all the kids surrounding me, listening to the girl
speaking English on the tree vine.

I reluctantly said goodbye, hung up, and headed back to
my house alone, feeling even lonelier. I wanted it to be Easter
here, too. While they did celebrate a Catholic mass that morning in the little open-air wooden church in town, the rest of
the day had been business as usual.

I stopped by the little *tienda*, which was just the window of
an enterprising townsperson's house with a couple of shelves
stocked with pasta, beans, vegetable oil, and sometimes toilet
paper. I bought two eggs, stowed them away in a little yellow-
and-red striped plastic bag, crossed a couple of streams and
climbed to my house. I asked Yolanda, the next-door neighbor, to hard boil the eggs, then called a few of the older kids
up to my house.

"Here." I handed two of the four kids the hard-boiled
eggs. "Want to color?"

"On the eggs?" they asked. But they gladly drew trees and
chickens and grass on them with crayons and pens.

I called the rest of the kids. About eighteen of them showed
up. I explained that in my family, back in the States, we celebrated Easter with an Easter egg hunt. I told them about the
Easter Bunny, and that we were going to do an egg hunt.

A couple of the older kids and I went and hid the eggs,
one under half of a coconut shell, and the other in the crook
of a banana tree. Chaos ensued as all eighteen kids burst out
of the door, competing to get down the narrow stairs to look
for eggs. The one under the coconut shell was found quickly.
One of the shorter kids found the other one in the banana tree
about a foot higher than he could reach. He was frantically
jumping up, reaching as high as he could, kicking his legs out

to the sides in an effort to reach the egg before the older kids noticed. I had a hard time walking over to him, doubled over laughing so hard, before I could get the egg down for him.

Then amazingly, the eighteen kids split the two eggs in a show of sharing and selflessness that I had never seen the equal of in the U.S. They each took a pinch of white and a pinch of yolk, the older kids pushing each other out of the way to make sure the younger ones got their pinches. Eggs were a delicacy.

I had done it. The Easter egg hunt made home seem a little bit closer to this strange land. It didn't all have to be foreign, just different, like eggs in banana trees.

The day after the Easter egg hunt, the kid who found the banana tree egg, one of my favorites, showed up at my door as usual. I could usually hear him stomping up the stairs that were each a tall reach for his little legs, especially with oversized boots on. He was the grandson of the chuckling coffee-drinking grandmother. He was always around, watching, offering to help me, other children, or his family members, following me around with his huge curious eyes. He was a short tyke about five years old, with a buzz cut that made his hair stand up on end. He was usually naked except for his blue underwear, and occasionally tall black mud boots and a machete. He always stood with his legs a little apart, and his little barrel chest stuck out. He used my name as punctuation. Except Jessi came out as "Yessi." "Yessi, what are you doing, Yessi?" "Yessi, could I have some milk, Yessi?" "Yessi, can we color, Yessi?" I called him, along with every other kid in the village, Chi, or ChiChi (for the smallest babies and kids), which is what all children before teenage years were generally called. *Chi* meant "small." This Chi was my first friend in town.

He came in, kicked his boots off, flopped on the floor, and flipped through the pictures in the *Newsweek* magazines I had, his brow furrowed.

"Yessi, can it be Easter again today, Yessi, so we can eat eggs again? Yessi, I have a question, Yessi."

"What is it?"

"Yessi. The Easter Bunny, Yessi. So he's a big white rabbit?"

"Yes, a big white rabbit. He's the Easter Bunny."

He paused, flipping through the magazine photos. "O.K., Yessi, and the rabbit. How does he get eggs? Does he steal eggs from a chicken, Yessi?"

"Um, yes, I guess so. Maybe he bought them. Or maybe the chicken gave them to him?"

He stared me down. "O.K., Yessi. And then the rabbit, after he gets the eggs, cooks the eggs?"

"Yes."

"How did he cook them, Yessi? Does he have his own fire, or did someone else have to cook them, Yessi?"

"Um, I don't know." I had never stopped to question the culinary skills of the Easter Bunny or if he even had a kitchen.

"O.K., Yessi. So he cooks the eggs, and then he paints them?"

"Yes."

"Then he hides the eggs, Yessi?"

"Yes."

"Then the kids get to find the eggs, Yessi?"

"Yes."

"Then the kids get to eat the eggs, Yessi?"

"Yes."

"Then, Yessi, why can't the rabbit just give the kids eggs to eat?"

"I don't know. It's just a story." I didn't quite know what to make of the fact that the five-year-old wasn't at all enamored with the Easter Bunny story.

"O.K., Yessi." He paused for awhile, the topic of the Easter Bunny clearly closed.

"Is Easter coming again soon?" he then asked with his two eyebrow muscles clear little question marks.

"Once a year," I told him.

"Oh." He hung his head dejectedly.

"But we can do another hunt next Easter, O.K.?" I offered.

That made him happy, running off on his stout little legs, leaving me to ponder how the Easter Bunny got eggs and cooked them. I couldn't wait for Halloween.

Jessi Flynn served as a Peace Corps Volunteer in Panama from 2002-04, in the indigenous Ngabe village of Norteno. She takes care of the dog she brought back from Norteno, who still understands Spanish better than English and stays involved with the mystery of international work. She currently works as a Regional Recruiter for the Peace Corps.

JANETTE K. HOPPER

The Bus Ride

*What begins as a simple bus ride to the city ends in an
unforgettable encounter with a grieving mother.*

EARLY IN THE MORNING, THE ROOSTERS BEGIN TO CROW BEFORE
first light comes. This is the *madrugada*: the time of day when
the men with their machetes head out for the *campo*. And on
this day the Peace Corps Volunteers will also head out of the
village, to the city, going to a meeting and to check on the
town's only refrigerator for keeping medicine at the hospital. Somehow, though absolutely essential, it has never been
repaired nor made it back to the village.

Thinking about a good meal in the city, the Volunteers
rise early at the first hint of morning light and eat a little day-
old bread with a black cup of coffee and walk holding hands
toward the outskirts of town to catch the bus to the coast.
(The villagers who don't know think they are brother and
sister because they have no children.) As they first pass the
cement houses with backyard stick fences and then the mud
huts along the main road away from the center of town, the
world comes alive with sound: children's voices and babies'
cries, the soft tones of lowered voices and the *cumbia* that will

be blaring loudly on the radio out of every door later on. As they continue out of town, the sounds and smells of the fields and jungle fill their lungs and ears. They remember how they learned in training that Colombia had two seasons: one hot and dry, the other hot and wet. Soon it will be hot, but for now it is the coolest part of the day. She is wearing a simple flowered cotton shift and sandals, he his Levis and cowboy boots. Anticipating insects, the two have light long-sleeve shirts covering their arms.

They walk towering over the few people they pass on the way. The road surface alternates between thick dust and hard clay ruts. The mosquitoes aren't bad, but the no-see-ums are the worst, and this is their season: quietly they make their burning presence felt on any bare spot of skin.

Upon reaching the stop, they see a few others have already gathered, waiting. A lady with a baby and small child constantly bats at the invisible but real tormenters with a small white scrap of sheet blanket. A man whom they visited about a family garden walks up and greets them patting them on the shoulders. Another villager they don't know joins the group and offers everyone cigarettes. They decline with apology. Another couple comes up toting a bag of clucking chickens. An old pickup drives by with a load of people in the back heading the other way. At last, the brightly colored striped bus comes, turns around and stops with a screech. Hoping for a seat on the aisle side, they board in turn. Given a choice, the Volunteers don't sit by the window, not since the time the child a few seats up vomited leaning out of the bus.

There are several seats left, but at the next stop the bus will be full to bursting. The driver has his front seat altar gaily decorated with fringe, hanging dolls, balls, a supply of guardian saints and Marias. This all will bring us all luck as the bus meanders through the countryside picking up people at rural stops and in villages and towns along the route. The people are stuffed into the tight space wearing freshly pressed clothes with splashes of white baby powder on their black skin, ready for the heat that will become oppressive as the day goes on. At one stop, the lady vendors come with baskets filled with "*arepas con huevos*" on their heads. They shout and rush to sell their wares, quickly reaching up to the window of the bus as folks, anxious to get something to eat, strain to squeeze with their fingers on the latches and slide the windows low enough to send a few pesos out and grab a cornmeal-covered egg.

As the bus takes off, tired of the bumps, she lays her head on the back of the seat in front of her trying not to awaken her stomach to nausea and sleeps a while to make the time go faster. Her young husband puts his arm around her resting his hand on her shoulder as he thinks about the ducks and how he will convince the *camposenos* to pen them up and feed them. At least it is not rainy so the bus won't get stuck. Soon they will arrive in the midst of the market, and the bus driver will throw off the heavy loads tied on the bus roof onto the ground. The Volunteers will be off to do their work, heading for the office then to lunch: a huge plate of pork and rice at the Chinese restaurant. Perhaps they will run into some other Volunteers, and they will go to the beach after lunch before their return to the village. After a day of business and pleasure, they will hurry to not miss the bus, edging their way through the market to find the right bus to return to the village.

The marketplace is booming and noisy with people, animals, baskets, cooked food, smelly fish, fruits, and vegetables. A vender carves ice off a block and adds purple coloring for the first child in a line-up for cones. A man stripped down to his loose pants walks by with three wooden chairs stacked up on his shoulders. A child chomps on a mango: thick orange-colored juice runs out the corners of his mouth and onto his distended stomach. Men push carts by the crowds, miraculously not crashing into the women turning sideways to get through. She remembers the day in rainy season when they arrived at the market to catch the bus in a downpour and how they sat hunched in a cart as it took them to the bus, thus avoiding murky waters up to their knees. People gesture and bargain at every stall.

A pregnant woman who sits on the ground selling her wares holds another baby. Attempting to fan the pesky flies away from the oozing eye of her baby girl, the swarm zeros in, and several reach their goal despite her efforts. The daughter cuddles into her mom's side with a big-eyed smile, ears already pierced and a *mal ojo* leather bracelet around her chubby little wrist to protect her from harm. Intense noisy bargaining fills the air with shouts and catcalling. A man leaning on the corner of a stall leers at her as she walks by and says something; she tries not to hear what he says under his breath. She stares ahead and doesn't acknowledge his presence and soon stops to buy some carrots. She starts to walk away saying, "Hey, too *caro*" but then returns, buys some limp carrots to drop in her bag. He calls out, "Here's the bus."

The two scurry up the bus steps, but they are too late as the seats are nearly full. They can't sit together, but at least they won't stand. He goes on toward the back, and she sits on the aisle in the middle of the bus with a young girl next to her and a skinny man by the window. A heavy woman, old and fat with dirty fingernails comes along, places the board between the two aisle seats with one hand and settles in, her buttocks up against the person on each side of her. The woman holds a bundle, which seemed to be more of a burden. Occasionally her flabby, rough-skinned arm would come to rest on the Volunteer's knee; they share the load.

The young white woman studies her face and would vividly remember it for the rest of her life. The Costenian woman's face was not ugly. Her face was stern, but not unkind. She held within it all that she had suffered. Her eyes were glazed with sadness and hopelessness. Her fat neck and lopping chin fell to her swelling breasts with exhaustion. Her dress had been new, but those were other days. It was cut low, but had a collar that exposed a hanky clinging there between her breasts. Her ears were pierced and her ear lobes seemed the only part of her that was slim and young, with little dainty turquoise jewels, their gaiety in stark contrast to the preoccupied sorrow smothered deep within the figure. The feet were large and covered in part by chartreuse tennis shoes meant for a man.

Her bundle was well covered with a green and white towel. It was shouldered with strength and pride. At last a few tears escaped across the nose and down the chin to be quietly wiped away upon the collar of her dress. The dust was thick on the road with an endless parade of bumps and lumps. The ride was eternal. At last the woman shifted positions; she hoisted her burden upon her shoulder taking care it stayed well covered. As she rose slowly the gringa looked back at her companion behind and smiled. She thought about how when she finished working with these villagers teaching health and nutrition here, he would ranch and she would be an artist when they returned to the States. The encumbered woman pushed off the bus. As her foot left the last step and she hit the ground firmly, she threw back the top of the towel, which revealed the baby's head. She began the whining chant of a woman who had lost her son. Other women took up the chant that met her cries, "Antonio Segundo Sanchez is dead."

Growing up in Idaho, Janette K. Hooper and her boyfriend joined the Peace Corps during the Vietnam War era, after two years as a student at the University of Idaho. After being married only days, she and her new husband (now ex-husband) David reported for training and served in the Peace Corp in Colombia with an Agriculture, Health and Nutrition Program from 1966-1968. Requesting mountains they got the coast. She is currently a Professor at the University of North Carolina at Pembroke. Her artwork has been shown extensively in major museums, at colleges and universities and in private galleries all over the U.S. and in many foreign countries. Check her website at janettekhopper.com.

PART FIVE

SUSTAINABLE PEACE

·JESSI FLYNN

Fishpond Justice

*Memories of a community project gone awry can both
darken and enlighten a life, even years later.*

IT STILL HURTS, FIVE YEARS LATER. THOSE LOOSE ENDS, THE
regrets, the "what ifs?" All those things that I could have done,
or seen through, seem so simple and straightforward with
hindsight and reflection.

An empty pool of dark reddish-brown mud, dug out of the
middle of the jungle. The memory of how it almost became
a fishpond, and wondering what happened to it, wakes me up
in the middle of the night, heart racing with regret. Strange.
That's not what I expected Peace Corps to leave me with. I
expected memories of poverty, birth, death, people. Instead,
what I remember first is loose ends.

The first thing I remember about meeting Justo was walking
toward his house through the village of Norteño. The village had some eighty houses, mostly wooden-slat huts with
palm-thatched or tin roofing. They were on stilts about five
or six feet off the ground to avoid the rainforest's rain, mud,
snakes, and bugs. The air was thick with moisture and warmth.

305

Threadbare clothes, thinned and stretched from being washed and beaten on river rocks, helped me learn who people were since they wore them reliably. One leader always wore an old political t-shirt, faded to a gray-white color, the first letter of the now ruling party's name just a hole in the shirt.

Justo's house was at the end of town, by the river. It was a rickety hut, very small, but filled with huge smiles on lots of kids. I would ask *"Dre kukwe?"* "What's new?" The responses there tended to be honest or negative in order to not boast, as opposed to the token U.S. response "All's well, and you?"

"Mro ñaka." There's no food.

Oh.

The hammock Justo sat in creaked, and the house swayed slightly with the weight shift. Justo looked down at me on the ground from his hammock up in the hut. What does one say to that?

"Why is there no food?" I asked. The logical question from a middle-class white girl fresh from the U.S., assigned to the village as an agricultural extension agent, thinking I had a new problem to solve, or a new project in this man's lack of food.

"Ti krene." I'm lazy.

Oh. I didn't expect that one.

"Well, why don't we go plant something then?" I optimistically offered.

"Ti krene."

Oh. I wasn't used to that either. I wasn't used to people settling for the situation they were in, especially when they could do something about it. I didn't understand how life could feel so uphill; they were defeated.

Justo's apathy filled me with such a mix of emotions: frustration, anger, confusion. I wanted to offer the help they had asked for in a Peace Corps Volunteer, but apathy was not what I wanted to work with. I also knew I could never understand where they came from, and what their battles were. All I could do was work with willing people.

So, yes, I had my successful projects. I planted gardens, worked with the women's artisan group, helped medicine men and women from different locations connect, encouraged tree plantings, organized youth groups, gave sanitation talks, and taught literacy and math classes. They were only small successes, but not failures. Small steps.

However, even five years later, those small steps are not what takes the breath out of me at random moments in the day. Small steps do not wake me up at night. It's the unfinished business.

Justo proved to be quite a mixed bag, even though he was one of the more honest people in town. He would say when he felt lazy, but he also picked a few big battles that no one else in town would. One battle he chose was to promote the use of latrines, which is not everyone's ideal way to make a mark. Justo believed in latrines because he understood the need to have people use them. The common method was to sneak down to a corner of a creek or stream and go to the bathroom in the water, which made sense. They could clean themselves with water, as toilet paper was too much a luxury. Most people saw latrines as full, smelly, cockroach-infested pits their kids could fall into. Justo, though, understood the health impacts of how the water affected everyone and the importance of getting that knowledge across to people. He called community meetings, got people involved, got a committee together, and wrote a grant request to build latrines in two communities along the river. He hauled 100-pound bags of cement through mud and tropical heat and built most of the latrines himself. A thankless job, though it came with small amounts of grant money, a coveted thing in a subsistence community.

After a year, Justo said he wanted to learn about fish farming. He asked about a lot of things, most of it just curiosity. We did some research and talked about what it took to build a fishpond and take care of the fish. Somewhere along the way, he decided he definitely wanted to do it. He brought his decision up at a funeral. We stood at the top of a hill skirted with a cow pasture, under a tree, overlooking a beautiful mountain valley in a traditional burial ground. Old women wailed *"Ti täre!"* which means "I love, I hurt, and I am," all in one. We took turns throwing handfuls of red dirt down onto the white-painted wooden box. She had been my host mother, and she died of leukemia.

Apparently, life goes on—quickly. On the way back down the hillside through the cow pasture Justo pulled me aside.

"Want to see where I want to dig the fishpond?"

"Now?" I thought. He insisted that it was on the way back to the village. So after a bit of a hike involving a river, the ever-present mud and trails, we arrived at a muddy area along a small stream. It was rather perfect. It had a feeder stream and a logical wider place for the pond. He had done a good job scouting a location, and we made plans to work on it.

We dug for days, a few men and me. We dug and dug. Justo didn't want just *any* fishpond; there would be no experimenting. He wanted to go big, no matter what I said. Manual labor was no obstacle for these men. I dug until my blisters bled, while they showed only mild sweat. Finally, it was almost done. One thing remained: the drainage tubes to be built into the dam end of the pond. The tubes were critical to maintaining water level, keeping fish in the pond, and for draining the pond to harvest the fish.

Clearly, Justo thought I should get the tubes. According to him, I had the money, or connections to money, and the ability to go get the tubes. Clearly, I thought Justo should get the tubes, as this seemed to me to be the ultimate "teach a man to fish" situation. We talked about using local resources such as making tubes out of bamboo. Nope. Justo wanted the best for his tank, only brand new PVC tubes. I gave him the phone numbers to the Ministry of Agriculture who offered free tubing to community fish farms. He said that since I knew them, I should call. I said that since he was the one building the tank, and would need to know this Ministry for any follow-up and to get the baby fish "seeds," he should call.

We never finished the tank. Justo said he tried to call the Ministry a couple of times from the town pay phone, but he seemed to be out-waiting me. He knew I wanted to help. Surely I would give in and say, "Fine, I'll go get you a $2.50 PVC tube." No way. For me, it wasn't about the money, and it wasn't about the time. It was about the principle of the matter. The fishpond was the most concrete example of my Peace Corps frustrations. It frustrated me then, and still does now, when people said they wanted to learn about something, or do something, but either they or I wouldn't or couldn't act when the opportunity arose.

Why didn't I just buy the tubing? This thought still bothers me. Did the tank, and the hours of backbreaking work just ease back into the ground because of one stupid tube? If I had bought the tube, would that have reinforced the reliance on outside funding and knowledge? Would I have given a man, or his children, fish to eat for a day, but not taught them to fish? Does it really matter? In the end, not only did I not teach a man to fish, I didn't give his children a fish either. I am afraid that I failed him. I am afraid that I gave up because I was stubborn and had my own internal arguments about international development work and about providing outside resources. I am afraid that I was stubborn while his kids were hungry.

I am tempted to fly back down to the village and ask Justo what he thought of that fishpond. For all I know, he found out how to continue it. The next town up the river had a fishpond. He could have asked them for help, or he could have eventually called the Ministry of Agriculture.

I am tempted to go back and build him a fishpond. To dig until my hands bleed to make up for all the unfulfilled projects I had. To make up for the teenage girl I thought I worked with enough to continue school who then got pregnant. To make up for the fact that the village welcomed me, and put me through the gauntlet at times, but ultimately made me a *"bosse"* or daughter-in-law. Yet I don't write letters or call the pay phone even on Mother's Day. I wish I could bury my regrets so the good days come to mind first and not the unfinished business.

I think it's ironic that the memory that haunts me most is Justo: Just. The memories I have, and the thoughts that tug at me for my unfinished business in Norteño. Justo's fishpond, and all the issues that come with it—hunger, natural forces, local politics, poverty, international development work—factor into my decisions today. In discussing issues with people, making decisions concerning daily issues such as riding my bike to work, and planning for the next steps in my life, the perspectives I gained with Justo and throughout my Peace Corps service influence me today. Those pangs hurt, but they also make me feel. A just sentence and a just reward that I wouldn't change for the world.

Jessi Flynn served as a Peace Corps Volunteer in Panama from 2001-04 in the indigenous Ngäbe village of Norteño. She has taken her fishpond frustrations out on a plethora of houseplants and gardens, taking care of the dog she brought back from Norteño, who still understands Spanish better than English, and staying involved with the mystery of international work. She currently works as a Regional Recruiter for the Peace Corps.

Acknowledgements

We can still remember that 2007 evening. Jane Albritton called to tell us she was coming to Washington and wanted to discuss a project she had in mind; Jane and Bernie had been in the same India Peace Corps group. After she explained her idea to honor Peace Corps' upcoming 50th anniversary by publishing a series of books containing stories written by Peace Corps Volunteers from around the world, we agreed to help. Little did we know how dedicated Jane was to the project, how much time she was willing to invest in making it happen, and how good she was at keeping us involved.

We would also like to thank all the Volunteers whose stories appear in this volume. Without their willingness to share the highs and lows, the boredom and exhilaration of a Peace Corps tour, there would be no book.

Story Acknowledgments

"Sink or Drown Proof" by Paul Vitale published with permission from the author. Copyright © 2011 by Paul Vitale.

"The Making of a Leftist" by Wynne Dimock published with permission from the author. Copyright © 2011 by Wynne Dimock.

"Pablo's Christmas" by W. W. Wales published with permission from the author. Copyright © 2011 by W. W. Wales.

"Some Never Forget" by Maria Altobelli published with permission from the author. Copyright © 2011 by Maria Altobelli.

"Homeland Buffet" by Brandon Louie published with permission from the author. Copyright © 2011 by Brandon Louie.

Special thanks to
The Jason and Lucy Greer Foundation
for the Arts for their generous support of
the Peace Corps@50 Project.

About the Editors

Co-editors Pat and Bernie Alter met in Denver, Colorado, between their respective Peace Corps experiences. Peace Corps in its wisdom assigned Bernie, New York City born and bred, to Central India as a Poultry Volunteer from 1967-69 and Pat, raised in suburban St. Louis, to Paraguay as a Public Health Volunteer from 1970-72.

Upon returning from India, Bernie received an M.A. in International Relations from the University of Denver in 1971 and joined the U.S. Foreign Service in 1975. Together, he and Pat have lived in Pakistan, India, Thailand, Canada, Hong Kong and Korea. Pat received an M.L.S. in Library Science during their four-year tour in Toronto.

Bernie and Pat now live in Arlington, Virginia. While Bernie retired from the Department of State in 2006, Pat works as a Librarian at the Arlington Public Library. They are the parents of two sons, one born in Lahore, Pakistan, and the other started in New Delhi, India.

They attribute their lifelong wanderlust and interest in cross-cultural encounters to Peace Corps.